MW00325001

Congress and the Media

Congress and the Media

Beyond Institutional Power

C. DANIELLE VINSON

FURMAN UNIVERSITY

OXFORD
UNIVERSITY PRESS

Oxford University Press is a department of the University of Oxford. It furthers
the University's objective of excellence in research, scholarship, and education
by publishing worldwide. Oxford is a registered trade mark of Oxford University
Press in the UK and certain other countries.

Published in the United States of America by Oxford University Press
198 Madison Avenue, New York, NY 10016, United States of America.

© Oxford University Press 2017

All rights reserved. No part of this publication may be reproduced, stored in
a retrieval system, or transmitted, in any form or by any means, without the
prior permission in writing of Oxford University Press, or as expressly permitted
by law, by license, or under terms agreed with the appropriate reproduction
rights organization. Inquiries concerning reproduction outside the scope of the
above should be sent to the Rights Department, Oxford University Press, at the
address above.

You must not circulate this work in any other form
and you must impose this same condition on any acquirer.

Library of Congress Cataloging-in-Publication Data
Names: Vinson, Danielle, author.
Title: Congress and the media : beyond institutional power / C. Danielle
   Vinson.
Description: Oxford ; New York, NY : Oxford University Press, 2017. |
   Includes bibliographical references and index.
Identifiers: LCCN 2016034529 | ISBN 9780190632250 (paperback) | ISBN 9780190632243 (hardback)
Subjects: LCSH: United States. Congress—Reporters and reporting. | United
   States. Congress—Public relations. | Communication in politics—United
   States. | Press and politics—United States | Mass media—Political
   aspects—United States. | BISAC: POLITICAL SCIENCE / Political Process /
   Political Parties.
Classification: LCC JK1128 .V56 2017 | DDC 328.73/0731—dc23
LC record available at https://lccn.loc.gov/2016034529

9 8 7 6 5 4 3 2 1

Paperback printed by Webcom Inc., Canada
Hardback printed by Bridgeport National Bindery, Inc., United States of America

In memory of my grandmothers, Bertha Vinson and Cornelia Hutto, for St. Louis Blues, *chocolate meringue pie, and all the other joys of life they shared with me.*

CONTENTS

List of Illustrations ix
Acknowledgments xi

1. Introduction: Congress Goes Public 1

2. Four Decades of Going Public in Congress 26

3. Why Congressional Members Go Public 53

4. New Paths to Influence: Broadcast and New Media 82

5. Congress Responds to the President: The Case of Social
   Security Reform 110
   Coauthored with Megan S. Remmel

6. Overcoming Institutional Weakness: The Congressional Black
   Caucus Goes Public 129

7. A Tale of Two Senators: Adapting Public Strategies
   to Different Goals 150

8. The Possibilities and Limits of Going Public in Congress 179

Appendix 203
Notes 207
References 223
Index 229

LIST OF ILLUSTRATIONS

TABLES

2.1 Issue Agendas 41

2.2 Work-Related Activities and Direct Contact in Going Public 50

3.1 Passing Policy vs. Stopping It 65

3.2 Reaction to the President 77

5.1 Reaction to the President on Social Security 118

5.2 Reaction to the President's Budget: Effects
of Presidential Approval 125

6.1 Factors Affecting the Congressional Black Caucus
Going Public 138

6.2 CBC Support for and Opposition to the President 145

FIGURES

2.1 Who Goes Public 32

3.1 Goals in Going Public 59

3.2 Impact of Polarization on Reaction to the President 75

4.1 Reaction to the President on Television 89

4.2 Who Is Tweeting in Congress 95

5.1 Who Went Public on Social Security 115

5.2 Support and Opposition by Party 116

6.1   Cases of the CBC Going Public per Year 136

6.2   Average CBC Cases per Year by President and Party 137

6.3   CBC Reaction to the President 143

7.1   Making News 153

7.2   Graham's Support for / Opposition to the President
      and Parties 156

7.3   Target Audience 162

7.4   DeMint's Criticism of the President and Parties 170

ACKNOWLEDGMENTS

At times research and writing can seem like a very solitary venture. But looking back over the years of data collection, analysis, and writing that went into this book, I find a lengthy list of folks whose contributions, large and small, helped make this project possible.

My interest in Congress and media was sparked by the writing of Tim Cook, who took an interest in the ways and reasons members of Congress used the media well before most people thought it was important. His idea that politicians use the media to compensate for their institutional weaknesses provides the theoretical foundation for much of my research.

Content analysis of the kind I have undertaken is not possible without capable research assistants. I am indebted to many of my students at Furman University for their work on this project over the years. Students in my two sections of Media and Politics in winter 2005 compiled and provided initial coding of the transition-year data as part of their research assignment for that class. Whitney Goodwin, Susan Williams, Megan Remmel, and Joe Watson all served as summer research assistants working on data collection and coding for various parts of the book. Megan also helped write Chapter 5. Meredith Toole assisted with intercoder reliability. Administrative assistant Amy Cockman also helped collect data. Students Meghan Kelly and Hannah Haas introduced me to Twitter and Facebook, and Hannah provided the initial content analysis of congressional twitter use for Chapter 4.

My research benefited greatly from interviews with several members of Congress and congressional staff. Congressman John Lewis and Senators Lindsey Graham and Jim DeMint graciously agreed to on-the-record interviews, and I appreciate their candor. Keiana Barrett, former communications director for the Congressional Black Caucus, provided information about the media relations efforts of the CBC. These interviews would not have been possible without Quentin James, Jessi Blake, and former Congressman Bob Inglis helping to arrange them. I'm also grateful for informal conversations with many of my former students who work in congressional offices, most notably Tate Zeigler, Patrick Barron, Gena Villari, Tom Andrews, and Will Miller. They and others provided me with insights about why and how members go public and their reasons for doing so. These conversations guided the questions I asked in the research and also provided a reality check as I went.

A number of colleagues and anonymous reviewers offered feedback on the project. David Paletz encouraged my early musings on the topic and offered substantial feedback on the book proposal that led to the chapter on broadcast and new media and the case studies. Tim Groeling, Pat Sellers, Tracy Sulkin, and Dan Lipinski read early versions of some chapters that I presented at conferences. Their suggestions have greatly improved the book. Of course, any mistakes are my own doing.

Furman University provided funding for my summer research assistants through the Furman Advantage program and provided me with a sabbatical that allowed time for data analysis and writing. My colleagues in the Political Science Department are a delight to work with and have been supportive in many ways. Mike Bressler has been particularly helpful as a sounding board for ideas and working through problems in the research. Jim Guth sent relevant articles and asked insightful questions along the way. During my time as department chair, all of my colleagues put up with my disappearing act on Thursdays and tried not to bother me with department business so I could dedicate one day a week uninterrupted to research. Our department administrative assistants, Lori Schoen and Paige Blankenship, made it possible for me to be department chair and still get research done. In addition to handling their considerable administrative responsibilities, they graciously volunteered to provide research assistance when their normal work was slow, and I happily accepted. Their competence and good humor are unfailing, and I appreciate them more than I can say.

The folks at Oxford University Press have patiently guided the manuscript through review and publication, improving it along the way. Alexandra Dauler and Kathleen Weaver were quick to respond to my questions, and Kathleen provided guidance in revisions. Editor David McBride offered helpful advice in the revision process and was a pleasure to work with. Cheryl Merritt and Thomas McCarthy took care of production and copy-editing. Many thanks to all of them.

Work can at times be consuming, but a project like this also reminds me that I have many personal debts of gratitude to people who have made my life easier and more enjoyable: to Dr. Cal Maddox and Mrs. Sandra Smith, whose lessons in grammar and writing continue to be among the most valuable that I learned in school at any level; to Angie Kirkland, the only person I trust to cut my hair and hide the gray this project has given me and who faithfully asks how the book is going and when it will be finished (Angie, it's done!); to my dear friends Trisha Bouknight Miller and Marian Vreman Boucher, who let me escape political science and never ask how the book is going; to Claire Saizan, Patty Watkins, and Ann Crowe, who make me laugh, let me vent, and feed me gluten-free food; and to the folks at Sanctuary Church in Greenville, who remind me what is important and provide me with community.

Finally, I am grateful to my family. My parents, Mike and Diane Vinson, help me keep things in perspective, remind me of the importance of a sense of humor, and entertain me with conversations about the farm, NASCAR, and Duke basketball. I'm pleased to offer them a new grand-book. While I was working on this project, both of my grandmothers passed away. They lived well into their nineties and helped me remember the importance of historical perspective and living joyfully. The book is dedicated to them.

Introduction

Congress Goes Public

In 1981 Congress began its traditional Easter recess with major budget and tax battles between Republican President Ronald Reagan and the Democratic majority in the House of Representatives looming ahead. There were fundamental differences in the policy proposals of the president and the Democratic congressional leaders. Before the break, Reagan gave a public address on his budget plan. During the recess, he continued to speak out on his proposed budget cuts, sent friendly members of Congress to hold news conferences on the issue in places where the president was personally popular, and lobbied members behind the scenes. Meanwhile, House Speaker Tip O'Neill, whose Democrats solidly controlled the House, spent the recess in Australia and New Zealand. When congressional members reconvened, the public had heard Reagan's message and, in key parts of the country, supported it, and conservative Democrats, feeling the public pressure, did not hesitate to abandon their own silent party leadership to support the president, giving him his first major victory in Congress. When asked if "he should have stayed home and mobilized opposition to the President's budget," the Speaker replied, "Who the hell knew that was going to happen while I was in New Zealand?"[1]

Fast-forward to May 2001. As the Memorial Day recess approached in Congress, President George W. Bush introduced his energy plan. Senate Republicans announced their "recess action plan" and encouraged their members to make appearances at gas stations in their states to emphasize high gas prices and talk up President Bush's plan.[2] Not to be outdone, the minority House Democrats bought advertising time to attack the president's energy policy in California and other states facing energy shortages and set up a website, grandoldpetroleum.com; they also arranged for House members to do radio and television interviews criticizing the president.[3] None of the congressional leaders went to New Zealand. The president's voice was not the only one heard during that congressional break. And Bush was never able to muster support to pass his energy bill.

These two episodes illustrate two important points about Congress. The first story reminds us that Congress as a whole is not often on the cutting edge of new trends. In 1982, the year after congressional Democrats ignored the importance of communicating to the public through the press, leaving the president to dominate the coverage, 179 congressional members had no press secretary or staff member listed with press responsibilities.[4] By contrast, presidents had been hiring press secretaries since Franklin Roosevelt was president, and the White House Office of Communications had been in existence since 1969. There is evidence that some in Congress had begun to recognize the usefulness of media relations in policymaking at least by 1977. That was the year Republican Senator Howard Baker became a surprise choice for minority leader. Party members chose him largely because they wanted "leaders who [could] act as effective spokesmen rather than as floor tacticians," and they saw Baker as more articulate than Senator Robert Griffin (R-MI) who ran against him.[5] However, Democrats, selecting Senator Robert Byrd as their leader, were apparently more interested in a tactician than a spokesperson. Even in the early 1980s, House Democrats continued to choose party leaders whose strength was moving legislation behind the scenes rather than dealing with the press. Change comes slowly to Congress.

But these stories also reveal that Congress does eventually catch on and evolve. At least partly in response to the budget disaster, Speaker O'Neill began holding daily press conferences that often included harsh attacks on President Reagan.[6] And the second story shows that by 2001, Congress clearly had learned the value of using the media to influence policymaking. Indeed, party leaders and individual members of Congress devoted considerable resources to media relations designed to attract and shape news coverage. Today, trying to influence media coverage is integral to both presidential and congressional efforts to shape, pass, and even implement policy. Although there is extensive research on the president's public strategies in policymaking,[7] surprisingly little has been written on Congress going public. The purpose of this book is to understand more about the evolution of going public in Congress over the last forty years and how political circumstances affect members' decisions to use the media and their ability to attract coverage to influence policymaking. Particularly, it examines how members have used public strategies to move beyond their institutional powers to supplement their formal powers and even overcome institutional weaknesses to influence national debates and policymaking.

DEFINING GOING PUBLIC IN CONGRESS

Before we go any further, I need to define exactly what I mean by going public in Congress. In his classic work, Samuel Kernell defined going public, in reference to the president, as "a class of activities that presidents engage in as they promote themselves and their policies before the American public ... in a way that enhances [their] chances of success in Washington."[8] As it applies to Congress, this definition requires some revision. While it is usually easy to distinguish the president's efforts to go public from his formal duties, that are often carried out in meetings behind closed doors, much of what members of Congress do is on display for television cameras, whether or not these activities are part of public strategies. Thus, our definition needs some qualification of intent to determine the class of activities that make up Congress's going public. And while this distinction is easy to see in theory, it does pose some problems in operationalizing the concept (which will be discussed later in the book).

A second aspect of the definition that raises concern in regard to Congress is the connection between promoting oneself and one's policy. It makes sense for a president to promote himself even if he is not eligible for re-election because higher approval ratings have been linked to success in Congress.[9] But for members of Congress, approval ratings matter mostly in the context of one's own constituents, not the public at large, making it less useful to talk about members of Congress going public to promote themselves. That would encompass a whole other set of activities designed primarily for re-election and directed toward a narrower audience, mostly their voting constituents.[10] Consequently, the definition of going public that I use in this book is a class of activities specifically intended to reach the public at large, generally by attracting media attention, that members of Congress engage in to promote their policies and/or to enhance their influence in the policymaking process.

Persuasion in the Public Sphere

Although the phrase "going public" has most often been used to describe the president's efforts to use the media to influence the policymaking process, the concept of public persuasion and its importance in the realm of politics is not original to modern American presidents. In Plato's *Gorgias*, Socrates and Gorgias discuss rhetoric as an important tool for persuasion and thus as essential for exercising power in a democracy.[11] Going public through the media merely expands the audience for political rhetoric.

Although going public to persuade is most closely associated with the presidency in American politics, the concept is not foreign to Congress. Typically, we think of members of Congress communicating with constituents for re-election purposes, claiming credit for what they have done for the district or state, taking positions on issues important to constituents, and just getting their names out to constituents.[12] But members do use the media to educate and persuade the public—not just constituents—and others in Congress and elsewhere in government.[13]

Members of Congress have always taken action intended to be noticed in the public sphere, though their methods have varied considerably over time.[14] In 1793, under the pseudonym Helvidius, Congressman James Madison penned a series of newspaper articles in response to Treasury Secretary Alexander Hamilton to attack President George Washington's Neutrality Proclamation. A few years later, Senator Pierce Butler leaked the Jay Treaty with Britain to Madison, and Senator S. T. Mason leaked it to the public, both hoping to encourage opposition to the policy and ultimately to change it.[15] In the early 1950s, Senator Joseph McCarthy publicized his allegations of communism through controversial hearings and investigations intended to reach an audience beyond Congress. And Senate Minority Leader Everett Dirksen and House Minority Leader Charlie Halleck resorted to frequent press conferences in the 1960s to shape public opinion and define the Republican Party's position on issues, especially in relation to the president.[16] In all of these cases, members wanted to make at least some part of the public aware of events and of the congressional members' or parties' positions on these issues.

Although we can find examples throughout congressional history of members trying to engage the public sphere to some extent, we cannot deny that members have taken it up a notch in recent decades, with their interest in using mass media to influence policymaking increasing dramatically over the last forty years. We can see the evidence in the growing number of press secretaries and communications staff on Capitol Hill and the policy role played by press relations staff in the offices of party and committee leaders.[17] And in just the last ten years, the number of congressional members taking to new media like Facebook and Twitter has exploded.[18] What accounts for the greater focus on going public? Why do members of Congress seek the media to influence policymaking? What do they hope to accomplish in going public?

Why Go Public?

The media have arguably become a political institution in their own right as the routine decisions reporters make about what is news and how to cover it affect political behavior and outcomes. Recognizing the media's central role in politics, Cook hypothesizes that political officials use the media to compensate for their own institutional weaknesses.[19] That is, they turn to the media to help them do what they cannot accomplish through their formal powers. This theory has the potential to explain the interest in the media for both Congress as an institution and also individual members of Congress, and it may offer insight into variations in congressional use of the media over time as power within Congress shifts with changes in rules and the political environment. Developments outside of Congress and within it over the last forty years have created not only disadvantages, weaknesses, or problems for Congress, its leaders, and rank-and-file members but also opportunities that may have encouraged congressional members to turn to the media to help cope with these challenges.

CHANGES OUTSIDE OF CONGRESS

The **decline of traditional intermediaries** as a primary way to communicate with the public, combined with the growing pervasiveness of the media, has changed communication within the political system. People have become less tied to political parties, with party identification weakening and campaigns becoming more candidate-centered,[20] and to interest groups and community groups than they were forty years ago.[21] At the same time, technological advances have made the media ubiquitous. Media are an efficient way to reach a national audience and are sufficiently diverse that various niche media can allow a politician to target specific audiences.[22] And the proliferation of media has created an appetite for political news, making members of Congress more in demand as sources.[23] Therefore, even as traditional intermediaries have declined, the media have readily filled the vacuum, providing an alternative avenue of communication for members of Congress who want or need to reach a national audience. The question then is why would members of Congress want to communicate nationally?

This brings us to a second important development outside of Congress—the well-documented increase in **presidents going public**. Presidents have long found the media a useful supplement to their formal powers,[24] and the integration of campaign-style media relations as a central tool in executive branch efforts to make policy is so complete that we now speak of the "permanent campaign."[25]

There are several ways going public can help the president. Talking through the media about an issue, which often increases public concern for the issue and puts it on the public agenda,[26] allows the president to raise the cost of congressional inaction and push the issue onto the legislative agenda as well. The president can also use the media to define or frame an issue, which can influence how the media cover it and in turn affect public opinion. People often have an array of competing considerations or values relevant to public issues.[27] The key to changing people's opinions may be to cue the "right" considerations that will cause them to re-evaluate their preferences and support the politician's preferred policy, a process referred to as priming.[28] In practice, political pundits often dismissively refer to this as spin, but there is a wealth of research that suggests agenda setting, framing, and priming have a real impact on public opinion and preferences for specific policies,[29] and presidents have certainly tried to reap the benefits of using media to bring about these effects.[30]

Presidential success with the media has not escaped the attention of congressional members. Given the possible benefits of going public, members of Congress can ill afford to allow the president to monopolize the media. Their experience with President Reagan "showed Democrats the danger of ceding the public forum to the president. . . . [As a result] congressional Democrats demanded that their leaders become more active participants in national debates."[31] Essentially, members of Congress have adopted more public strategies to compete with the president in educating the public and reaping the potential benefits of shaping media coverage.

Members of Congress may especially find public opposition to the president necessary when their own institutional powers fail to put them on an equal footing with the president to shape policy. This is particularly true in the realm of foreign policy, where the president's formal powers are considerable in comparison to Congress's. Members of Congress may try to influence the president's foreign policy, especially his use of military force, by taking public stands, conducting investigative hearings, publicly opposing the president, and introducing or debating legislation even when it has little chance of passing, all in an effort to influence both domestic and international public opinion.[32] Even during the initial stages of military conflict, when public opinion is often supportive of the president, scholars have found more media coverage of criticism of the president than praise as members of Congress attempt to influence the president's policy and subsequent levels of public support the president is able to obtain.[33]

In the realm of domestic issues, members of Congress often have more formal powers to influence policy, but they still find it useful to go public in opposition to the president. Understandably, those who are not in the president's party may choose to publicly oppose his policy proposals. In fact, if the opposition party is in the minority, it may have few formal powers to block the president's initiatives and thus may rely heavily on the media to generate public opposition to the president.[34] But members of the president's own party also oppose him publicly, though possibly for different reasons. One scholar noted that the president's own party was as likely to be a source of opposition as the other party over time, particularly when it was in the majority in Congress,[35] and others found that the president gets more public criticism than praise from his own party even though members of his own party are usually highly supportive of his proposals when it comes to voting for them in Congress.[36] These findings suggest that members of the president's party may publicly oppose his policies in an effort to change them *before* they are actually voted on in Congress.

CHANGES WITHIN CONGRESS

There is no doubt that presidents' increased reliance on going public has caused members of Congress to pay more attention to using the media to influence policymaking. But members of Congress are vying not just with the president to frame and shape policy; they must also compete with others in Congress. Developments within Congress have made inside strategies alone more difficult and perhaps less effective. Particularly, going public may help members cope with two growing trends, individualism and polarization, that have emerged in Congress over the last forty years.

Increasing **individualism** is evident in the demands of individual members of Congress for more freedom to pursue their own policy goals.[37] The American political system in general, not just Congress, has shifted from institutionalized pluralism, where policymaking took place largely among a handful of leaders in a particular policy area, to individualized pluralism, where leaders often speak with certainty only for themselves.[38] In Congress, the practical effect of this shift has been increased independence of members. And even though there has been a resurgence in party leadership within Congress (partly as a result of the demands and expectations of rank-and-file members, as we will see), the leaders have been limited by threats of revolts by factions within their parties. The network of congressional committees and subcommittees has also created little fiefdoms that pose challenges to the leadership. In addition, there are many other organized groups, such as the Congressional Black Caucus and the Freedom Caucus. These various power centers and sometimes conflicting attachments have made it difficult to know where to start building winning coalitions.

Consistent with the theory that political actors use the media "to help counter the main deficiencies they encounter in accomplishing their tasks,"[39] going public is one way to overcome the obstacle of communicating across these affiliations to signal potential coalition partners. In her study of congressional media entrepreneurs—members of Congress who seek to use the media to influence legislation—Karen Kedrowski found that these members see going public as a way to reach not only the public but also others in Congress, especially party leaders and congressional staff.[40] Her work suggests that media are a primary means of communicating within issue networks that include experts from interest groups, the bureaucracy, think tanks, and Congress.[41]

The second trend in Congress we need to consider is increasing **political polarization**. Congress has witnessed a striking decline in the number of moderates in both parties over the last thirty years, leaving the parties farther apart ideologically.[42] With common ground harder to find, making it more difficult to resolve policy differences through behind-the-scenes negotiation, members have turned to the media to shape policy, frame debate, and influence public opinion.[43]

One result of polarization has been the centralization of power in the hands of party leaders. Along with their enhanced powers in relation to committee chairs and their influence over members' committee assignments and party and campaign resources, party leaders have also added an important communications element to their jobs: what some have called message politics.[44] Led by Congressman Newt Gingrich (R-GA), Republicans began to embrace this idea in the early 1980s, as they made television an integral part of their strategy to confront Democrats rather than try to cooperate with them.[45] Senate leaders began to act as national party spokespersons on television. It is now standard for party leaders to be charged with promoting the image of the party and its message to help individual members reach collective goals. And in some cases, leaders "may not even be concerned with passing legislation but merely making debating points or forcing awkward votes for the other party's members with an eye to the next Senate [or House] election campaign."[46] As an aid to then Minority Leader Nancy Pelosi said, "'It's not about governing. We're focused on message.'"[47] In this way, going public has become an important tool for party leaders, one that links electoral and policy goals of the party and rank-and-file members.

A byproduct of polarization and possibly going public has been declining civility in Congress. Polarization makes it more difficult for members to compromise because of the gulf that exists between the parties. As a result, the parties are interested in either maintaining their majority or becoming the majority. Politics becomes a zero-sum game, where one party's victory is the other party's loss.[48] Their communications strategies reflect this reality as parties attack each other's policies, leadership, and motivations. For example, as negotiations over raising the debt limit broke down between Republicans and Democrats during the summer of 2011, Speaker John Boehner said, "I know the president's worried about his next election. But, my God, shouldn't we be worried about the country?" while Senate Democratic Leader Harry Reid put the blame on Boehner, saying the Speaker took a "'my way or the highway' approach."[49] This kind of rhetoric, while effective at attracting news coverage, undermines civility in Congress, which may make it harder to build relationships with members of the other party and can create obstacles to communication within Congress. Thus, going public may be needed as a way to communicate between parties. As journalist Juliet Eilperin reported, often in the 109th Congress when Minority Leader Nancy Pelosi wanted to communicate with Speaker Denny Hastert, she drafted a letter and released it to the press.[50]

BEYOND INSTITUTIONAL POWER

While going public is a way for members to cope with increasing individualism and polarization in Congress, it may also be the natural progression of changing norms in Congress and a new kind of member of Congress. Today's congressional members (think Senators Ted Cruz of Texas and Elizabeth Warren of Massachusetts) are often not content to wait until they have sufficient formal power to have an impact on policy. They are less willing to defer to seniority and committee chairs, and the plethora of media outlets allows both individuals and parties to take more initiative to accomplish their goals even when their formal powers are limited. Many of today's members are media-savvy individuals who see going public as one more tool to influence policy and enhance their own credibility in a policy area.[51] We see them using the media to supplement their formal power in several ways.

Members of Congress who find themselves in the minority, especially in the House of Representatives, have limited powers with which to influence policy. As one congressman who was in the minority once explained to students in my Congress class, "The question is not whether the majority will run over [the minority] but how many times they'll back the train up and run over you again." Certainly in the House, if the majority party is unified, its leaders have the powers to accomplish the majority's will, and they use those powers.[52] Scholars have found that the media have become an important resource for the minority party to oppose the majority in these situations. Political scientist Lawrence Dodd argues that the minority party's lack of power provides an incentive to pose a united front against the majority and facilitates "centralized coordination" by pursuing a national campaign with a coherent party agenda that focuses on current governing issues and highlights the "policy problems and perceived crises" that remain unsolved or perhaps are even caused by the majority.[53] And because of the media's interest in conflict, the minority party may find the media more receptive to its criticism of the majority than praise for the minority's own ideas.[54] These unified attacks on the majority party may serve two purposes for the minority—to stop legislation from passing and to improve the minority's electoral prospects.

Members of the majority party may also find it necessary to go public against their own party. It is typically more difficult for the majority party to speak with a unified voice. It is natural for majorities to become less cohesive over time as members begin to pursue their own constituent interests,[55] and this is certainly reflected in the coherence of the party's message.[56] Members may begin to oppose their own party publicly. But unlike *inter*party opposition, which is often intended to stop policy from passing, *intra*party opposition may stem from members using the media to "compete to define the party message" to bring it in line with a member's own position or that of her constituents.[57] Such criticism of the majority party from within may well be intended to communicate with the party leaders who shape the party message and image.[58]

Even in the Senate, where individuals and the minority party have more procedural tools, most notably the filibuster, to influence policy or at least to stop legislation from passing, members in the minority have found going public an important supplement to procedure. Those who use holds or filibusters alone to stop legislation run the risk of being labeled obstructionist. Therefore, senators have increasingly combined the threat of a filibuster with full-blown public relations campaigns that attempt to explain and justify their procedural strategies.[59]

Going public is not just an outlet to voice opposition to the majority. It can also be a way for those who are losing the debate to gain influence by bringing others into the discussion, often referred to as expanding the scope of conflict.[60] It may be difficult for members of Congress to change minds, but they can reframe an issue and shift attention to new dimensions of the conflict to bring in people and groups who were not previously interested in the issue.[61] "[I]ssue definition largely structures the coalitions of actors in a policy community."[62] In some cases, redefining the issue may not just result in a counter mobilization to stop a course of action; it may generate enthusiasm for a new idea that leads to policy change.[63]

At the very least, going public may enable members to increase the traceability or visibility of the actions taken by the majority so that members will be held accountable for the policy. Traceability is an important component in members' voting decisions in Congress.[64] If nonleaders or members of the minority in Congress can increase the awareness of a controversial vote, they may be able to influence votes or shape the legislation even if they are excluded from the formal markups and committee discussions surrounding the issue.

Sometimes members of Congress find themselves with no institutional platform to initiate or influence policy. In these circumstances, the media can be an important alternative in both the short and long term.[65] Committees are still the primary way for most members of Congress to influence the policy process, but members may have policy interests beyond their committee assignments. Media can help these members in two ways. First, in the short term, getting coverage of a particular issue may be a way to bypass the leadership and formal process to put issues on the legislative agenda and force members who do have power to take action. In the long term, many members find that getting coverage in conjunction with a particular issue is a way "to establish themselves as 'players.' "[66] If the media view them as credible spokespersons on an issue, others in Congress may be more likely to involve them on that issue to enhance their own credibility.

Another situation in which members need to supplement their formal powers through going public may be their efforts to influence action in the other house of Congress. The only formal process involving members of both the House and Senate is the conference committee. But before legislation can get to conference, it must be acted on in both houses, and individual members have no formal power to force the other house of Congress to act. Thus, going public to gain support for action may be the best way to pressure the other house to act. Congressman Dan Lipinski (D-IL) acknowledged using this tactic when he and Congressman Bob Inglis (R-SC) held a press conference with Senator Lindsey Graham (R-SC) after the passage of their H-Prize legislation in the House primarily to build support and pressure the Senate to pass the bill.[67]

Deciding to Go Public

As we have seen, members of Congress might want to go public for a variety of reasons. It facilitates communication within Congress and with policymakers outside of Congress. It can be used to build public support to shape and pass legislation or to build public opposition to stop legislation. It can be used to get around limited formal powers to accomplish policy and power goals as well as re-election goals. But going public is not and cannot be used in every situation or on every issue. We turn our attention now to the strategic context in which going public occurs and consider the factors that might affect members' decisions to go public. What challenges to going public are imposed by the media and what they are willing to cover? What impact do the political environment and polarization have in determining who can go public and on what issues they choose to do so?

WHAT THE MEDIA WILL COVER

Wanting to use the media is no guarantee that a politician will get media coverage.[68] The way the media cover Congress (or don't, as the case may be) creates obstacles members must overcome to go public. Perhaps the biggest problem is that coverage of Congress has declined over time, especially on network television.[69] And when the press does cover Congress, journalists often do not expect Congress to lead, just react.[70] This means that to go public, congressional members must overcome the media's lack of interest in Congress as an institution.

But that is just the first challenge. Members must also convince the media that they themselves are newsworthy. When a president wants to communicate to policymakers in Washington, he can hold a news conference or other event that the Washington media are likely to report. And if he decides he needs more direct appeals to the public, he can travel to congressional members' own backyards, where the local media are sure to relay his message. Because he is the president, he is newsworthy. However, for most members of Congress, this strategy will not work. National media are not interested in most members. The press tends to focus on members who have authority—primarily party and committee leaders—and those who have credibility as policy experts.[71] Journalists are also interested in mavericks who buck their party.[72] Members might try to gain attention in their state or district media, but this would reach only a limited audience, and they are not guaranteed coverage, even locally.[73]

The nature of news coverage of Congress presents additional challenges for members of Congress hoping to use the media to influence policymaking. Coverage of Congress is overwhelmingly focused on conflict.[74] By design, conflict is inherent in Congress. We find it among committees, between the two houses of Congress, between the two parties in Congress, among regional and ideological factions in Congress, and between Congress and the executive branch. Unfortunately for members of Congress, the media's preference for drama combined with the abundance of conflict in Congress often leads to coverage that amplifies the conflicts themselves and ignores or downplays the more substantive aspects of the disagreements. Scholars have found that policy coverage of Congress has declined while the focus on conflict has increased.[75] This may complicate members' efforts to go public to gain support for a policy or create a favorable image of their party. Members might find the media more receptive to going public as a means to refute, oppose, or obstruct someone else's policy, which capitalizes on the news value of conflict.

A second aspect of congressional coverage that may affect if and how members go public is the increasingly negative tone of coverage. The press does not just portray conflict in Congress; it also focuses on scandal and interbranch rivalry that frequently paint Congress and its members unfavorably.[76] Even when Congress is shown exercising oversight or launching investigations, its efforts are depicted as incompetent, grandstanding, and feeble.[77] Members may view the press as a source of power, but coverage often comes with a price. Former Speaker Newt Gingrich used the press to gain power, but as Speaker, his coverage was "relentlessly negative."[78] Members of Congress have to decide if they are willing to cater to the news values of the media in going public and also if they are ready to accept the potential consequences of going public in the form of negative attention to themselves.

THE POLITICAL CONTEXT

The political context in which members operate will shape the political calculus members use to determine if and how they decide to go public. Whether one is in the majority or minority party and how narrow the majority is, whether there is unified or divided government, and which party controls the White House all may influence how individual members and parties in Congress deploy public strategies. Let's consider the possible impact of each of these.

Members of the majority party have more formal resources to influence policymaking than do those in the minority. For this reason, members of the minority may be quicker to go public. But they may also face a higher hurdle for gaining coverage because they have less authority than members of the majority and thus may be of less interest to the media. As a result, they may need to restrict going public to issues on which the minority is united and more likely to attract media interest. While members of the minority may be more reliant on public strategies, the majority party members still have plenty of reasons for going public, as we have seen. They have an interest in framing issues and influencing the public agenda. This suggests that we might expect a difference in the goals the minority and majority parties have in going public. The majority may try to use the media to shape debate and pass legislation, while the minority may be more interested in going public to stop legislation.

How members go public may also be affected by how narrow the majority in Congress is. People in an institution are unlikely to challenge the status quo if there is little chance of success. But if expectations of success improve, we can expect more challenges.[79] Applying this to going public, we might expect minority members to use the media to pressure moderates in the other party to defect to defeat legislation or to change it. Narrow margins might also embolden factions within the majority to go public to pressure the leadership to make concessions.

Whether there is divided government or unified government and which party controls the White House are also likely to affect decisions to go public because these contexts change the various power structures for members of Congress. For example, the minority party in Congress is in a better position during divided government when it controls the White House than in unified government when both Congress and the presidency are controlled by the other party. In the latter situation, going public may literally be the only way for the minority to be heard, depending of course on how closely divided the Senate is. The majority party may find more reason to go public in divided government as it competes with the president than in unified government where the president may speak for the majority. A public relations campaign to influence policy may be more important during divided government because the majority party in Congress is in competition with the White House to frame the debate in a way that gives it an advantage in negotiating with the president.[80]

POLITICAL POLARIZATION

In addition to the periodic shifts in the political environment brought
about by congressional and presidential elections, long-term changes such
as polarization and the subsequent strengthening of party leaders might
also affect how going public is practiced over time. As some scholars have
argued, institutions are not fixed; they evolve in response to other institutions and processes.[81] Therefore, we would expect the changes polarization
has created in Congress to be evident in the ways members use the media
to work within Congress. Three specific aspects of going public may be
most affected by polarization: the issues members choose to publicize, the
impact on committee chairs' use of the strategy, and the partisan nature of
public messages.

As discussed earlier, polarization has enhanced the role of party leaders in coordinating and presenting the party's message in the media—
what some refer to as message politics.[82] But what issues do party leaders
choose to highlight in the press? In his important work on party communications, Patrick Sellers[83] has argued that party leaders will look for
issues on which their caucus has a consensus and issues the party owns;
that is, issues with which the public favorably associates the party.[84] Party
leaders will find it easier to coordinate their members' communication
on such issues. Lawrence Evans fleshes this out further by incorporating
the distinct roles of the majority and minority parties in Congress.[85] He
explains that minority party issues are those on which the public is favorable, the minority is united, but the majority is divided. Minority leaders
will use procedural and public avenues to push the majority into dealing with these issues. Majority party leaders will try to keep these off the
public agenda or find ways to link them to issues owned by the majority.
Leaders in both parties will have to deal with shared issues, such as the
budget, but both will try to frame these issues favorably by linking them
to issues favorable to the party.[86]

A second change in Congress that has accompanied increasing polarization is the subjugation of committee chairs to party leaders. Beginning
in the 1980s, party leaders began to take a more active role in shaping

policy, sometimes coordinating committee activities or, in some cases, bypassing committees to push their party's policy goals.[87] The 1994 elections that installed new Republican majorities in both the House and Senate enhanced the party leaders' power even further as they limited the terms of committee chairs and in the House increased the Speaker's power over committee chairs.[88] This ebb and flow of power between committee chairs and party leaders could have an impact on public strategies in Congress. The electoral concerns, message politics (communication), and legislative agendas of the parties are inextricably linked, and party leaders are likely to be highly involved in issues that are matters of message politics.[89] Becoming more active in policy and eclipsing committee chairs in their power would also make the party leaders more attractive to the media even on policy-related matters where committee chairs had been the center of power in the past. Therefore, we might expect committee chairs to find it more difficult over time to go public to influence policy except on issues that party leaders do not consider part of their message politics.[90]

Finally, as polarization has focused more attention on the parties in Congress, we might expect a partisan tone in going public, with fewer members using public strategies to oppose their own party or tout bipartisan efforts in policymaking. Competitive parties (associated with polarization) are likely to promote disagreement even if compromise or consensus is possible, especially if the majority is narrow.[91] This attention to disagreement may manifest itself in the way members of Congress respond not only to each other but also to the president through the media. Indeed, research shows that a coherent party message "is more achievable through negative commentary about the opposition" than communication about the party's policy preferences.[92] And certainly this bitter partisan conflict coincides well with current news values, perhaps making it easier to attract media attention.[93] The result may be that members of Congress are less likely to voice publicly criticisms of their own party or president than they once were. Members may also face more pressure to follow their party rather than working with members or presidents across party lines. To the extent that they do engage in such bipartisan policymaking, members may choose to avoid the public spotlight and the subsequent suspicion or ire of their fellow partisans.

Understanding Going Public in Congress

Members of Congress have clear incentives to go public by using the media during the policymaking process, and there is evidence that they devote extensive resources to media relations. Furthermore, much of the existing research on Congress suggests the importance of communications and the media to members' accomplishing their policy goals. We see claims that Congressman Gingrich and the Republicans "challenged" House Democrats or congressional members "pushed issues" and "mounted sustained assaults."[94] Such statements imply that members did this publicly through the press, but the communications aspect remains implicit in most scholarly research on Congress; explicit and systematic consideration of going public in Congress is relatively infrequent with a few notable exceptions.[95] And most textbooks on Congress make little mention of media and Congress. Even as scholars acknowledge that members of Congress can influence policymaking by reframing issues or changing the way we discuss issues, they admit that how this occurs is not well understood.[96] This is in stark contrast to the explicit central role of media and communications strategy in understanding the presidency, its power, and success.

Why have members' efforts to use public strategies to influence the policy process often been neglected? First, scholars have dismissed this strategy as being uncertain and too complex, and its success is hard to measure.[97] We do not have the kind of concrete data that are readily available in congressional voting studies or presidential archives, for example. And how can we tell when going public has changed the trajectory of a policy? A second major problem is the perception that this does not really help predict outcomes or behavior in Congress, and until recently, many believed that only a small percent of members of Congress were involved in public strategies.[98] This may also be a consequence of the tendency to treat institutions as fixed over time.

Some scholars, however, have argued that we need to recognize that institutions do "evolve over time in response to new issues and the actions of competing institutions."[99] Although in the 1970s Congress may not have been interested in going public, by the 1980s it found itself having to adapt to media-savvy presidents. Members adjusted their strategies to take into account the strategies of other players in the policy process and changes in the media themselves. In David Mayhew's words, members of Congress "operat[e] in the public sphere with consequence," but much of political science has overlooked this idea.[100]

This book accepts the invitation to consider Congress in the public sphere and explores explicitly and systematically how members use the media to influence national policy and debate and how this may have changed over time. In doing so, it attempts to answer several questions: who in Congress has successfully gone public and for what purposes?[101] How has this strategy evolved over the last forty years? What are the strategic decisions that members make about when and on what issues to go public? And what impact does the political environment have on members' decisions to go public or the media's willingness to cover these efforts? What evidence is there that members can use public strategies to supplement their institutional power or overcome institutional weakness?

DATA AND METHODS

To study going public and how it has changed over the last forty years, I rely primarily on news coverage of congressional members' public statements. Specifically, I used coverage of Congress in the *New York Times* from 1977 to 2015 and interviews with congressional members on NBC's Sunday morning talk show *Meet the Press* from 1990 to 2009.[102] The *New York Times* has been an important and respected contributor to national policy debates throughout the time period I wanted to study, and it is generally reflective of mainstream news media throughout this era. *Meet the Press* has often been the leading voice among the Sunday talk shows, and its complete transcripts went back farther than other talk shows at the time I was gathering data.

From the *New York Times'* coverage, I created two data sets that look at successful cases of going public in Congress generally. The first (referred to as the full data set) consists of a random sample of three days when Congress was in session in each year from 1977 to 2015 and includes 921 cases of going public. The purpose of this data set is to see what is covered about Congress and who in Congress has success in going public on a *typical* day in each year of the study. The second data set (referred to as the transition year data) focuses on transition years between 1977 and 2001. With the help of students in my media and politics courses in 2005, I analyzed two months of coverage (January and May) of each year that marked the first year of a new presidential administration (1977, 1981, 1989, 1993, and 2001) or that followed a shift in partisan control of either house of Congress (1987 and 1995). I chose transition years because these are times of high congressional activity and a likely time that members would be using public strategies for a variety of reasons. I focused on January and May because they tend to be active months in Congress and they encompass different points in the legislative cycle.[103] This data set includes 3,713 cases of going public and allows us to follow congressional public strategies over a more sustained period of time to see how they develop.

For both data sets, my research assistants and I selected all articles from the days we observed coverage that quoted or paraphrased a member of Congress commenting on a public issue, policy, or event related to his or her job in Congress. Because this book is interested in how congressional members use the media to influence policymaking and the national debate in the interest of shaping policy, we did not include articles focused only on campaign-related issues or the members' private lives unless they were related to their work in Congress. Similarly, the *Meet the Press* data included all interviews with members of Congress unless they focused exclusively on elections. That yielded 915 interviews over the twenty-year period. In all data sets, each member of Congress quoted or paraphrased constituted a case. For details about coding, see the Appendix.

I supplemented the analysis of the general news coverage with several additional data sets. Chapter 4 includes discussion of a small sample of congressional members' communication via Twitter, Facebook, and YouTube that allows for comparisons between how members use traditional news media and the unfiltered new media. And Chapters 5 through 7 provide more in-depth case studies of congressional efforts to going public over time on particular issues or by specific groups or individuals. These data will be discussed in more detail in those chapters.

Some may question the use of news coverage to study going public. After all, it does not tell us who attempted to go public, only who received coverage. One might argue that press releases or media events would be a better way to study what members of Congress have tried to do to go public. While there is some validity to this argument, there are several problems with this kind of data. First, they are not readily available for any period of time beyond the last couple of years. Recent press releases for some members of Congress and the parties can be found on their websites, but there is no accessible archive of press releases or record of congressional press events that dates back forty years. Second, congressional members do many things that are important in getting news coverage that are not captured in a press release—for example, impromptu conversations with reporters and personal efforts to cultivate reporters. Third, press releases and archives of media events would tell us nothing about which statements or events actually received coverage. Focusing on news coverage of members' public statements is a more manageable way to see the public efforts that were actually successful in gaining news coverage over more than three decades whether they stemmed from press releases, media events, or conversations with reporters, and it allows us to see what was communicated.

Furthermore, other studies have found that news coverage does reflect what elites are doing even if it does not fully report every event or statement.[104] As Lawrence Jacobs and Robert Shapiro argue, "the overall pattern of the media's reporting mirrors the intensity, content, and relative degree of dissensus in ongoing policy debates among authoritative government officials."[105] Their evidence supports their claims that coverage is driven by the "statements, behavior, and events in the political world."[106] Research on Congress by Sellers offers substantial evidence that politicians' public statements "appeared to shape news coverage" as public relations efforts increased coverage of members' messages and differences in the promotional efforts of parties were reflected in coverage.[107] His study also found that messages that were promoted more frequently received more coverage. Of course, both studies acknowledge that media coverage is not an exact reproduction of reality. Jacobs and Shapiro note that the media's own interests lead them to emphasize or exaggerate the level of conflict, and Sellers finds that reporters did try to balance the more frequent messages with coverage of competing messages, even when it meant giving "more coverage to the disadvantaged party than their promotional efforts would" lead us to expect.[108] Overall, however, there appears to be strong evidence that media coverage of politics reflects the reality of politics and the strategies of politicians, making news coverage an acceptable means to study successful cases of going public. Recognizing the limitations of this approach, however, where possible, I will draw on other existing data and interviews to determine whether coverage is an accurate representation of what congressional members were trying to do in the press.

PLAN OF THE BOOK

Guided by the theory laid out here in Chapter 1, the next three chapters look systematically at how members of Congress have gone public through the media and how this has changed during the last forty years. In Chapter 2, I look at who in Congress has successfully gone public on what issues and how they have gone public. Chapter 3 is concerned with why members go public. Chapter 4 looks at members' presence on television over time and their more recent use of new media, including Twitter and Facebook. These three chapters offer evidence that the institutional power of congressional members (or the lack of it) and the political context are related to members' ability to go public and what they communicate and try to accomplish through their public strategies.

Chapters 5 through 7 examine three case studies of going public in Congress that provide evidence that members do use the media to compensate for their institutional weaknesses. Chapter 5 takes an institutional perspective in looking at how congressional members have used public strategies to respond to presidential proposals to reform Social Security and how these have changed over time in response to developments in Congress. Chapter 6 focuses on how groups in Congress can employ the media, examining how the Congressional Black Caucus has used the media over the last four decades through changes in the political environment and its own institutional power. Chapter 7 moves to the individual level with a study of two relatively junior senators to see how they have used media to compensate for their institutional weaknesses and adapted media strategies to different goals, ultimately extending their influence well beyond what their institutional powers could accomplish.

In the final chapter, I consider the effectiveness of going public and offer a final assessment of going public as a way for members of Congress to move beyond their institutional power in Congress to influence policy.

Four Decades of Going Public in Congress

In 1977 Senate Majority Whip Alan Cranston (D-CA) announced he would discontinue briefing the press following Democratic leaders' meetings with President Jimmy Carter after other Democratic congressional leaders criticized him for revealing their private disagreements with President Carter.[1] But times change. In 1995, new House Speaker Newt Gingrich (R-GA) held daily news conferences with reporters and frequently criticized President Bill Clinton and Democrats in the press. Today it is quite common for congressional leaders in either party to brief the press and freely air their criticisms or reservations following (or even before) meetings with the president, and in many cases, they do so on the White House driveway rather than waiting till they get back to Capitol Hill.

And it is not just party leaders who have resorted to the media to try to influence public opinion and policymaking over the last forty years. Committee leaders have learned that celebrity witnesses at committee hearings draw more press (and sometimes more committee members) than experts and bureaucrats. So actor Ben Affleck is invited to speak at a hearing on the Congo, and comedian Stephen Colbert testifies at a hearing on immigration reform. Rank-and-file members too have turned to the press to help influence the legislative agenda and policymaking. From Congressman Tony Hall (D-OH) going on a hunger strike in 1993 to call attention to hunger in the United States and advocate for a permanent committee on hunger to Senators Jim DeMint (R-SC) and Tom Coburn (R-OK) denouncing pork projects in legislation to force leaders in both parties to get serious about earmark reform in 2007, members of both parties in both houses of Congress have found public strategies useful. The advent of new media has expanded their options, as Twitter now allows members to respond immediately and publicly to presidential speeches, meetings, and other events.

But while we know going public has become an important part of policymaking over the last forty years, we know little about how it has developed—who uses it successfully, on what issues, or how they go public and how any of this varies over time or is affected by changing political environments or long-term trends in polarization and political power in Congress. That is the subject of this chapter.

GOING PUBLIC OVER TIME

Looking at the big picture, we find in the *New York Times* coverage from the full data set that sampled three days each year from 1977 to 2015 that the number of successful cases of going public each year varied greatly, with a low of 7 in 2008 and a high of 67 in 1987. Dividing the time period into thirds, we find the average number of cases of going public that made the news each year remained relatively stable: it was 24 annually from 1977 to 2002 and went up slightly to 25 cases from 2003 to 2015. One important caveat about the increase during the most recent thirteen-year period is in order: in 2011, the *New York Times* began running regular online content and blogs that did not appear in the print edition of the newspaper. If we drop the cases that appeared only in the online content, the average number of cases per year from 2003 to 2015 falls to 21. This decline confirms what others have found: traditional media coverage of Congress has declined during the last thirty years,[2] which would make it harder for members to get coverage for their public strategies over time in traditional media. But it appears that the online content of traditional newspapers may mitigate the trend somewhat.

If we shift our attention to the transition-year data, the time periods where Congress was perhaps more newsworthy because of changes in partisan control of the presidency or Congress, we see a slightly different picture. The average number of cases of going public that made the news in January and May during the transition years before 1994, before party leaders began to focus so much attention on media strategies, was 509; that number went up to 583 in the transition years after 1994, when public strategies became central to the party organizations and increasingly important to most rank-and-file members. When the patterns of the two data sets are combined, they suggest that it may be harder to get traditional print news coverage of Congress today than it once was, making it more difficult to employ public strategies successfully; but at times where the political situation makes Congress more newsworthy, concerted efforts to gain media attention can be successful in attracting coverage for congressional members. In short, the media's interest in Congress may well play a role in when members of Congress might reasonably plan to go public and the amount of effort required to do so successfully.

There is additional evidence that the political context has an important influence on public strategies or their success in getting covered. Coverage of going public in Congress was highest in years following midterm elections—about 30 cases per year compared to 22 in other years. The contrast was even starker in the transition-year data where the years after midterm elections contained on average almost 150 more cases (635) than the years following presidential elections (489). Overall, cases of going public were most common in nonelection years, with an average of 27 cases per year in the full data set compared to only 20 per year during elections. Presidential election years were least amenable to congressional going public, with 15 cases per year. Additionally, cases were more frequent in times of divided government (26 per year) than unified government (19). This pattern was also true of transition years, which averaged 549 cases a year in divided government compared to 491 during unified government.

The interaction we see between the political context and the successful cases of going public suggests some limitations members of Congress may face in going public. First, members may find it difficult to compete with elections for the media's attention. Cases of going public clearly dropped during both midterm and presidential election years, but there is no reason to suspect that members are less interested in trying to shape policy debates during election years. In fact, they may be keenly interested in framing debates during an election, but the available news space may be substantially reduced as reporters focus on campaigns. Second, divided government may offer more opportunities than unified government for members of Congress to go public: the media are more interested in conflict that inevitably arises when different parties control the legislative and executive branches of government or the two houses of Congress.

But before we declare members of Congress to be completely at the mercy of the predilections of journalists, we should also consider the possibility that the patterns we see in coverage of going public are a reflection of reality. Members of Congress may actually be going public less during election years if for no other reason than they are focused on their own re-election back home in their district or state. And during unified government, the majority party may have less incentive to go public because it has more power to enact its policies through legislative processes it controls and because it defers to the president to communicate the party's message. That leaves the minority party or disgruntled members of the majority as the ones most likely to need to resort to public strategies during times of unified government, possibly reducing the number of cases of going public that the media could cover. The next section looks more closely at these possibilities, examining who in Congress goes public and when they succeed in doing so.

WHO GOES PUBLIC?

Clearly, some members of Congress have more incentive to go public than others. And there is reason to suspect some may be more successful at it. So who has gone public successfully? Rank-and-file members of Congress made up a slight majority of those whose public efforts made the news, with 53 percent of the cases over thirty-nine years in the full data set. Committee leaders accounted for just under a third of the cases, and party leaders about 16 percent. Two-thirds of the cases involved majority party members, while minority members made up only one-third. Democrats went public in 57 percent of the cases, and Republicans did so in 40 percent, perhaps the result of Democrats controlling one or both houses of Congress in twenty-seven of the thirty-nine years compared to just twenty-three years of congressional control for Republicans. Just under half of the cases involved members of the president's party. And senators went public in a little more than half of the cases. Although the exact percentages differed slightly, these patterns held in transition years.

Overall, the trends in coverage of who has gone public in Congress have remained remarkably consistent over time. In all but six years, rank-and-file members received the most coverage of their public efforts, usually followed by committee leaders and then party leaders. And if we divide the thirty-nine-year time period into thirds, we see only slight changes over time in the percent of cases involving party leaders, committee leaders, and rank-and-file members. However, when we look more at the contexts that might affect who chooses to go public and who gets covered, we find some interesting and significant changes over time. The cases involving members of Congress in the president's own party have declined over time as have the cases involving Democrats. And the cases in which members in the congressional minority go public have steadily increased over time.

The changes we see in who goes public are consistent with several important developments over the last three decades and with distinctions linked to changes in the political context. As we examine these more closely, we will see that the centralization of power in the hands of party leaders and their subsequent focus on communication over time is evident in the patterns of who goes public, and we will find that members have learned to use the media to compensate for institutional weaknesses as public strategies have become a valuable resource for minority members of Congress. We will also examine the impact of the political environment on members' ability to employ public strategies.

Congressional Leaders

It is not particularly surprising that rank-and-file members account for more of the cases of going public covered by the news. After all, they do substantially outnumber congressional leaders. But when we look at the specific members who received media attention for their public statements, we find congressional leaders dominating the list of those covered most frequently. Of the nine House members who were covered at least five times in the sample of coverage from the thirty-nine-year period, only one, Stephen Solarz, did not hold committee or party leadership positions at the times he was quoted. In the Senate, nineteen members were quoted in six or more articles. Only one of these senators held no leadership position at the time: Daniel Patrick Moynihan from New York—thus the hometown senator for the *New York Times*.

What is somewhat puzzling about congressional leaders in the coverage is that their cases of going public have not increased over time in relation to the public efforts of rank-and-file members. The enhanced powers given to party leaders and the increasing polarization of Congress during the last forty years would lead us to expect more coordinated communication led especially by party leaders. Have these changes in Congress simply failed to influence members' public efforts or the media's coverage of them? The transition-year data set may be more useful for answering this question because it allows us to analyze sustained coverage collected over month-long periods of time, something that coverage from three random, nonconsecutive days during a year does not permit. And because these transition years follow elections with major consequences for partisan control and the direction of policy, we would expect them to be times where congressional leaders would be more important for setting the agenda and framing policy debates.

THE INCREASING PUBLIC ROLE OF PARTY LEADERS

Indeed, the coverage from the transition years indicates that over time congressional leaders have made up a larger share of those going public. In 1977 party and committee leaders accounted for just over one-third of the cases. In the 1980s through 1993, that number rose to between 40 and 43 percent. In the final two years of the analysis, leaders were involved in nearly 48 percent of the cases.

Much of the increase in going public over time by congressional leaders can be attributed to the increasing focus of party leaders on communication. Figure 2.1 shows the percent of cases by party leaders, committee leaders, and rank-and-file members over time. Although party leaders rarely exceeded the number of cases involving committee leaders, they did narrow the gap over time. Coinciding with increasing polarization in Congress, party leaders have become even more prominent as the percent of going public done by party leaders rose significantly in the years after 1994. The variation in behavior of committee leaders is less consistent and shows no overall change from the periods before and after 1994. Analysis of the correlation between leaders and the year of coverage reveals that party leaders going public significantly increased in the coverage over time, while there was no significant change for committee leaders' coverage over time.

The evolution of public strategies as a tool for party leaders is even more interesting when we look at differences between the parties.[3] Chapter 1 noted that Republicans were the first to choose their party leaders based primarily on their ability to interact with the media rather than their

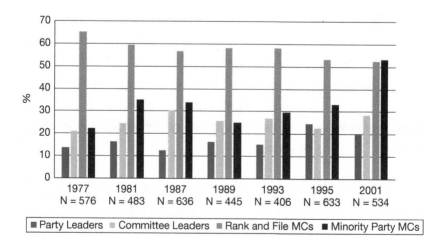

Figure 2.1 Who Goes Public

knowledge of parliamentary procedure, as evidenced by their selection of Howard Baker as minority leader in 1977. And certainly Republican Newt Gingrich took the communications role of party leaders to a new level—in both the minority and majority. He is often credited with popularizing the strategy of "being as outrageous as possible" to get publicity while he was still in the minority as he encouraged his fellow partisans to demonize opponents in their floor speeches and use the rhetoric of good and evil to dramatize issues.[4]

The Republicans' emphasis on their leaders going public and Gingrich's personal influence is clear in the transition-year data. In 1977 Republicans accounted for only 20 percent of all party leaders going public. That jumped to 29 percent in 1981, with no mentions of Gingrich appearing yet. Perhaps this increase was just a result of Republicans gaining the majority in the Senate that year, but their percentage climbed even higher, to 32 percent, in 1987 despite their loss of the Senate, and still Gingrich accounted for only two cases that year. Republicans continued increasing their percentage of the cases of going public until it peaked at 69 percent in 1995, the year Gingrich became House Speaker, and dropped back to 54 percent in 2001, a year where the Senate was evenly split and Republican leaders had to compete for attention with a new president from their own party. The full thirty-nine-year data set corroborates this pattern, with the Republicans' share of the cases significantly rising in the later years of coverage. Further evidence that going public has become more centralized among Republicans compared to Democrats can be found in the increasingly larger share of cases involving Republican Party leaders compared to others in their own party during the transition periods from 1989 forward. The same trend does not exist among Democrats.

THE IMPORTANCE OF POLITICAL CONTEXT

Thus far we have seen that going public has become a more common tool for party leaders over time, especially among Republicans, but as is the case with most political tools, going public is used strategically. It is not equally needed by all members, nor is it universally useful. And because it comes with some potential costs, leaders may use it more in some situations than in others. Another important consideration for congressional members is when the media are willing to cover public strategies. The question we consider next is in what political contexts party leaders are most likely to need and be able to use public strategies.

As suggested in Chapter 1, members of Congress are most likely to turn to the media to augment their institutional powers and particularly to compensate for institutional weaknesses. Although the formal powers of party leaders are determined by the party caucuses and the rules of each house of Congress, the relative strength and weakness of party leaders depends in part on the overall political context—specifically, whether the party leaders are in the majority or minority in the House or Senate, whether their party controls the White House, and whether there is unified government, with one party controlling both Congress and the White House, or divided government, where each party controls one branch, or even whether control of Congress itself is split between the two parties.

Minority party leaders are certainly in the most disadvantageous position in terms of their institutional powers to influence policymaking. In the House they may have no input in crafting legislation in an era of unorthodox lawmaking where major bills may not go through normal committee processes.[5] And if the majority party is unified in the House, the minority is powerless even to stop the legislation given the majority's tight control over the rules for debate.[6] Although the Senate rules offer a little more protection for the minority, Senate minority party leaders may be limited to using the filibuster as their only real formal power to influence policy. And if the majority controls close to the sixty votes needed to invoke cloture, the position of minority party leaders may be little better than that of their House counterparts. In such climates, minority party leaders may adopt the strategy of going public to enlarge the scope of conflict to try to change their relative bargaining position. It may be the only way to influence policy given the limits of their institutional power. However, the media may be less interested in covering the minority precisely because of this lack of power. Indeed, although minority party leaders became a slightly larger percentage of those going public over time in both the full data set and the transition-year data, their numbers remained quite small compared to coverage of others going public.

Times of unified government only magnify the problem for the minority because they do not have a president of their own party to represent their interests in policymaking as they would in divided government. Going public may become even more necessary under such conditions. The good news for minority leaders is that, though they have less formal power, they may be more newsworthy in unified government as the voice of opposition to both the president and the majority in Congress. In fact, minority party leaders made up a greater percentage of leaders going public in unified government compared to divided government (47 versus 30 percent over the thirty-nine-year time period), a trend that held in transition years as well.

Although minority party leaders may have the greatest need for public strategies, leaders in both parties go public, and the political context appears to figure into their abilities to do so. Coverage of public strategies was greater during divided government than in unified government. Across thirty-nine years, this averaged to 9 more cases a year when control of Congress was divided and 5 more cases a year when one party controlled Congress and the other held the presidency compared to years with unified government. Party leaders seemed best able to get coverage when control of Congress was split as they averaged 2 cases more per year than in unified or divided government. Committee leaders were most covered during a split Congress or divided government (2 cases more per year than in unified government in both data sets).

In the transition-year coverage, the impact of the political context was even more apparent. Nearly half the cases involving party leaders occurred during divided government compared to 39 percent in unified government. That is, 103 cases of leaders going public per year in divided government and only 83 per year in unified government. Fifty-seven percent of cases with committee leaders occurred during divided government, and only one-third took place during unified government—an average of 217 cases per year in divided government and only 126 per year under unified control.

This pattern makes sense theoretically. During unified government, with one party controlling Congress and the White House, there is presumably less disagreement between the legislative and executive branches, especially early in the president's term, when the transition-year data were mostly collected. Thus, members in the majority in Congress may find it less necessary (or prudent) to battle publicly with the president. Similarly with one party controlling both houses of Congress, differences can be worked out behind the scenes among majority party and committee leaders. In contrast, divided government often pits the majority party against the president in a battle for public support of each side's preferred policies. This theory finds support in the fact that party leaders in the president's party were somewhat less likely to go public than leaders in the opposing party (43 to 55 percent). It is not clear whether leaders simply deferred to a president in their own party or whether they found it difficult to compete with him for news attention because journalists typically find the president more newsworthy, but the result is the same: going public may be both easier and more necessary when control of the government is divided between the two parties. The political context matters.

Minority Members

One of the most interesting developments in going public we see in the coverage over the last three decades is the growing attention to members in the congressional minority. Their share of the cases went from 28 percent in the first thirteen years to 33 percent in the next thirteen and up to 39 percent in the final thirteen years. Only four times in the twenty-six years from 1977 through 2002 did minority members account for more than 40 percent of the cases covered. That threshold occurred seven times in the thirteen years from 2003 through 2015. This pattern is equally evident in transition years, where new presidents or new majorities might be expected to steal the media spotlight. Instead, the cases of minority members going public trended up over time, with a low of 22 percent of all cases in 1977 up to a third of all cases in 1995 and more than half in 2001 (see Figure 2.1).

There are no obvious reasons the media would have become more interested in minority members over time, so something else appears to be at work here. Two explanations, both related to increasing political polarization in Congress, seem plausible. First, as polarization has left the parties more internally homogeneous, there may be less public dissension within each party. Therefore, although the media may be more interested in covering members who are in the majority because they have more power to influence policy, reporters may have to look to the minority to provide the conflict and drama that reporters crave in their stories. If majority party members are less likely to oppose each other, the minority party may find it can get coverage if it is willing to criticize the majority publicly. Second, the polarization in Congress has made it less likely the majority will make legislative concessions to the minority party, especially in the House, where the majority rarely needs minority votes to pass legislation. Therefore, minority members who once were able to influence policy through legislative processes may now find those routes closed to them, making public strategies not only a more attractive option but possibly the only option. Their increased efforts to go public would reasonably result in more coverage of minority messages.

The transition-year coverage lends further validity to these explanations if we look at how the political context relates to coverage of minority members' efforts to go public. In unified government, when the minority party is at its weakest, minority members make up 4 percent more of the cases of going public than they do in times of divided government. The increase is small but statistically significant.

Looking at who has had success in going public and how this has changed over time has provided evidence that the political context—both the periodic shifts from unified to divided government and the long-term growth of political polarization—has some impact on members' ability and possibly desire to go public. In addition, we have seen that members have been able to use the strategy when they lack institutional power. The next section looks more closely at the issues on which they have been able to go public.

GOING PUBLIC ON WHAT ISSUES?

A public strategy does not suit all issues. Some may be too complex, some too sensitive, possibly involving classified information. Some policy questions may affect too small a segment of society to be helped by a public strategy, or the necessary policy solutions might be unpopular and a public strategy would bring unwanted attention. Furthermore, it is not just members of Congress who determine which issues are ripe for a public strategy. The reality is that journalists are not interested in covering all issues. Some topics are simply considered more newsworthy than others, especially those affecting large numbers of people and those involving conflict or controversy. Reporters also prefer issues that are relatively easy to understand or that can be simplified.

Consistency on Issues

Given these considerations, there is incredible consistency in which issues members were able to go public on over time. In the *New York Times* over the full thirty-nine years, budgets and taxes,[7] foreign policy, and government affairs—which includes such topics as campaign finance reform, investigations into government agencies, and congressional ethics or scandals—were the most frequently covered subjects of members' public statements with 14 percent each. Just behind those with 11 percent of the cases were defense or national security issues. The next most common issues, each making up 6 to 8 percent of the cases, were executive and judicial appointments, health care, and business and regulation. The final issues that were covered somewhat regularly (3 to 5 percent of cases) included the economy, crime, energy, the environment, and social policy.

The picture in transition years is quite similar. Budgets and taxes were the subject of a fifth of all cases of going public. Government affairs was second at 16 percent. Because the time periods studied included a disproportionate number of new presidential administrations, appointments received somewhat more attention than they did in the full data set (nearly 11 percent). Foreign policy followed closely with about 10 percent of the cases. In addition to these topics, health care, social welfare policies, business and regulation, defense and national security, and party politics received regular attention in the press. Of the issues most covered in transition years, only party politics received little attention in the full data set.

The consistency with which budgets and taxes, foreign policy, and government affairs appear as issues for going public raises the question of whether this was merely the result of media interest in the subject or a true reflection of congressional interest. The Policy Agendas Project offers a way to answer this question.[8] The data compiled on the project website indicate that the most common topics seen in the transition-year coverage were among the top five subjects of congressional hearings held during the same time periods, suggesting that the media accurately reflected what was going on in Congress.

So why would members of Congress use public strategies most frequently on these issues? Many of these subjects are a predictable and recurring part of the legislative cycle, and that makes it easy to attract the attention of reporters who like to follow routines and predictable storylines. Members have to debate the budget every year. Presidential appointments occur routinely, particularly at the beginning of each administration. In foreign policy, the particular countries and situations may change, but as a superpower, the United States is always involved in foreign policy. In 1977, it was Israel and the Middle East (OK, some things don't change), the Iran-Contra affair in 1987, the North American Free Trade Agreement (NAFTA) in 1993, and the US war on terror following the September 11 attacks in 2001. Other issues members chose to go public on resulted from persistent problems, like the rising costs of health care or the solvency of Social Security, which are much debated but rarely permanently resolved. All of these issues may be easy for members to get covered on because they fit the media's definition of newsworthiness in that they have a major impact on a large number of people. Other issues that appeared frequently, such as government affairs and appointments, satisfy another news value: conflict and controversy.

What Determines the Issues?

When we move beyond the most covered issues and look at what members were talking about in each year, we see shifts from year to year and over the larger time span. Issues seem to come and go in Congress, with one topic being a major focus in some years and practically disappearing in others. For example, within the transition years, energy was the fifth most mentioned issue in 1977, but it did not account for even 1 percent of the cases in any other year except 2001. And across the full thirteen years, 85 percent of the cases related to energy issues occurred between 1977 and 1992; only 15 percent occurred in the following twenty-three years. Thirty-five percent of the cases related to defense and national security issues took place from 1977 to 1989, but only 17 percent occurred over the next thirteen years; that jumped up to 48 percent from 2003 to 2015. What explains such variations from year to year or longer? Several possibilities stand out: the president's agenda, real-world events, and changes over time in the political landscape.

Scholars have long noted the influence of the president's agenda on congressional behavior.[9] Presidents have a range of venues in which to introduce their legislative priorities—from the State of the Union address to major addresses and political travel around the country to press conferences and direct communication with Congress. If the president's party controls all or part of Congress, his agenda is likely to be given top priority in Congress, especially early in his tenure. But even in times of divided government, the president's concerns are likely to be considered by Congress even if his specific proposals go nowhere.[10] If for no other reason, media interest in what the president is talking about may force members of Congress, particularly those in leadership positions, to respond to the president's concerns and proposals.

Because the transition-year data include two full months of coverage in each year, they allow us to see what factors likely affected the issues members chose to go public on and which ones were covered. Table 2.1 lists the top issues members of Congress talked about publicly in the *New York Times* for each year of the study. The issues in bold were not a top issue of

Table 2.1 ISSUE AGENDAS

Year	*New York Times*	Hearings	President
1977	Gov't affairs	Appointments	Budget/taxes
	Budget/taxes	Energy	Economy
	Appointments	Gov't affairs	Energy
	Foreign policy[1]	Business	Social policy
	Energy	Budget/taxes	Environment
	Environment	Environment	Gov't affairs (ethics)
	Economy	Defense	
		Economy	
1981	Budget/taxes	Budget/taxes	Budget/taxes
	Appointments	Gov't affairs	Economy
	Social policy	Business	Defense
	Foreign policy	Environment	Business (deregulation)
	Gov't affairs	Appointments	
	Civil rights	Defense	
		Social policy	
1987	Gov't affairs	Foreign policy	Budget/taxes
	Budget/taxes	Budget/taxes	Defense
	Foreign policy	Business	Social policy (welfare)
	Defense	Health care	Agriculture
	Business	Gov't affairs	Foreign policy
	Health care	Social policy	
		Energy	
1989	**Gov't affairs**	Budget/taxes	Budget/taxes
	Foreign policy	Environment	Crime
	Business	Foreign policy	Environment
	Budget/taxes	Appointments	Business
	Party politics	Business	
	Appointments	Social policy	

(continued)

Table 2.1 CONTINUED

Year	New York Times	Hearings	President
1993	Budget/taxes	Budget/taxes	Budget/taxes
	Civil rights	Appointments	Economy
	Appointments	Business	Health care
	Business	Foreign policy	Social policy
	Foreign policy	Health care	Crime
	Gov't affairs	Social policy	Civil rights
		Defense	
		Gov't affairs	
1995	Budget/taxes	Budget/taxes	Budget/taxes
	Gov't affairs	Gov't affairs	Gov't affairs
	Foreign policy	Foreign policy	Social policy
	Social policy	Defense	Health care
	Health care	Business	Immigration
	Business	Social policy	Foreign policy
2001	Appointments	Budget/taxes	Budget/taxes
	Budget/taxes	Appointments	Education
	Party politics	Foreign policy	Health care
	Gov't affairs	Health care	Social policy
	Foreign policy	Business	
	Defense	Energy	
	Education	Defense	
Total	Budget/taxes	Budget/taxes	Budget/taxes
	Gov't affairs	Business	Social policy
	Appointments	Appointments	Economy
	Foreign policy	Foreign policy	Health care
	Business	Gov't affairs	Gov't affairs
	Defense	Environment	Defense
	Party politics	Social policy	Business
		Defense	Foreign policy

[1] Issues in bold were not among the top issues of congressional hearings or the president's agenda.

congressional hearings or the president's agenda. The second column after each year lists the top subjects of congressional hearings, obtained from the Policy Agenda Project, during those same months and years, and the third column lists the issues mentioned by the president in his State of the Union address (or first address to Congress) during the year and in other public addresses during the time periods.

The impact of the president's agenda is readily apparent, especially on the substantive policy issues that are not among the four most consistently prominent issues during transition years (budget, government affairs, appointments, and foreign policy). In 1977, energy, the environment, and the economy were all among President Jimmy Carter's top concerns, and they were among the issues members of Congress most discussed publicly. No other presidents made the environment or energy top priorities during the transition periods in this study, and those issues do not appear again among the issues members of Congress discussed most frequently in the *New York Times*. In fact, we find that 53 percent of the cases of going public that focused on energy occurred in 1977, with another 31 percent coming in 2001, when President George W. Bush charged Vice President Dick Cheney with leading a task force to come up with an energy policy. Nearly one-third of the cases involving the environment occurred in 1977, with the remainder spread in smaller numbers across the other years. In 1981 President Ronald Reagan's top three priorities—budget and tax cuts, defense spending increases, and economic recovery—were mostly subsumed under congressional debate on the budget and taxes.

With the shift back to Democratic control of the Senate in 1987, we might expect Congress to be more independent of the president, and there is some evidence that Democrats pursued some health care issues, such as catastrophic health care insurance, that were not among Reagan's top priorities, but they also went public frequently on defense matters, as Reagan made public his own interest in preserving the increases he had made in defense spending. In 1993, congressional focus on civil rights was a direct response to President Bill Clinton's decision in his first week in office to consider repealing the ban on gays in the military. And in 1995, members of Congress picked up on two issues that were presidential priorities—health care (a patient's bill of rights) and social policy (welfare reform). Finally in 2001, education appeared for the first time as a top issue for members of Congress to go public on largely because President Bush made it one of his top two issues. Half of the cases of members going public on this issue occurred in 2001.

Helping to drive the agendas of presidents, members of Congress, and the media are real-world events. As is the case with presidential agendas, the impact of events is most readily seen in the substantive policy areas apart from the more process-related topics of government affairs, budgets and taxes, and appointments. The focus of the president and members of Congress on the economy and energy issues in 1977 was directly related to an economic recession and high energy costs and shortages. The pattern held across the full thirty-nine years, with economic issues receiving much attention during economic recessions and little or no attention during times of prosperity. Both were issues the public expected Congress and the president to solve. We see similar examples throughout the data. Members' interest in social policy in 1981 was largely the result of their concerns about the solvency of Social Security, which went through major changes just two years later. The public discussions on business in 1987 and 1989 were in part prompted by the savings and loan collapses in the late 1980s. And no doubt the good economy and relative peace made it possible for the president and Congress to focus on education in early 2001.

Finally, some issues appeared to be tied to long-term changes in politics. Most notably, the increase in going public on the issue of party politics fits this description. Party politics was an issue in less than 3 percent of the cases each year before 1989. In 1989 it was the fifth most discussed issue, and after a drop in 1993, it went back up in 1995 and was the third most discussed issue in 2001. Although only 54 percent of the cases of going public occurred in 1989 or later, 71 percent of the cases involving party politics took place in 1989 or later years. The full data set corroborates this, with 88 percent of the cases involving party politics occurring after 2000. This reflects the growing polarization that has been evident in Congress over time.

Which Members Choose Which Issues?

Looking at what issues different groups of members go public on reveals that some issues are important for all members. Over thirty-nine years, majority and minority party leaders, committee leaders, and rank-and-file members all went public most on the same four issues—budget and taxes, government affairs, foreign policy, and defense. During transition periods, appointments were added to that list. The only real differences are, first, that during transition years party leaders went public on party politics, an issue largely absent from the public comments of committee leaders and rank-and-file members; and second, that committee leaders and rank-and-file members were more likely to go public on substantive business and financial regulation issues than party leaders during the entire thirty-nine-year period.

These two distinctions make sense intuitively. Party leaders have become the spokespersons for their party, and they are the logical ones to weigh in on party affairs—as, for example, was the case when party leaders reacted to Republican Senator Jim Jeffords's decision in May 2001 to become an independent and caucus with the Democrats, a move that cost Republicans control of the Senate. Because business policy and financial regulation are often complex issues likely to be found on the business pages, it is understandable that party leaders would leave discussion of those issues to members with more expertise—the committee leaders and members of the relevant committees. But with these exceptions noted, members of Congress, regardless of their position in Congress, tend to find success in the media speaking out on the same issues.

Party leaders, however, appear to be more narrowly focused on the top four issues than other members of Congress. Nearly 65 percent of cases involving party leaders dealt with the top four issues. The same was true of ranking minority committee members. But for committee chairs and rank-and-file minority members, the top four issues accounted for just over half of their public statements in the press (55 and 50 percent, respectively). And for majority party rank-and-file members, the top four issues dropped to less than half of their successful public efforts. Instead of the heavy concentration on budget and tax policy, foreign affairs, defense, and government affairs, committee leaders and rank-and-file members seemed to attract attention on a wider range of substantive policy issues including health care, energy, business, the environment, and social policy. This suggests two important factors in going public. Party leaders are likely to focus on the big picture (budget and tax policy), processes in government (party politics and government affairs), and controversies with the president (foreign policy and defense). Other members of Congress with expertise and relevant committee positions may be able to employ public strategies in conjunction with these issues in support of their party leaders or in opposition to them, but they also have considerable latitude to go public on narrower substantive issues where they have expertise or experience and where party leaders may have less consistent interest.

HOW DO MEMBERS GO PUBLIC?

Often we equate going public with events designed specifically to attract press attention. Presidents, for example, go public through news conferences, televised addresses, public appearances, and political travel.[11] Likewise, members of Congress have a variety of options to make news. There are direct methods of contacting the press, including news conferences, interviews with reporters, press releases, and letters to the editor or op-ed pieces for newspapers. But members can also go public through their regular work-related activities. Unlike much of the president's work schedule, congressional members' work-related activities—committee hearings, filibusters, and floor debate, for example—are typically conducted in public.

For members of Congress, direct contact with the press is at least somewhat intentional. Even if they do not seek out a reporter, members do not have to respond to reporters' queries; silence or a "no comment" are options. In contrast, members may or may not be trying to attract media attention through their work activities. Some floor speeches or questions at committee hearings are crafted, even coordinated with other members or outside events, with news values in mind and are intended to convey a particular message. For example, members in the minority party of the House often coordinate special orders speeches to call into question the actions or policies of the majority party after the day's business on the floor has ended.[12] Newt Gingrich and other young Republicans did this in a well-publicized incident in 1984 that led to a confrontation with House Speaker Tip O'Neill. Their intended audience was C-SPAN viewers and the press. But some floor speeches, amendments, and committee questions are merely members doing their jobs. In a committee hearing, a congressional member may ask a witness a question not to gain publicity but because he genuinely needs the information to create legislation to address a problem.

In most cases, news coverage allows us to determine whether members' comments were the result of direct contact or work-related activity, but it usually does not tell us if the work-related activity was intentionally designed for coverage. When reporters cover what members said at a news conference, we know the members intended to go public, but when reporters tell us what members asked a witness at a congressional hearing, we have no way of knowing if the member intended to go public or was merely trying to get information from the witness. In the content analysis of the *New York Times* coverage, I recorded whether each member's statement was the result of direct contact with the press or a work-related activity.[13] Although this does not completely clear up the intentionality of members' public statements, it allows us to see how members' direct contacts compare to their work-related activities in generating coverage of their messages.

Work-Related Activities versus Direct Contact

The coverage is revealing about how members go public and how this has changed over time. Eighty-two percent of the cases over thirty-nine years involved direct contact with the press, and nearly a third were the result of work-related activities.[14] For the first twenty-six years of coverage, direct contact with the press was evident in about 78 percent of cases, and work-related contact was evident in about 34 percent, with little change over that time period. But in the last thirteen years of coverage, there was a dramatic shift away from work-related public statements toward direct contact with the press. From 2003 to 2015, work-related activities accounted for only 25 percent of cases of going public, while direct contact was evident in 90 percent of cases. In the transition years, the differences are not quite so stark, but the trends of declining coverage of work-related instances of going public and increasing coverage of direct efforts to go public are still evident. In both data sets, the correlation between the year and coverage of direct or work-related activities was significant, with direct contact increasing over time and work-related activities declining. This suggests that members of Congress may need to be more intentional about their public strategies to get coverage today than they once were.

In addition to changes over time, we should consider whether work-related going public or direct contact with the press is more of a possibility for some groups than others in Congress or in some political contexts. Senators are often better known to the public and to the media because they represent larger constituencies than most House members, which would make it easier for them to use direct contact with the press than for House members. At the same time, however, senators have more work-related options for attracting media given the greater freedom of individuals in the Senate to influence floor debate through filibusters and amendments than in the House, where the majority party, through the use of the Rules Committee, can control floor debate. Thus, House members may be more constrained to make direct contact with the press. It also seems likely that party leaders would tend to use direct contact to go public rather than work-related activities because they are viewed as newsworthy by the press. Work-related activities may appeal more to rank-and-file members and members of the minority who might find it easier to attract media attention if they can obstruct the process than if they merely hold a press conference. Because such members do not have the obvious power of party or committee leaders, they may have to demonstrate their ability to influence the process before the press finds them newsworthy. And it seems likely that such calculations by both members of Congress and the media may depend on the political context and whether one party enjoys unified control over government or whether power is divided between the parties.

Influences on How Members Go Public

To sort out these relationships and their potential significance, I turned to statistical analysis. Table 2.2 shows the results of logistic regression models for work-related activities and direct contact in both the full thirty-nine-year data set and the transition-year data set. Although this analysis cannot explain all or most of the use of direct contact versus work-related activities to go public, it does allow us to see the relative influence of the political context and the positions of members on the ways they are able to go public. Looking at the results in the first two columns, we see a significant 2.3 to 3.5 percent decline in coverage of work-related going public over time. On the flip side, the last two columns show a significant increase in cases of direct contact over time. This does not necessarily mean that members engage in fewer work-related activities to go public today than they once did. Members continue to conduct hearings and speak during floor debates. What seems more likely is that it is more difficult to get coverage for these activities unless they are particularly controversial. It is evident in reading coverage of Congress over the last thirty-nine years that fewer articles appear to be eyewitness accounts by reporters of congressional hearings or debates. Articles in the last ten years that report on hearings and debates tend to be shorter and include fewer quotes from hearings and debates. Instead, they summarize the events and offer a few reactions from congressional members from both sides.

In addition to these changes over time, evidence suggests that different members receive coverage for different kinds of activities. Party leaders were about 58 percent *less* likely than other members to be covered in work-related activities but much more likely to be seen using direct contact. By

Table 2.2 WORK-RELATED ACTIVITIES AND DIRECT CONTACT
IN GOING PUBLIC

Independent Variables	39-Year Work-Related Coefficient	Transition Year Work-Related Coefficient	39-Year Direct Contact Coefficient	Transition Year Direct Contact Coefficient
Year	−.023***[a]	−.036***	.036***	.020***
	(−.023)[b]	(−.035)	(.037)	(.020)
Divided	.328	.084*	−.615**	−.007
Government	(.388)	(.088)	(−.459)	(−.007)
Senate	.093	.325***	.283	−.275***
	(.098)	(.384)	(.327)	(−.241)
Minority	.195*	.132	−.211	−.343***
	(.215)	(.141)	(−.190)	(−.290)
Party Leader	−.894***	−.870***	.822**	.834***
	(−.591)	(−.581)	(1.276)	(1.302)
Committee	.002	−.180*	.143	.203*
Leader	(.002)	(−.165)	(.154)	(.225)
Constant	45.563***	70.330***	−70.992***	−38.502***
	N = 889	N = 3,620	N = 889	N = 3,620
	R^2 = .053	R^2 = .061	R^2 = .072	R^2 = .042

[a] Significant at ***$p<.001$, **$p<.01$, *$p<.05$.

[b] Likelihood change in the dependent variable given a change in the independent variable, holding all other variables constant.

contrast, minority members were somewhat more likely than majority members to be covered while engaged in work-related activities, but they were much less successful with their direct contact with the press, particularly in transition years. We also see that senators were somewhat more likely than House members to get coverage for work-related activities and less likely to be covered as a result of direct contact in transition years, though there were no significant differences in the full data set. The evidence further reveals that committee leaders were significantly less likely to be covered for work-related activities than direct activities during transition years.

The political context also appears to be linked to the use or coverage of work-related and direct efforts to go public. In both data sets, work-related activities appear more likely to be covered in times of divided government than of unified government (the coefficient barely missed statistical significance in the full data set). In contrast, direct contact appears to decline during divided government. This makes sense intuitively because in unified government, the majority party has little need to use work-related activities to call attention to an issue, and the minority party has limited control over the routine processes of Congress, so it is constrained in using work-related activities to gain attention except for the filibuster in the Senate, which cannot be used in all situations. In divided government or with a divided Congress, the majority may use congressional hearings, floor debate, or amendments to try to influence public support of legislation proposed by the president or the other house of Congress.

It is a little less clear why direct contact would decline in divided government. It may be that the congressional minority defers to or is upstaged by its president during divided government when it comes to direct contact with the press. And during divided government or split control of Congress, both sides may do more to coordinate their communication with their work-related activities to compete for the media's attention.

During the transition years, we do see more combining of work-related activities and direct contact with the press, which suggests fewer distinctions in when and how the two types of activities are employed.

CONCLUSIONS

There have indeed been changes in going public in Congress and the coverage of such strategies over the last forty years. Although rank-and-file members have consistently accounted for the majority of cases of going public that make the news, the attention paid to party leaders has increased, particularly during times of transition. It is also clear that minority party members have increasingly found success in going public over time at the same time their institutional powers have been diminished.

These developments lend support to the idea that public strategies are a way to enhance institutional power or compensate for a lack of it.

We have seen that context matters for who can capture media attention when going public. Party and committee leaders may find it both more necessary and easier to get media attention in times of divided government or when the parties split control over Congress. For the minority party, going public has become a necessity during unified government, and it appears easier to obtain coverage in that circumstance. Greater polarization also seems to coincide with the increased interest and success of party leaders and the minority party in getting coverage.

How members go public appears to have changed. As reporters seem less interested in covering committee hearings, floor debates, or other work-related activities, members have to be more intentional, using direct contact with the press to go public. Here, too, the political context has some impact on the likelihood that work-related activities will successfully attract coverage, with this happening more frequently in divided government than unified government.

Finally, some things have changed little over time. Four issues have dominated going public—budgets and taxes, government affairs, defense, and foreign policy—and these have remained at the top in both transition and nontransition periods for all members of Congress.

The next chapter goes beyond who goes public to consider their reasons for doing so. In that discussion, we will not only see how media help members go beyond their institutional powers but also begin to see the impact of growing political polarization on members' public strategies.

Why Congressional Members Go Public

When presidents go public, they often do so to try to sell their issues and policy preferences to the public to get what they want in the policy process. Members of Congress certainly use the media for those same reasons, but they also go public when they have no chance of passing their preferred policies. In June of 1999, three women in the House of Representatives—Carolyn McCarthy (D-NY), Nita Lowey (D-NY), and Rosa DeLauro (D-CT)—led a public campaign for a strict gun-control measure in the House. With majority Republicans mostly opposed to their proposal and Democrats divided, they faced impossible odds, but that did not stop them from holding almost daily news conferences, conducting frequent interviews with reporters, and inviting press cameras to cover their "behind the scenes" phone calls to lobby their House colleagues. In the end, their efforts to pass legislation failed, as everyone knew they would, but they had succeeded in making headlines and raising awareness of the issue and the vote in Congress. This example suggests a wider range of goals may be accomplished by going public in Congress.

Unlike the president, who even at his weakest has the power to influence policymaking directly through his ability to sign or veto legislation or go around Congress with executive orders, individual members of Congress often do not have the institutional power to shape or influence legislation. Members in the minority do not have the votes in committee or on the floor to pass their own policies or perhaps even to amend the majority's legislation. Even members within the majority may not be on the relevant committee to help craft legislation, or they may find themselves in opposition to their party's leadership on an issue, leaving them with limited input in the process. And in some cases, members of the majority—leaders and rank and file alike—may find themselves at odds with the president, making it difficult for them to do what they want on a policy. Where their institutional powers fail them, members may turn to the media to try to influence policy—preferably to pass legislation they like or, barring that, to stop undesirable policy from passing or, when passage is inevitable, to mitigate the effects or call attention to the deficiencies of the impending policy in an effort to hold the perpetrators accountable.

This chapter considers why members of Congress go public. It pays particular attention to the connection between members' institutional roles and power and what they try to accomplish through their public comments. After examining the goals members have in going public, I look at the reactive nature of public strategies in Congress and how members use them to respond to the president.

MEMBERS' GOALS IN GOING PUBLIC

Members' goals in going public are often evident in the media coverage of their public statements. In some cases, a congressman's own words make it clear that he is trying to pass or stop legislation. For example, during debate on a 2006 bill governing detainee interrogation and trials for terror suspects, Congressman Ike Skelton (D-MO) made clear his intention to stop the legislation, saying, "If you want to be tough on terrorism, let's not pass something that rushes to judgment and has legal loopholes that will reverse a conviction."[1] Sometimes the context or the reporter provides information about what the member hopes to accomplish with a public strategy. In coverage of the automakers' bailout in 2009, before quoting several Republican members of Congress, the reporters explained, "Many conservative Republicans remain staunchly opposed to any further corporate bailouts by the government, and some are openly calling for Congress to let one or more of the automakers go into bankruptcy."[2]

For each case in the transition years and the full *New York Times* data sets, my research assistants and I categorized the member's apparent goal in going public as one of three possibilities—passing policy, stopping policy, and other (everything else).[3] Although not an exact measure of members' goals, these categories do offer a glimpse at the diverse ends for which members employ public strategies, and they allow us to see the connections between a member's purpose in going public and his or her own position in Congress and the political context. The patterns we are able to observe offer further evidence that congressional members do indeed use public strategies to go beyond their institutional power.

Passing or Stopping Policy

The two most obvious goals members have when going public are to enact their preferences through legislation, confirmations, or other actions considered by Congress and others in government and to stop policies and actions they do not like. For simplicity's sake, I refer to these two goals as passing policy and stopping policy, even though the actions members hope to take or block may extend beyond legislation and actual policy to confirmations or resolutions that might simply influence policy.

Nearly all members of Congress have some interest in passing policy, and many believe the media can assist in this effort. Public strategies can aid in passing legislation by making the public aware of a policy that is already popular and thus alerting others in Congress to the proposal's public support and the potential costs of not passing it. Going public can also be used to frame a proposal in a way that will attract public support. The battle over the "death tax" versus the "estate tax" illustrates the point. While many people ignore debates about estate taxes because they do not see themselves as having an estate to tax, they take great exception to the death tax because everyone faces death.[4] Almost a quarter of the cases in the sample of *New York Times* coverage over thirty-nine years were attempts to pass policy. That was slightly higher during transition periods.

Stopping legislation from passing or nominations from being confirmed is also a goal of going public. Members of Congress who find themselves on the losing side of a debate may turn to the press to expand the scope of conflict by letting more people, especially the public and interest groups, know what is at stake. In some cases, this may simply mean calling attention to an unpopular policy that is being moved quietly through Congress. Members may try to use the press to raise the visibility or "traceability" of votes and issues in Congress that they oppose, hoping the public will also disapprove and pressure Congress to stop the legislative process.[5] Other situations may require members who want to stop the legislation to persuade the public by educating citizens about the negative consequences of the policy or reframing the debate to trigger different considerations among citizens that would shift support away from the policy. South Carolina Senator Jim DeMint did this during the 2007 debate on immigration reform when he used the word "amnesty" to characterize the bipartisan compromise to create a pathway to citizenship for illegal immigrants already in the United States. That word sparked a public outcry that caused the compromise to collapse. Twelve percent of the cases of going public were, like this one, efforts to stop policy.

Other Goals

Although passing policy and stopping it are the two easiest goals to identify, there are a number of other reasons members of Congress go public, and together these other goals account, over thirty-nine years, for 64 percent of all cases of going public (57 percent in transition periods). Some members of Congress attempted to use the media to further debate, hoping that they could make changes to the policy before it came to a vote. For example, in 1993 Senator David Boren (D-OK) and other conservative Democrats, along with some moderate Republicans, primarily from oil-producing states, announced that they would not vote for President Bill Clinton's energy tax *in its present form*. Armed with an alternative proposal and a persistent public relations campaign, the group ultimately persuaded their colleagues and the President Clinton to settle for a small gas tax rather than the more ambitious BTU tax the president had originally sought. Many such efforts to further debate seemed to be in response to a proposal from the president or a member's own party or leadership where the member's objection was not to the entire proposal but only a small piece of it. In other cases, members went public simply to raise awareness of an issue and to get it on the agenda.

Members also used public strategies to explain a policy and their reasons for supporting or opposing it. Sometimes members may have been thinking about the electoral implications of their support or opposition, and in others their interest may have been directed toward influencing implementation of a policy. The continued debate after the passage of the Affordable Care Act (Obamacare) in 2010 illustrates both of these purposes. Republicans took every opportunity to portray the legislation as a step toward socialized medicine and a violation of the Constitution and vowed to repeal it, giving them an effective line of attack against Democrats in the 2010 midterm elections. Their public attacks also encouraged some governors to challenge the legislation in court and drag their feet in implementing key parts of it at the state level.

Finally, members used the media to improve accountability. Even in a losing cause, as we saw in the case of the three women urging gun control, where members knew they could not pass their policy or stop a policy, they used public strategies to call attention to the issue as a way of increasing traceability and making it easier for voters who agreed with them to hold their members accountable for the vote.

Goals and a Member's Position in Congress

Although, as we can see, there are many reasons members of Congress might go public, all members of Congress do not use public strategies equally for the same purposes, and those that want to do so may find it difficult to get coverage in their pursuit of some goals. If a minority member in the House goes public to try to pass a bill the majority opposes, the media may have no interest in covering the quixotic effort because the minority member has no chance of success. Thus, a member's purpose in going public and likelihood of getting covered may vary depending on his or her position in Congress (and subsequent institutional power) and the political context.

If members use the media to supplement their institutional powers or to compensate for a lack of power and if media are interested in members' public efforts to varying degrees, depending in part on the political context, who would we expect to see going public in pursuit of which goals? Congressional members in the majority party would be likely to employ public strategies more often as part of their efforts to pass policy than would minority party members, whose formal powers limit their ability to pass legislation. Conversely, we would expect minority party members to rely more on the media to help block bills and nominations than would majority members. Majority party members have a variety of institutional powers and leverage with their leaders controlling the political process that would allow them to change legislation or keep it from coming to the floor; thus, they would be less likely to need to expand the scope of conflict by going public to try to stop the process outright. In contrast, minority members may have no other alternative but to go public to stop legislation. Indeed, we see in Figure 3.1 that over thirty-nine years the majority was much more likely to be covered trying to pass policy than to stop it (24 to 10 percent of cases, respectively). And though the minority was nearly evenly divided between passing policy and stopping it, minority members were covered less often trying to pass policy and more often trying to stop it than majority party members.

By the same logic, we would expect to see similar distinctions between the goals of leaders and rank-and-file members. Given their advantage in institutional power, both party and committee leaders may be more interested in using public strategies to pass policy rather than stop it compared to their rank-and-file counterparts. Although we see in Figure 3.1 that party and committee leaders went public to pass policy more than to

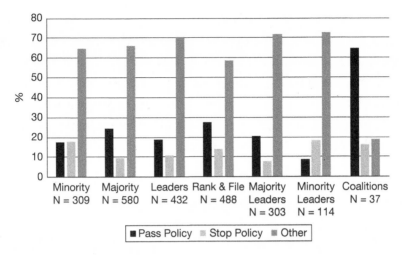

Figure 3.1 Goals in Going Public

stop it, we find a similar pattern for rank-and-file members, indicating that going public to pass legislation is an option for members of Congress even without the power of leadership. Where we do encounter a big difference between leaders and nonleaders is their ability to pursue other goals with a public strategy. That nonleaders were covered going public for reasons other than passing policy or stopping it in 12 percent fewer stories than leaders (the difference fell slightly, to 8 percent, in transition years) suggests that rank-and-file members may find it more challenging to use public strategies to frame debate, push leaders in their preferred direction, or explain their own positions.

Of course, we must also consider the special case of party and committee leaders in the minority. Because of their minority status, they have a greater need to go public to stop policy than do majority party leaders or committee chairs. In fact in the full data set and transition years, minority leaders were two to three times more likely to go public to stop policy than were leaders of the majority and about two to three times less likely to use the media to try to pass policy as their majority counterparts.

One relatively small set of cases also deserves attention. For all groups in Congress, more than half the cases of going public were used for some reason other than passing or stopping policy, except for ad hoc coalitions. For these groups of members coming together to work on a specific issue, often outside of formal institutions like committees and across party lines, the goal in 65 percent of their efforts to go public was to pass policy. A typical example of this occurred in May 2001, when a bipartisan group of four senators went public to announce they were combining their election reform plans into one bill to improve the chances that legislation would pass to insure that the 2002 elections would not be a repeat of the controversies that occurred in the 2000 presidential election.

Goals and the Political Environment

The political environment adds to the strategic calculations members make in determining what they can hope to accomplish through public strategies and their prospects for getting covered.

THE PRESIDENT

Being in the president's party strengthens members' hands in the policy process, assuming they share the president's policy preferences. In both unified and divided government, the Congress often looks to the president to set the agenda and even provide a starting point for debate on a policy. Members of the president's party can go public to encourage passage of the president's proposals, and even if they are in the minority in Congress, they know the president's ability to threaten to veto legislation that does not incorporate his ideas gives congressional members a chance to get the policy they and the president want passed.

That same veto power means congressional members in the president's party may not have to go public to stop policy as often as those in the opposing party. Again, if the president shares their convictions, they can trust him to reject the legislation, whereas those who are not in the president's party, especially if they are in the minority, may need the media to help turn public sentiment against the president's proposal to stop it in Congress so that it never reaches his desk.

Interestingly, the data bear this out only in transition periods. During these times, at the beginning of a new presidency or change in partisan control of Congress, members in the president's party went public to pass policy just over 30 percent of the time, while those not in his party used the media to pass policy just under 25 percent of the time. And members of the president's party were slightly less likely to resort to public strategies to stop policy than those not in the president's party (13 to 17 percent, respectively). However, in the thirty-nine-year period, there were no distinctions between members of the president's party and those in the opposition in their efforts to stop policy.

But if we break down the cases by the year of the president's term, we start to see more clearly what may be going on. In the first year of a president's term, his party members' efforts to pass policy accounted for 30 percent of their cases of going public, and their efforts to stop policy were less than half that (12 percent). But going public to pass policy declined as a proportion of the president's party's total cases in each subsequent year of the president's term—dropping to only 18 percent in the fourth year of his administration. And although the cases of going public to stop policy fluctuated less predictably, during the last two years of the administration, the cases involving members of the president's party were more evenly divided between passing policy and stopping it. Thus, it appears that as the president's power declines over his term in office, his own party becomes less well positioned to pass policy and more vulnerable to passage of policies it opposes. This change makes the party less able to use the media to pass policy, or perhaps its agenda simply shrinks as the next election approaches.

The opposing party's goals moved in the opposite direction. As the cases of going public to pass policy declined by more than half for the president's party over his term, those for the opposing party more than doubled, from 14 percent the president's first year to 30 percent in his fourth year, and the percentage of cases attempting to pass policy compared to stopping it moved from nearly even to a 21 percent advantage for passing policy in the fourth year. This suggests that while the opposing party and media may look to the president to set the agenda in his first year, the opposition begins to assert itself more easily through the media as the midterm election approaches, and it continues for the final two years of the presidential term.

UNIFIED VERSUS DIVIDED GOVERNMENT

Whether there is unified or divided government may also affect the reasons members of Congress go public and the media's interest in them. In unified government, the minority has no control over Congress or the White House and thus has little power to influence policy. Its members are, therefore, most likely to need the media to help block the policies of the majority party and the president. Fortunately for them, the media may be more interested in the minority in unified government to balance the majority views. In divided government, members of the minority are in the president's party and can often rely on his veto to stop legislation. In the transition periods, when legislative activity may be greatest, cases involving the minority going public to stop legislation dropped from 28 percent during unified government to 16 percent during divided government. In both unified and divided government, the majority was less likely than the minority to use the media to stop legislation, and the percentage of cases aimed at stopping policy fell only slightly, from 12 to 9 percent.

Also evident in the political context is that divided government requires some degree of compromise across parties, as both the majority and the minority have some hope of influencing policy—the majority through its control of Congress and the minority through the president. Members need to craft legislation that the president will sign or that will attract sufficient support from minority party members to override a veto. This dynamic shows up in the data in two ways. First, in the transition periods, there was a significant increase in the number of cases of both majority and minority members that were focused on the third category of goals. Members in divided government were not covered primarily going public to pass policy or stop it; they were going public to try to influence the debate to shape the final legislation. The percent of cases devoted to these other goals rose from 55 percent among both majority and minority members in unified government to 65 and 63 percent, respectively, during divided government.

Second, over the full thirty-nine years, the need for compromise and, perhaps, evidence that it is hard to come by were apparent in the increase in the percent of cases aimed at stopping policy during divided government compared to unified government for both majority and minority members, though it remained largest for the minority in every political context. Additionally, the minority members' public efforts to pass policy grew significantly during divided government. Thus in divided government, both parties appeared to be playing offense (passing policy) and defense (stopping it).

POLITICAL POLARIZATION

Finally, there are two ways in which the increasing political polarization in Congress may affect what members can hope to accomplish by going public. First, members of the minority will find the majority less willing to allow them to participate in shaping legislation as partisanship has increased, leaving minority members with even fewer opportunities to pass legislation and more reliant on public strategies to stop legislation with which they disagree. The news coverage in transition periods confirms this: the percent of cases in which the minority tried to pass policy declined after 1992, and in each year after 1992, stopping policy exceeded passing policy as a goal of the minority members, a reversal from the years prior to 1992. But coverage from the full thirty-nine years shows little change in the goals of minority members who received coverage for their public efforts before and after 1992.

Second, for the majority party, polarization means there is more pressure from party leaders for members to support the party's position. Members who disagree with their caucus may be encouraged to air their concerns privately rather than in the press, and therefore, we would expect to see a smaller percent of cases in which the majority goes public to stop policy over time. In the thirty-nine-year span and to a lesser extent in the transition periods, the percent of cases in the majority party's efforts to stop policy fell after 1992—13 percent down to 6 percent for the thirty-nine-year period and 13 percent down to 9 percent in transitions—an indication of the majority party's greater institutional power as polarization has increased.

One word of caution is in order. We cannot be sure, based on the news coverage alone, whether members of the minority really choose to use the media less to pass policy over time or whether the press is simply less interested in covering such efforts than in highlighting the differences between the parties that were clear in minority members going public to stop the majority's proposals. The latter possibility plays into the media values of conflict and drama. The case that majority members are less likely to go public to stop policies since 1994 is stronger; research indicates that the media are certainly more interested in intraparty squabbles that would be found in majority members going public to stop their own party's policies.[6]

Determinants of Members' Goals in Going Public

How the position of congressional members, majority or minority and leadership or rank and file, interacts with the political context—whether the member is in the president's party, divided or unified government, and whether it is before or during the era of polarization in Congress—is important for determining the reasons members choose to go public or their likelihood of getting coverage of their public efforts. But because of the complex interactions, we need to employ something other than simple correlations to measure the strength and significance of these factors on members' goals in going public. Dropping the "other goals" category and focusing exclusively on cases involving passing policy or stopping it, I used logistic regression to determine the impact of being in the minority, in the president's party, and in party or committee leadership on the likelihood that a member would be going public to stop policy rather than pass it in news coverage. In addition, I included measures for which house of Congress and which party the member was in, and I incorporated political context variables to measure the impact of a split Congress or divided government in comparison to unified government, the impact of polarization measured with a dummy variable for cases occurring after 1992, and in the case of the thirty-nine-year data set, the year of the president's term.

The results appear in Table 3.1. The first two columns of results use no interactive terms, and for the full thirty-nine-year time period, only one variable is significant. Being in the minority did increase the likelihood

Table 3.1 Passing Policy vs. Stopping It

Independent Variables	Model 1 39-Years Coefficient	Transition Coefficient	Model 2 39-Years Coefficient	Transition Coefficient
Minority	1.080****[a]	1.054****	.077	.370**
	(1.946)[b]	(1.870)	(.080)	(.448)
Party Leader	.362	−.036	.263	−.156
	(.436)	(−.035)	(.300)	(−.144)
Committee Leader	.336	−.278**	−.213	−.557***
	(.399)	(−.243)	(−.192)	(−.427)
President's Party	−.154	−.201****	−.607*	−.135*
	(−.143)	(−.182)	(−.455)	(−.126)
Party	.147	−.312***	.387	−.111
	(.158)	(−.268)	(.473)	(−.105)
Senate	.385	−.158	.340	−.188*
	(.470)	(−.146)	(.404)	(−.171)
Split Congress	.148	.168	.277	.198
	(.160)	(.183)	(.319)	(.219)
Divided Government	.269	−.313**	.554	−.271**
	(.308)	(−.269)	(.740)	(−.237)
Post-1992	−.376*	.295**	−.705**	−.055
	(−.313)	(.343)	(−.506)	(−.053)
Year of President's Term	−.088		−.330*	
	(−.084)		(−.281)	
Minority Party × Party Leader			1.651*	1.009***
			(4.213)	(1.743)
Minority Party × Committee Leader			.707	.681**
			(1.027)	(.975)
Minority Party × post-1992			.923	.907****
			(1.517)	(1.477)
President's Party × Party Leader			−.537	−.374**
			(−.416)	(−.312)
President's Party × Committee Leader			.402	.071
			(.495)	(.073)

(continued)

Table 3.1 CONTINUED

Independent Variables	Model 1		Model 2	
	39-Years Coefficient	Transition Coefficient	39-Years Coefficient	Transition Coefficient
President's Party ×			.216	
President's Term			(.240)	
Constant	−1.570	−.065	−1.572	−.142
	(−.792)	(−.063)	(−.671)	(−.133)
	N = 303	N = 1,540	N = 303	N = 1,540
	$R^2 = .105$	$R^2 = .118$	$R^2 = .150$	$R^2 = .141$

[a] Significant at ****p<.001, *** p<.01, **p<.05, *p<.10.

[b] Likelihood change in the dependent variable given a change in the independent variable, holding all other variables constant.

that members were going public to stop policy rather than pass it. The transition periods provided more significant results. Minority members were dramatically more likely than majority members to be covered trying to stop policy, while committee leaders, members of the president's party, and Republicans were less likely to be covered trying to stop policy. Cases during divided government were less likely to be aimed at stopping policy than those in unified government, but those in the more polarized post-1992 era were more likely to focus on stopping policy than those in less polarized times.

The last two columns of results take a more complex look at the data by including interactive terms that allow us to distinguish between minority and majority members and those in the president's party in party or committee leadership positions and in the era of increasing polarization. Starting with the full thirty-nine-year period, we find that while being in the minority by itself is no longer significant, being a minority party leader was associated with a much greater likelihood of going public to stop policy. Going public to stop policy actually declined after 1992, possibly the result of the majority being less likely to go public to stop policy as their party leaders more successfully maintained party unity. And we see an increased likelihood of coverage of efforts to pass policy over the course of the president's term in office. Being in the president's party was significantly related to fewer public efforts to stop policy, but this appeared to reverse over the course of the president's term in office, with members of his party being 24 percent more likely to get coverage for trying to stop policy with each additional year of the president's term, an increase that just missed being statistically significant.

During the transition periods, several factors were connected to members' goals in going public. The independent influence of being in the minority was significant in transition periods, as the minority's rank and file and party leaders were more likely to be seen trying to stop policy, a pattern that was further strengthened in the polarized period after 1992. And as expected, we find members of the president's party, particular its party leaders, more focused on passing policy than stopping it. Passing policy also appeared to be more likely for senators and during times of divided government.

Members use the media for a variety of reasons, and it is clear that their goals and their ability to attract coverage in pursuit of these goals vary with the political context and their own institutional power. The next section considers another reason members go public: to react to events and others in government.

GOING PUBLIC TO REACT

When presidents go public, they are as likely to be introducing a new agenda or initiating a policy discussion as they are to be reacting to some event or action by other policymakers. For Congress, however, going public usually means reacting. Eighty-six percent of the cases in the thirty-nine-year period and in transition years involved members of Congress reacting to something. For example, in 1995, Democrats in Congress reacted negatively to the congressional Republicans' introduction of a balanced budget amendment to the Constitution.[7] In some cases, members reacted to something the president had done, as when

in 1995 Senator Bob Dole (R-KS) introduced legislation to allow the
United States to sell arms to Bosnia despite the UN embargo of arms
sales. The article and Dole's comments made clear that the bill was a reaction against the Clinton administration's refusal to get the United Nations
to lift the embargo.[8] In most years of the study, 70 to 90 percent of the
cases of going public were in reaction to events or other policymakers.
In only five years did fewer than 70 percent of cases involve reaction,
and even then they never fell below 60 percent. Only 14 percent of the
cases involved members of Congress going public to initiate some action
without a clear antecedent. Often these cases were members of Congress
introducing new legislation or trying to raise awareness of an issue not
already on the national agenda.

Going public to initiate discussion on an issue was not only less common than reacting but also declined significantly over time. There was a
particularly substantial drop over the last thirteen years of the coverage.
Close to one-fifth of all cases in the first twenty-six years involved members initiating discussion, but only 5 percent did so in the last thirteen
years. A similar pattern of decline in initiating action was evident in transition periods, with the exception of an increase in 1995, when the new
Republican majority armed with the Contract with America clearly set the
agenda in the first five months of that year.

Why Congress Reacts

It should come as no surprise that the majority of going public in Congress
is reactive. Several factors make this outcome likely. First, in the era of
the modern presidency, presidents are the focus of American government. They are expected to try to set the agenda. Part of the reason 1995
was seen as an unusual year is that the new Republican majority did have
such a unified agenda, at least in the House, for the first hundred days. If
presidents typically provide the starting point for debate, much of what
Congress does will be in reaction to that even if the reaction is to criticize what the president proposed and offer a different policy in response.

In this political system characterized by proposals and counterproposals, the president usually moves first.

Associated with this is a second factor that leads to Congress being reactive. Congress is not structured to initiate action easily in a coherent way. Although members belong to parties, they often have their own agendas, and thus, they attempt to influence those with the power to craft policy by reacting to what the leaders suggest. The situation is compounded by the presence of the two parties, whose members frequently react to each other. Given congressional members' dependence on their constituents, they are also likely to react to whatever events and issues have captured the attention of the public.

Finally, the news values of the media reinforce the idea of Congress as a reactive institution and may in fact make it difficult for members to gain media attention for their efforts to initiate policy or discussion. As the only nationally elected political figure, the president is inherently newsworthy. As most members of Congress, however, are barely known outside their district or state, if they are even known there, they are less attractive subjects for the national press. Many studies have shown that coverage of members of Congress is often woven into other stories, and the members are sought out primarily for their reactions to other policymakers or to events.[9] Members may tailor their public strategies to tap into current stories or debates because they are more likely to receive attention for their reaction than if they try to introduce new topics without some sort of existing hook.

This last argument suggests that the decline in cases in which members initiate discussion rather than react to events may be more a reflection of how media coverage of Congress has changed over time, as reporters turn to Congress primarily for reaction, rather than an actual change in congressional behavior. However, one could also reasonably argue that as polarization has increased, members have become more aware of the costs of failing to respond to the president or the other party, and they have become more adept at responding. If so, coverage would reflect that reality. The existing research that finds that members of Congress adapt to media values to get coverage and that coverage usually reflects what elites are actually doing offers the likelihood that the two patterns have emerged somewhat simultaneously and reinforced each other.[10] The press covers members reacting, which fits well with the news value of conflict; because they have success in getting covered when they react, members do more of it.

Members Who Initiate Action

Although most members of Congress use the media to react in policymaking, we would expect some members by virtue of their position to have more success in initiating discussion by going public. Not surprisingly, majority members appeared to use public strategies to initiate policy more often and to react less often than those in the minority. The difference was considerable among leaders, with majority leaders initiating discussion in 10 to 20 percent more cases than their minority counterparts. In transition periods, this difference extended to rank-and-file members, but such distinctions disappeared across the full thirty-nine-year period.

Among the rank and file, those most likely to receive coverage for trying to initiate a policy or discussion were coalitions involving members from both parties or both houses of Congress. If we look at the cases involving joint statements from members from both the House and Senate, we find they initiated policy in nearly one-fifth of the cases (rising to 42 percent during the transition periods) compared to cases involving just senators (14 percent) or just House members (13 percent). Likewise, Republicans and Democrats differed very little from each other, with 12 to 14 percent of the cases involving them focused on initiating policy, but 27 percent of the cases that included members from both parties were intended to initiate policy (44 percent in the transition periods). Though these ad hoc coalitions are only a small percentage of cases of going public that get covered, when they form, they are often designed to address a policy neglected by the parties or by the majority or to resolve some sort of congressional stalemate, and members who want to call attention to the issue unite with others to project a louder voice, one the media might notice. For example, the bipartisan public efforts of Senators John McCain (R-AZ) and Russ Feingold (D-WI) over several years forced the majority party to consider serious campaign finance legislation and eventually led to the passage of that legislation. Incorporating members from both chambers and both parties lends credibility to a coalition and may enhance the group's newsworthiness in the eyes of the press.

Thus far we have seen that when members of Congress get covered going public, it is mostly to react. Their reaction to the president merits special attention. The next section looks at members' support or opposition to the president in their public statements.

REACTING TO THE PRESIDENT

As Chapter 1 noted, one of the primary reasons members of Congress developed an interest in going public in the first place was to respond to the president and keep him from dominating the news and subsequent political debate. About one-fourth of the cases from 1977 to 2015 and one-fifth of the cases during transition periods involved members of Congress reacting to the president, and opposition to him outnumbered support about two to one. For the most part, the members of Congress who reacted to the president did not differ from those who went public for other reasons. About two-thirds were in the majority, a little more than half were from the Senate, and 55 percent were not in the president's party, mirroring the overall percentages of members who went public. The exception to this pattern was the party leaders. They went from about 15 percent of all members going public to 23 percent of those reacting to the president, and the increase occurred among both majority and minority party leaders. Intuitively, this pattern makes sense, as party leaders are looked to by their own members to lead the party in supporting or opposing the president and by the media as the closest thing to an institutional voice that Congress has to compete with the executive.

President's Party versus the Opposition

More important than who reacts to the president is *how* they react. Supporting or opposing a president privately or even on a congressional vote is one thing, but going public to announce one's support or opposition involves some strategic calculations of costs and benefits. Perhaps the most important factor in members' decisions is whether they are in the president's party. Members of the president's party may have more at stake than those in the opposition party when reacting publicly to the president. Because of their shared party label, the fates of the president and his copartisans in Congress are inextricably linked. When the president enjoys high approval and is able to enact policy and address national problems, his party often enjoys higher approval and success in elections than when he is unpopular and unable to get his policies through Congress.[11] Therefore, members of the president's party in Congress have some incentive to help him succeed by publicly supporting his policies and actions. This is particularly true of party leaders in the president's party because they are often more concerned with the party's collective goals than rank-and-file members.[12]

Furthermore, members of the president's party may find it very costly to oppose the president publicly when they disagree with him. The president can be a valuable resource for members of Congress, enhancing their power in the policy process, especially if their party is in the minority in Congress or if members are not in a position in Congress to influence policy on some issues that are important to them. Publicly opposing the president on an issue might make it more difficult for a member of the president's party to secure the president's support on an issue of importance to the congressional member later on. The future costs to the member might well outweigh any immediate benefits of publicly opposing the president.

Conversely, those who are not in the president's party have little incentive to support him publicly and several reasons to oppose him. Just as the president's copartisans have an electoral interest in his success, his opponents are more likely to benefit in public opinion and at the polls from the president's failure, though few of them will publicly admit this. If he and his party are unable to pass legislation or take action to solve the nation's problems or if his solutions are unpopular with the public, the opposition stands to gain and, therefore, may be likely to oppose the president's plans publicly. In addition, the other party may go public to oppose the president as a way of drawing distinctions between the two parties that members hope will benefit their party in the next election. An excellent example of this strategy in action was congressional Republicans' very public wholesale opposition to President Obama's health care reform bill in 2009 and 2010 that helped them reclaim a majority in the House in 2010.

Beyond their electoral concerns, members of the opposition may go public against the president for genuine disagreements over policy. In unified government, the opposition party, being in the minority, may adopt a public strategy opposing the president in an effort to turn public opinion against the president and possibly block his action or policy. Republicans did this on the issue of economic stimulus during President Obama's first year in office, explaining that they preferred tax cuts to increased spending. Although Republicans did not have the numbers to stop the president, they could shape opinion of the stimulus spending and bailouts. In divided government, the opposition party members may be inclined to go public against the president as a way of forcing him to compromise with them.

The evidence supports this theory that how members react to the president is linked to whether they share his party affiliation. Members of the president's party were more likely to go public in support of him than were members of the opposition. Of the cases in which members publicly supported the president, 69 percent were members of his own party (75 percent in transition periods), and just under a third (a fourth in transitions) were from the opposing party. Among those who were not in the president's party, 83 percent (89 percent in transition periods) went public to oppose the president. The special concerns of party leaders in the president's party were also evident, as these leaders went public to support him in nearly two-thirds of the cases and to oppose him in only one-third. By comparison, other members in the president's party were divided somewhat more evenly between opposition in just over half the cases and support in just under half. Among members of the opposing party, the difference between leaders and rank-and-file members was nonexistent during transition periods, with both groups opposing the president around 89 percent of the time, and the differences during the thirty-nine-year period were merely a matter of degrees of opposition, with the leaders continuing to oppose the president in 91 percent of the cases, while rank-and-file members in their party opposed the president 80 percent of the time.

Although members of the president's party appeared more likely to support him publicly than those who did not share his party label, the coverage also reveals that members of the president's party were not shy about opposing him. Half of the cases involving the president's copartisans were reactions *against* the president. This is not completely unexpected: existing research shows that members of the president's party may go public against him as a way of pulling their party in their preferred direction.[13] A closer look at the coverage suggests additional reasons. In times of divided government, members of the president's party reacted against him if he compromised too much with the opposition majority in Congress. A typical example of this occurred when Democratic Senator Daniel Patrick Moynihan announced his plans to introduce his own welfare proposal in 1995. He explained that he disagreed with the Republicans' plan and found too much overlap between the Republicans' and President Bill Clinton's proposals. Moynihan "said Mr. Clinton bore some responsibility for the conservative drift of the welfare dispute."[14] During unified government, members of the president's party may find public opposition to the president a necessary strategy to shape policy, particularly if their party leaders in cooperating with the president have blocked them from the process. Congressman Jim DeMint made the news in May of 2001 when he publicly complained that President George W. Bush's No Child Left Behind legislation was turning into "leave no Democrat behind," as Bush and Republican committee leaders made compromises with the Democrats while pushing aside some of the concerns of conservative opponents.[15]

Polarization in Reactions to the President

Another factor that we would expect to influence whether members publicly support or oppose the president is the growing polarization of Congress. Not only might the decline in moderates in both parties reduce cross-partisan support for or opposition to the president, but there may be more pressure from party leaders on rank-and-file members to toe the party line at least in their public communications. As polarization has increased, members who go public in support of a president of the other party or against a president of their own party may incur the wrath of party leaders and thus may be less inclined to do so. If they cannot agree with their party caucus's public position with regard to the president, they may be encouraged to remain quiet. Therefore, over time we would expect to see members of the president's own party being more supportive when they go public and less likely to oppose the president in the media.

The patterns in the coverage shown in Figure 3.2 offer striking evidence of polarization. From 1977 to 1989, members of the president's own party received coverage for opposing him in 57 percent of the cases in which they reacted to the president. That dropped to 37 percent over the next thirteen years and moved back up to 49 percent in the last thirteen

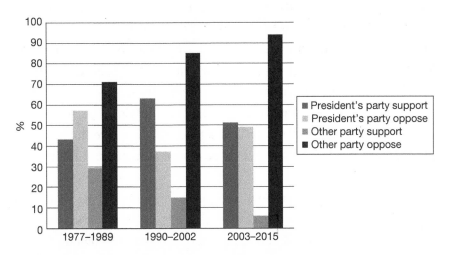

Figure 3.2 The Impact of Polarization on Reaction to the President

years. At the same time, the cases in which they supported the president increased from 43 percent in the first thirteen years to just over 50 percent in the last thirteen. The changes in the party opposing the president were even more dramatic. Opposition to the president from those in the other party went from 71 to 94 percent, and support dropped from 29 to 6 percent of the cases. What is more, these trends are most likely evidence of changes in behavior of congressional members rather than changes in media coverage. The media's interest in conflict and the unexpected has increased over time, which would make opposition to the president by his own party or support from the opposing party more newsworthy, not less. And yet it is these counterintuitive cases that have declined over time.

Determinants of Reaction to the President

Given the various ways a member's position in Congress and party can interact with the political context to affect his or her willingness to publicly oppose or support the president, we again need to turn to multivariate analysis. Including only the cases in which members reacted against or in support of the president, the logistic regression models reported in Table 3.2 use a dummy variable for support for the president as the dependent variable. The first two columns of results show the impact of whether members were in the president's party, party leadership, and committee leadership, as well as the impact of the political party and the house of Congress members were in. In addition, the model includes political context variables—dummy variables for split control of Congress, for divided government, and for cases occurring after 1992 to capture the impact of polarization. Finally, the model includes the year to account for any factors unique to the year.

It is immediately evident that being in the president's party is the key determinant in members' supporting the president, as it was significantly related to an increased likelihood of support for the president during the thirty-nine-year period and the transition periods. In fact, it was the only significant factor in the thirty-nine-year period. As expected, the data

Table 3.2 REACTION TO THE PRESIDENT

Independent Variables	Model 1 39-Years Coefficient	Transition Coefficient	Model 2 39-Years Coefficient	Transition Coefficient
Party	−.075	.521***	−.292	1.883*
	(.072)[a]	(.683)	(−.253)	(5.574)
President's Party	.901****[b]	1.052****	−.418	2.697*
	(1.461)	(1.863)	(−.342)	(13.834)
Senate	−.360	−.479***	.287	−.289
	(−.302)	(−.381)	(.332)	(−.251)
Split Congress	−.681	−.313	−2.361**	−.423
	(−.494)	(−.269)	(−.906)	(−.345)
Divided Government	.543	−.621**	−.945	−.762
	(.721)	(−.463)	(−.611)	(−.533)
Minority	−.228	.156	−.305	.631
	(−.204)	(.169)	(−.263)	(.879)
Party Leader	.294	.922****	−.792	.358
	(.342)	(1.514)	(−.457)	(.430)
Committee Leader	.271	.500**	.445	.290
	(.311)	(.649)	(.560)	(.336)
Post-1992	−.314	−.378	−1.237	−3.886*
	(−.270)	(−.315)	(−.710)	(−.979)
Year	.005	.021	−.308	.182
	(.005)	(.021)	(−.037)	(.199)
Year of President's Term	−.191		−.109	
	(−.174)		(−.103)	
President's Party × post-1992			1.388***	.693***
			(2.812)	(1.000)
President's Party × Party Leader			.857*	.587**
			(1.355)	(.799)
President's Party × Committee Leader			−.178	.203
			(−.163)	(.225)
President's Party × Party			.614	−1.372
			(.848)	(−.747)

(continued)

Table 3.2 CONTINUED

Independent Variables	Model 1		Model 2	
	39-Years Coefficient	Transition Coefficient	39-Years Coefficient	Transition Coefficient
President's Party × Senate			−.629 (−.467)	−.104 (−.099)
President's Party × Split Gov't			1.084* (1.955)	.696* (1.005)
President's Party × Divided Gov't			.814 (1.257)	−.306 (−.264)
Constant	−10.627	−44.345	76.064	−364.675
	N = 230	N = 797	N = 230	N = 797
	R² =.231	R² =.304	R² =.346	R² =.348

[a] Likelihood change in the dependent variable given a change in the independent variable, holding all other variables constant.

[b] Significant at ****p<.001, *** p<.01, **p<.05, *p<.10.

from the transition periods suggest that other factors may be important in public support for or opposition to the president. Being a Republican, a House member, or a party or committee leader also led to a higher likelihood of supporting the president, while Democrats, senators, and rank-and-file members were more likely to oppose him. We also see evidence that opposition to the president did indeed increase during times of divided government compared to unified government.

What we do not see in Model 1 is the influence of polarization, but to observe that requires a distinction between the president's party and members of the opposition within the various positions in Congress and the possible political contexts. Therefore, we look to Model 2, which includes interactive variables for the president's party with each of the other factors. The influence of polarization becomes obvious as we look at the results in the last two columns. First, it is clear in both the thirty-nine-year period and in times of transition that the president's own partisans became much more likely to support him after 1992 than they were prior to that. The transition years are particularly interesting on this point: they reveal that even though the period after 1992 was associated with more opposition to presidents, members of his own party were even more supportive of the president after 1992 than before, indicating that partisan polarization has indeed had an impact on members' decisions to oppose or support the president publicly, particularly among his copartisans. This finding is especially strong in light of the fact that the media, interested in conflict and the unusual, would be particularly likely to highlight intraparty squabbles between presidents and their copartisans if they occurred.[16] We can, therefore, be certain that increased support from the president's copartisans is a reflection of actual behavior, not just a consequence of media news values. In addition, we find in both data sets that party leaders in the president's party were more likely than nonleaders to support him.

There is also some indication of a connection between political context and support for the president. In the thirty-nine-year period, support for the president declined when control of Congress was split between the two parties compared to unified government. However, both data sets show a somewhat significant increased likelihood of support for the president among members of his own party when control of Congress was divided. It seems likely that in times where control of Congress was split, the media have been more inclined to focus on the president and the opposition party to provide two sides of the conflict. The president's own partisans may have found it more difficult to go public for any reason during these times, but they also knew they did not need to go public to oppose the president if they disagreed with him because their own control over one house of Congress gave them sufficient power over the policymaking process to alter or stop policies. Given their institutional power in such situations, they did not need to incur the costs of irking the president further by opposing him publicly when he was already battling the opposition party.

One more interesting finding emerges from the transition period data in Table 3.2. Once we control for the president's party, it appears that Republicans were somewhat significantly more likely to support the president than Democrats. In fact, a closer look reveals that Democrats were much tougher on their own presidents than were Republicans in transition years. In two of the three years in which a Democrat was in the White House (1977 and 1995), Democrats publicly opposed their presidents in more than 55 percent of the cases involving Democrats, and in the third year (1993), Democrats were supportive of their president in only slightly more than half the cases. In contrast, only in one of the four years with a Republican president did Republicans oppose their president more than 50 percent of the time (1987). In two of the other three years, their support was 60 percent or better. This would seem to support the conventional wisdom that Democrats have been a less cohesive party in general than Republicans.

CONCLUSIONS

I began this chapter asking why members of Congress go public. We have found several answers to this question. Members pursue a variety of goals through public strategies—passing policy, stopping it, and trying to shape the public debate, among others. They go public to react to events and other politicians, most notably the president. Perhaps most importantly, we have found evidence that members go public to enhance their power in Congress by trying to rally public support to help them shape or pass legislation and to compensate for institutional weakness by rousing public opposition when they cannot stop policy on their own.

We have also learned that the political context and growing polarization in Congress have influenced members' public strategies and their ability to attract coverage of them. During unified government, the minority party tends to be covered much more frequently for its efforts to stop legislation. In contrast, in divided government, both majority and minority members find it necessary to go public to stop legislation, and they also receive more attention for their efforts to frame the debate and shape policy. The different stages of the president's term in office also appear to affect members' efforts to go public. Over the president's term, his own party's public efforts to pass legislation decline, while the opposing party's efforts to do so increase. Polarization is linked to a growth in coverage of the minority party's attempts to stop policy and a drop in its public efforts to pass policy, while the majority party's use of public strategies to stop policy appears to decline, perhaps in an effort to maintain party unity. The impact of polarization is most keenly observed in members' reactions to the president. His own party's support for him has increased dramatically with heightened polarization while its public opposition has declined. At the same time those who are not in the president's party have nearly ceased their public support for him.

Chapter 4 moves beyond print media to consider how members of Congress have used television and new media to expand their opportunities to go public. It examines whether the political context plays the same role in members' public strategies in these other types of media.

New Paths to Influence

Broadcast and New Media

On June 10, 2010, *Politico* reporter Ben Smith highlighted what he called the best media advisory of the day. It was an electronic release from the offices of Congressmen Anthony Weiner (D-NY) and Jason Chaffetz (R-UT) entitled, "Weiner, Chaffetz, Goat," announcing a press event that the congressmen planned to hold to call attention to their efforts to kill outdated mohair subsidies.[1] To illustrate the issue, the congressmen would be joined by two angora goats, Lancelot and Arthur. The event was well conceived to attract a variety of media. It was connected to the larger issue of the federal budget and wasteful spending, a perennial favorite of the national media. With the addition of the goats, it had the potential for interesting video, important for television and new media, and a quirky dimension that might entice a variety of websites to pick up the story, not to mention countless opportunities for bad puns. Neither the politicians nor the goats disappointed. As Congressman Weiner decried earmarks, he held up the goat's ear which was indeed marked with a tag, and Congressman Chaffetz complained about the "fleecing of America."[2] But Lancelot got the last laugh when he literally stole the headlines by goring Congressman Weiner's hand. Lancelot's protest notwithstanding, Weiner and Chaffetz, two junior members of Congress, ultimately succeeded in gaining attention on national television, including nearly four minutes on the Fox News show *Fox and Friends*, and across the Internet for their efforts to cut mohair subsidies.[3]

As noted earlier, the opportunities for members of Congress to make national print news are limited and have declined as newspapers have reduced their coverage of politics over time. We saw in Chapters 2 and 3 that the attention to party leaders has increased over time in comparison to others in Congress, but attention even to specific party leaders in newspapers is still limited. And although rank-and-file members make up the largest percentage of members whose public efforts are covered in the *New York Times*, the amount of coverage that any single rank-and-file member receives is quite small. However, there have been significant developments in the media environment over the last two decades that have expanded opportunities for members of Congress—both leaders and nonleaders—to go public.

Two changes stand out. First, the advent of cable television with twenty-four-hour news channels and public affairs programming on non-news channels, like Comedy Central, has increased the need for political stories and commentary. Media-savvy members of Congress have happily stepped in to fill the void as it allows them to reach specific audiences.[4] Second, new media have given members more outlets for making news and new avenues for producing their own news. The example of Congressmen Weiner and Chaffetz illustrates the possibilities provided by the Internet. Typically, print media would not (and in fact did not) have the space to cover something like the mohair subsidy press event, but the online versions of national newspapers and exclusively online publications and blogs were free to cover it. Many did, some at surprising length. Furthermore, even without the coverage on various websites, new media—particularly social media like Twitter, YouTube, and Facebook—have removed the journalistic gatekeepers and allowed members of Congress to communicate whatever they like in a variety of formats. The initial information about the mohair subsidy event was published online on the congressmen's websites and emailed to the press. And whether reporters had chosen to cover the event or not, the members could post it to Facebook and YouTube and comment on it via Twitter.

This chapter looks at how congressional members have been able to use television and new media to go public to influence policymaking. As in earlier chapters, I consider the impact of the political context and members' own institutional positions on what and how they are able to communicate through television news and what they choose to communicate through new media.

TELEVISION

Prior to cable television and the explosion of channels that came with it, television news may have been the most challenging medium for members of Congress to use in going public. There were a limited number of news broadcasts each day, and congressional news had to compete with other issues and events, not all of them political. On political issues, members of Congress had to contend with not just each other but also the president and executive branch. Not widely known outside their state or district, most members of Congress were at a serious disadvantage because they were unlikely to attract the national audience network television news coveted. In a study of House members mentioned on network television news from 1969 to 1986, even in the best years fewer than half made the evening news even once during the year.[5] The same study found that party and committee leaders had a much better chance of making television news than rank-and-file members. In a study of the national media's attention to senators, author Stephen Hess also noted that leaders got most of the attention and concluded that most senators received so little national press that it was "irrelevant in affecting their elections or promoting their policies."[6] Even if they made the news, congressional members were likely to be heard only a few seconds as sound bites became shorter. Sunday morning news talk shows expanded the possibilities for members somewhat. The hour-long format dedicated primarily to public affairs and politics made some congressional members attractive guests because of their involvement in these issues. And the format lent itself to longer discussions than typical news stories afforded.

Sunday Talk Shows

To understand more about how congressional members have been able to use television news to go public and how this has changed over time, I analyzed all interviews with congressional members on NBC's Sunday morning talk show *Meet the Press* from 1990 to 2009.[7] There were 915 congressional interviews over the twenty-year period. They were relatively evenly divided between Democrats and Republicans. Reflecting national media's preference for the executive branch, members of the president's party in Congress accounted for only 44 percent of the interviews.

BIAS TOWARDS THOSE IN POWER

Television's bias toward those with power was evident. Nearly 60 percent of the interviews were with members of the majority party, only slightly less than in the *New York Times* coverage. Senators outnumbered House members two to one, somewhat more of an advantage than they had in print news. As evidence of the power individual senators have compared to House members, minority party senators had a much easier time getting covered than their House counterparts. In fact, minority party senators were interviewed nearly as often as those in the majority (47 and 53 percent, respectively). By contrast, only a third of House interviews were with the minority party. *Meet the Press* was particularly interested in congressional leaders, who accounted for just under half of the interviews, a bit more attention than they received from print media and quite out of proportion to their small numbers compared to rank-and-file members. The leadership interviews were nearly evenly split between party and committee leaders. Perhaps even more important than the number of interviews leaders had was the time they were given on the show. It typically exceeded what rank-and-file members received. When party leaders were on the show, they were the only guests during that particular block, and their interviews extended over several segments of the show. Interviews with rank-and-file members were usually just one segment of the show or involved multiple members being interviewed at once.

It is clear that *Meet the Press* had its favorites among individual members of Congress. Over the entire time period, just twenty-six congressional members accounted for 50 percent of the interviews. All of these members appeared on the show ten or more times. Senator John McCain (R-AZ) led with thirty-five appearances, nearly two per year. Senator Bob Dole (R-KS) was second with twenty-nine overall visits to the show, but he accumulated all of these appearances in just seven years, an average of four per year that outpaced all other members. Nine of the top twenty-six members were party leaders during this time period. During all of his seven years in the Senate over this time period, Dole was his party's leader, and his presidential aspirations combined with his wit help explain why he received more attention that other party leaders. Thirteen of the top twenty-six were committee leaders during at least part of this time period, often on key budget or tax committees. McCain was among this group, but like Dole he had added news value as a presidential hopeful, and he was something of a maverick who was not afraid to stand up to his party and was forthright with the press. The only two of the top twenty-six that held no party or committee leadership position and were not potential presidential candidates during the years studied were Charles Schumer (D-NY) and Lindsey Graham (R-SC). Both men made going public a conscious strategy to gain influence within the House and Senate, and they knew how to make themselves interesting to the media. In addition to being accessible to the media, both were highly quotable and sometimes unpredictable. It is perhaps a testament to the benefits of going public that Senator Schumer is expected to become his party's leader following Senator Harry Reid's retirement at the end of 2016. We'll learn more about Senator Graham's public strategies and their effects in Chapter 7.

SIMILARITIES TO PRINT MEDIA

As we saw in the earlier analysis of the *New York Times*, context mattered for congressional members' ability to get television coverage. There appeared to be fewer opportunities for members to go public on work-related issues during presidential and midterm election years. On average, fifty-seven members were interviewed in nonelection years. That number dropped to forty-seven per year during midterm elections and only twenty-two per year in presidential elections. The division of political power was also significant. Nearly two-thirds of the interviews occurred during divided government, when Congress is often a counterpoint to the executive. That trend was particularly unfortunate for minority party members who made up only 39 percent of the interviews in divided government, perhaps because media turned to the White House for their party's perspective. However, during unified government, the minority party fared better, accounting for 48 percent of the cases despite its lack of power. In that context, network television, if it wanted to maintain some balance, needed the minority as the primary voice of opposition to the majority in Congress and the White House.

There was striking consistency between television and print media on the issues members discussed in the press.[8] Government affairs, particularly scandals and investigations, was the most discussed issue, appearing in 35 percent of the interviews. This subject was followed by the budget and taxes (30 percent) and foreign affairs and national security in just over a quarter of the interviews each. Other issues came up regularly over time, including health care, civil rights, judicial and executive appointments, and social policy—all were mentioned in at least 10 percent of the interviews. Party politics was a topic in 10 percent of the television interviews, considerably more than in print media. The issue arose primarily after elections, as party leaders assessed their parties' gains or losses and the probable impact on legislation.

CHANGES OVER TIME

The *Meet the Press* interviews add to the evidence we saw in earlier chapters that going public in Congress has changed over time. Some of those changes may be driven by the media's changing interest, but some are no doubt prompted by members of Congress. The data reveal two major shifts in who was able to go public over time through television. First, in contrast to what we saw in the newspaper coverage, the proportion of *Meet the Press* interviews with congressional leaders compared to rank-and-file members declined over time. Congressional leaders accounted for more than 50 percent of the interviews in six of the first ten years of the *Meet the Press* analysis, but they rose above 50 percent only once in the second decade. A number of factors could account for the increased opportunities for rank-and-file members to go public on television. It might have been efforts by party leaders to involve more of their rank-and-file members in coordinating communication of the parties' messages. Certainly Congressman Dennis Hastert (R-IL), who was Speaker from 1999 to 2008, was quite happy to leave the television spotlight to others in his party. Or media-savvy rank-and-file members of Congress may have helped themselves by figuring out how to be more attractive to national television's news values. Whatever the reason, going public via television became significantly more likely for rank-and-file members over time.

A second change over time was the increased presence of minority party members going public, a development we also saw in newspaper coverage. In only one year from 1990 to 1999 did minority party members make up at least 50 percent of the interviews. But between 2000 and 2009, the minority party accounted for more than 50 percent of the congressional interviews in six years. Part of the reason for the increase may be the higher coincidence of unified government in the second decade. Indeed. half of the years in which the minority was interviewed at least as often as the majority occurred during unified government, but that also means that half the cases occurred during divided government, which suggests minority members may be making a greater effort to be heard even in situations where the media might not find them inherently newsworthy.

Most of the television data is from the era of polarization, and the evidence of partisanship is abundant. I selected five years from across the time period (about 25 percent of the total cases) to look at whether members of Congress were supporting or opposing the president in their comments on *Meet the Press*. The years were chosen to capture a range of political contexts (unified and divided government, election and non-election years, and various points within a president's term). More than half (57 percent) of the 234 cases in these years involved members reacting to the president. Consistently, the president's party was significantly more likely to support him than the opposition party did (see Figure 4.1).

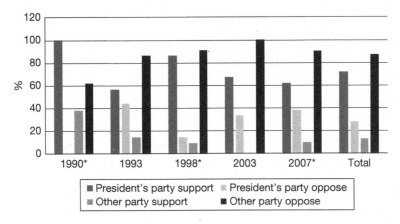

Figure 4.1 Reaction to the President on Television
*Indicates years with divided government.

In cases where members were reacting to the president, 73 percent of his copartisans supported him compared to only 13 percent of opposition party members. In fact, 83 percent of the opposition to the president came from those in the other party. Support among his copartisans was particularly strong from party leaders and increased during divided government, when the party would need to unite to accomplish its goals.

Not captured by the quantitative data but striking to me as I read the transcripts chronologically is a change over time in the show's format that encouraged more partisan debate. While the show made an obvious effort to provide balanced perspectives by interviewing members of different parties or members on different sides of an issue during the same show, during the earlier years the show's host and other journalists most often interviewed members of Congress, particularly party leaders, separately. Exceptions to this pattern were the frequent joint appearances by Senate leaders George Mitchell (D-ME) and Bob Dole (R-KS) in the early 1990s. While not afraid to discuss their differences, their joint interviews were quite civil. In the later years, however, the host would have more than one congressional member on at a time and often let them argue with each other. The later transcripts are rife with members talking over each other and using more combative rhetoric. The earlier transcripts provide evidence of more cerebral and orderly discussions of issues, while the later episodes more closely resemble the free-for-alls we have come to expect on cable television.

Cable Television

Although it is clear some members of Congress have figured out how to succeed in using network television news shows to go public, most still find this avenue closed to them because of the limited space for political news on these shows and the competition from the executive branch. However, cable television and twenty-four-hour news channels have opened a whole new world, one that many members of Congress have found more hospitable than traditional media. The daytime and evening programming on these channels, particularly Fox News and MSNBC, requires a steady stream of political news and commentary. In theory, this expanded political coverage might increase the number of issues that could be covered, allowing more members of Congress a chance to pursue public strategies for the issues on their personal agenda. In practice, however, it is not clear that cable news has really been open to more issues or has given members much more latitude to influence what issues get covered. Instead, these media organizations tend to focus on a limited number of major issues each day,[9] often those that fit the ideological agenda of the organization or the host of a particular show.

But cable news has expanded opportunities for members of Congress to talk about the issues cable news chooses to cover. Congressional members are involved in two ways. First, most cable news shows rely on news reporters to provide basic information on important stories and frequent updates and insight into how the issue or story is developing. Congressional members can serve as sources for these reporters. Second, members can appear directly on the shows to provide commentary on events and to debate each other or pundits. This latter option has become quite popular with those rank-and-file members who have a knack for speaking in sound bites and using highly charged rhetoric. Their combativeness is welcome on cable news, which is at least as interested in entertaining as informing its audience. Indeed some of the rank-and-file members, often relatively new to Congress, may be more sought after than party or committee leaders, who, out of necessity, may be somewhat more restrained in their rhetoric.

Congressional members' YouTube channels provide evidence of this new dynamic and the opportunities available on cable news channels. On July 1, 2013, there were no television appearances posted by House Speaker John Boehner or Minority Leader Nancy Pelosi in the "Recent Uploads" section of either leader's YouTube channel. But for three rank-and-file members I looked at on the same day, each had multiple cable television news appearances that had occurred within the previous month. Congressman Jared Polis (D-CO) had four television appearances among his twelve most recent videos—three on MSNBC and one on ABC. Congressman Jason Chaffetz (R-UT) had six appearances on Fox News, one on CNN, and one on the CBS Sunday show *Face the Nation*. Finally, Congressman Trey Gowdy (R-SC) had made seven Fox News appearances on various shows within three weeks.

Two things stand out about these videos. First, the Republicans appearing on Fox and the Democrat appearing on MSNBC suggest that the ideological leanings of each of these media organizations may offer more opportunities to similarly ideological members than more traditional news media and those like CNN that continue to resist ideological assignment. A quick search of Lexis Nexis transcripts for Fox News, MSNBC, and CNN programs during one month (July 2013) supports this ideological advantage, revealing that interviews are overwhelmingly conducted with congressional members who share the network's ideology. Fox programs included twenty-nine interviews with Republicans during the month but only three with Democrats, while MSNBC had thirty-one interviews with Democrats to just two with Republicans. And although CNN is more evenly balanced between Democrats (eight interviews) and Republicans (eleven interviews), overall CNN had fewer congressional interviews. Second, in all of the appearances posted on YouTube, the congressional members discussed issues the press was already covering. All three members went on television to talk about the recent IRS scandal in which the

IRS had targeted certain political groups, including Tea Party organizations, for special scrutiny in granting tax-exempt status. Other issues that came up in these videos included the 2012 attack on the American consulate in Benghazi, Libya, an issue to which Fox was particularly attentive, and the recent Supreme Court rulings on gay marriage, to which MSNBC gave considerable attention.

Beyond the typical news shows and public affairs talk shows that members have taken advantage of, cable television has provided additional opportunities for congressional members to go public. Most notably, two of Comedy Central's public affairs satire shows, *The Daily Show* and *The Colbert Report*, have featured members of Congress. Beginning in 2005, Stephen Colbert did a series of interviews with members of Congress on a regularly occurring segment called "Better Know a District." In addition to covering routinely what is going on in Congress through a satirical lens, *The Daily Show* hosts also interview members of Congress from time to time. Members' appearances on these shows are often among the most popular videos on their YouTube channels. However, while such shows give members exposure, they do not provide members with a consistent avenue for going public to influence policy.

NEW MEDIA

What have offered a more consistent means of going public are new media. Members have constructed their own official websites and email to communicate to constituents and the broader public for more than a decade now. They have invested more resources and staff to create "cyberoffices" that communicate frequently with constituents and mainstream media.[10] Members have also learned how to use blogs to influence public debate on issues.[11] Some have created their own blogs, while others, like former Senator Jim DeMint (R-SC), have fed information to friendly bloggers. During the 2007 immigration reform debate, DeMint sent parts of the bipartisan bill negotiated by President George W. Bush and congressional leaders to bloggers who began to criticize the legislation before it had been officially made public, helping to generate public opposition to the bill that scared many Republican senators away from supporting it.[12]

More recently, the unfiltered and immediate channels of communication offered by Twitter, Facebook, and YouTube have given congressional members a predictable and direct way to speak to the public on any subject members choose. Most members are now somewhat active on some, if not all, of these three social media platforms. In summer of 2012, only one senator and three House members were not on any of these social media.[13] Only twelve House members used just one. The rest of the House and Senate were active to some extent on at least two of these platforms. The next section looks at how members are using social media and compares this to their use of traditional print and broadcast media to go public to influence policymaking.

Twitter

Republicans in Congress were the first members to take to Twitter. Following the GOP's loss of its majority in the 2006 midterm elections, House Speaker John Boehner encouraged his members to open Twitter accounts to get the party's message out. In one example of the minority's Twitter use from 2008, several House members, including Congressman John Culberson (R-TX), used Twitter to publicize the Republicans' protest against Speaker Nancy Pelosi's decision to adjourn the House for its August recess without voting on a domestic offshore oil drilling bill. The Republicans stayed on the darkened House floor to make speeches criticizing the Democrats' refusal to vote on the issue, but without the benefit of C-SPAN cameras, which the Speaker had ordered turned off, members relied on Twitter to report on their protest, resulting in diverse coverage from States News Service to Agence France Press.

Some of the early studies of congressional Twitter use conducted by scholars at the Congressional Research Service in 2009 found that congressional forays into Twitter were undertaken by those who lacked institutional power. House members tweeted more frequently than senators, and minority party members were much more active on Twitter than members of the majority.[14] Much of what members communicated via Twitter called attention to their media events, their official duties, and their positions on issues. Only a small percentage of the tweets were personal. These patterns suggest that members turn to new media to compensate for and move beyond their institutional weakness, much as they try to do with traditional media. The big difference is that the new social media can accommodate all members, not just the ones that fit the traditional media's idea of newsworthiness.

CURRENT CONGRESSIONAL TWITTER LANDSCAPE

Since this initial research on congressional use of Twitter was done, 497 members (93 percent) have acquired Twitter accounts,[15] and Twitter use among the public and media has exploded. A sample of congressional tweets allows us to see how congressional Twitter use has evolved since 2009. Using the Tweet Congress website, which at the time contained a live feed of all tweets from members of Congress, my research assistant and I selected one daytime hour on nine nonconsecutive days in 2013 during February and March. Days were chosen to include times when Congress was in session and when members were in recess and back in the district, as well as weekdays and weekends; the times of day were varied. We analyzed all of the 324 congressional tweets that occurred during the nine selected hours. In quite a turnaround from the early days of Twitter, congressional Democrats outnumbered Republicans in tweets, 60 percent to 40 percent. House members, however, still outpaced senators in their Twitter activity, 80 percent to 20 percent.

Based on who is tweeting in Congress, as reported in Figure 4.2, it is clear that those with little institutional power have turned to social media to find their voice. In addition to House members drastically outnumbering senators in the use of Twitter in our sample, members of the minority accounted for 55 percent of the tweets, with minority House Democrats out-tweeting House Republicans 60 percent to 40 percent. And in stark contrast to what we saw on the Sunday morning talk shows or even in print media, party and committee leaders accounted for only one in four tweets,

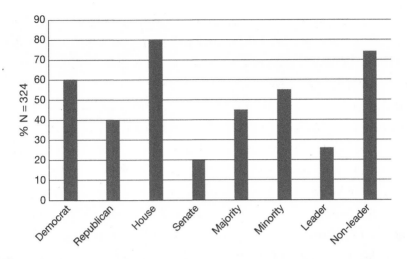

Figure 4.2 Who Is Tweeting in Congress

with the rest coming from rank-and-file members. When we looked at the most prolific tweeters in our sample, we found few in leadership positions. Fourteen members had at least four tweets. Congresswoman Louise Slaughter (D-NY) led the way with eleven. House Minority Leader Nancy Pelosi (D-CA) followed with seven, but she was the only party leader with more than three tweets in our sample. Six of the top fourteen members were relatively obscure House members, and only three were senators.

So what are members communicating via Twitter? We divided tweets into seven categories. *Position taking* involved members stating their position on legislation or an issue or introducing their own bill. *Advertising* included announcements of members' appearances in the district or state, meetings with constituents, and media appearances. *District outreach* announced events in the district or state that did not mention the member being there (e.g., job fairs), accomplishments of those in the district or state, invitations to constituents to offer feedback or participate in town hall events, and information about online newsletters. *Credit-claiming* tweets touted the accomplishments of the congressional member, such as passage of his or her bill. Some tweets *provided information* to followers or constituents without the member explicitly taking a position on the issue. The information provided varied widely—for example, on February

20, several members called attention to a government report that showed only a small percentage of those detained by Immigration and Customs Enforcement were serious criminals, and one member reminded residents in his district, where a major snowstorm was forecast, to bring in pets and check on elderly neighbors. However, a large majority of these tweets provided policy-related information, often tailored to the district, such as the ways budget sequestration would affect the member's state. *Response* tweets replied to another tweet. And *personal* tweets included anything that was not job-related, such as a member wishing people a happy Lunar New Year, tweeting pictures of the scenery as he was driving down the highway, or expressing his choice for pope.

The kinds of messages members tweet have not changed much during the time Twitter has been around. Activities that were simultaneously useful for influencing policy and re-election were most prevalent. Position taking was the most common reason members tweeted (40 percent of all tweets), and advertising came in second (25 percent), followed by providing information (12 percent). Activities more purely related to re-election followed: district outreach (10 percent) and credit claiming (5 percent). Personal tweets and responses combined for just 8 percent of all tweets. House members and senators devoted the majority of their tweets to more policy-related purposes (63 and 74 percent, respectively), but House members were more inclined than senators toward constituent-oriented tweets that might help with re-election. There were few major differences between the parties in the types of tweets. Most significant were that Republicans had a somewhat higher percentage of tweets advertising their media appearances (9 percent more), while Democrats had 9 percent more tweets providing other information. Two key differences between majority and minority party tweets lend further evidence that social media may be used to overcome institutional weakness. Because minority members may have a more difficult time attracting traditional media coverage, it is not surprising to see them tweeting less than half as often as the majority about their appearances on other media and using tweets more frequently to provide information directly to constituents and followers.

THREE OBSERVATIONS ABOUT CONGRESSIONAL TWITTER

The issues members tweeted about reveal three things. First, twitter is event-driven. On any given day, a large number of tweets often cluster around an issue linked to a specific event. Six tweets on health care on February 5 all reacted to the twentieth anniversary of passage of the Family Medical Leave Act. On February 28, forty-one of sixty-six tweets were on the House passage of the Violence against Women Act that day, and those accounted for 82 percent of all the crime-related tweets in the sample. President's Day generated multiple tweets. On March 6 the automatic budget cuts known as sequestration going into effect elicited thirty-six tweets on the budget and the effects of sequestration. Even the quite varied "other" category, which accounted for a third of the tweets, was often prompted by events: a festival in a district, a severe weather event that led congressional members to provide a link for storm information, or an anniversary of an event.

Second, members do have more control over the issue agenda on Twitter than they do in more traditional media. In print and television, five issues dominated what members discussed—budget/taxes, foreign policy, defense, government affairs, and appointments. Only one of those topics was the subject of more than 5 percent of the tweets; budget and taxes was the second-most tweeted issue, appearing in one in four tweets.[16] The most frequent issue category for the tweets was "other," accounting for 33 percent of all issues in the Twitter sample. In the print and television data combined, the "other" category made up only 2 percent of all issues across nearly 6,000 cases. Most of these other issues on Twitter were local: members touting the accomplishments of constituents, businesses, and sports teams in the state; mourning the passing of a local hero; or warning about impending weather events, among others. Crime was the only additional issue category that accounted for more than 5 percent of tweets; it was the subject of 15 percent of tweets, mostly because of the passage of the Violence against Women Act on one of the days in our sample. The other 27 percent of the tweets were divided among the remaining issue categories, with health care, immigration, civil rights, national security, business, foreign policy, and government affairs all mentioned in 2 to 4 percent of the tweets. On Twitter, members were free to discuss whatever national issues interested them, as well as many local issues, and they did.

Third, we find that coordinated communication is alive and well on social media. Members of Congress, often led by their party leaders, have learned that coordinating their communication—that is, multiple members focusing on one issue and using the same language to frame it and discuss it—is an effective way of trying to shape news coverage and thus debate on an issue.[17] Some of the tweets we observed showed evidence of such coordination. On February 28, the House passed the reauthorization of the Violence against Women Act, and five tweets had nearly identical language about giving victims of domestic violence the "support and protections they deserve." On March 6, numerous Democratic women, led by Congresswoman Louise Slaughter, tweeted about the budget sequester's effects on women as part of a Twitter town hall; all used the hashtag #standupforwomen. Coordination not only expands the number of people likely to see the message because different congressional members have their own followers; it also makes it more likely the press might pick up the message because journalists are often following multiple politicians and the repetition may catch their attention.

PARTISANSHIP ON TWITTER

Earlier in this chapter and in preceding chapters, we saw that members' public messages in traditional media have reflected the growing partisan polarization over time. Signs of partisanship were also evident on Twitter in the choice and framing of issues and in the political targets of many of the tweets. Just under 30 percent of the tweets involved issues that had a clear partisan perspective—either the issue was owned by one party or was framed in a way that favored one party. A few examples serve to illustrate. Tax cuts are a Republican-owned issue, while voting rights belongs to Democrats. Many issues not clearly owned by a party can be framed in ways that favor each party. For example, the budget issue does not inherently belong to one party; indeed, 35 percent of the tweets regarding the budget had no discernible partisan perspective. But Republicans can turn it toward their perspective by focusing on the need to cut wasteful

spending, while Democrats can use a frame that stresses the need to protect the disadvantaged from harsh cuts and to expect the wealthy to share
in the sacrifice of balancing the budget. In fact, about one-third of the
tweets on the budget used the Republican frame, and just under a third
used the Democratic frame. Across all tweets and issues, 17 percent were
obviously from the Democratic point of view, while 11 percent took the
Republican view.

The real partisanship becomes clear in looking at the members who
adopted these partisan perspectives. Nearly all (96 percent) of the tweets
on issues owned by Democrats or framed in their favor came from
Democrats, and 95 percent of tweets espousing Republican-oriented
frames came from Republicans. There were not many members of either
party venturing to adopt the other side's viewpoint. Even on the Violence
against Women Act, an issue that on paper was bipartisan and received
support from most Democrats and significant numbers of Republicans
in the House and Senate, few Republicans opted to tweet even generic
praise for the passage of the legislation that Democrats had embraced.
In contrast, nearly forty Democrats tweeted about the protections for
women. For Democrats, the issue clearly fit their message that they are
the defenders of women's rights, and some of their tweets on this issue
raised questions about whether Republicans were equally committed to
protecting women.

Beyond the issues and how they were framed, partisanship could also
be found in tweets that had a clear political target like the president or a
political party. Although only 9 percent of tweets explicitly referenced the
president or a party or party leader, an overwhelming 86 percent of those
that did expressed opposition to the target. And those voicing that opposition were from the opposing party in all cases. All opposition to President
Obama and to Democrats came from Republicans, and all opposition to
Republicans came from Democrats. For example, Republicans criticized
Obama for not offering a budget and changing positions on the sequester: from Congresswoman Virginia Foxx (R-NC) on February 5, 2013, "If
Pres. Obama is serious about lifting the sequester, why hasn't he offered
a budget? #ObamaAboutFace." Senator Johnny Isakson (R-GA) hit both

the president and Democrats in his tweet on March 6, 2013: "POTUS is a mo. late on his budget & Senate Dems haven't passed one in 1,400+ days. This is no way to run a country." On the other side, several Democrats criticized the GOP version of the Violence against Women Act. Minority Leader Nancy Pelosi (D-CA) tweeted, "House Republican VAWA bill is a non-starter for our nation's women. America's mothers and daughters deserve better" (February 22, 2013). What support there was for each party came only from members of that party. Thus, between the issues and how they were framed and the political targets of some tweets, the partisan divisions we saw in traditional media during the current era of polarization were also apparent on Twitter, though most tweets remained relatively free of blatant partisan rhetoric.

Facebook

A second social media platform that members have embraced is Facebook. Mostly we have heard about Facebook in the context of campaigns, as the 2008 presidential campaigns began to experiment with social media to connect supporters and communicate with them. By 2012 all but eighteen House members and three senators had official Facebook pages of some sort. To get a sense of how congressional members use their Facebook pages beyond the context of campaigning, particularly the extent to which they use them to influence policy debates, I looked at the Facebook pages of thirteen members of Congress all within a one-week period in June 2013. I chose *majority and minority party leaders* from each house—Senate Majority Leader Harry Reid (D-NV), Senate Minority Leader Mitch McConnell (R-KY), House Speaker John Boehner (R-OH), House Majority Leader Eric Cantor (R-VA), and House Minority Leader Nancy Pelosi (D-CA)—and the *chairs and ranking minority members* from the House and Senate Judiciary Committees—Senators Patrick Leahy (D-VT) and Charles Grassley (R-IA) and Congressmen Robert Goodlatte (R-VA) and John Conyers (D-MI). I also included a relatively junior rank-and-file member from each party on the Judiciary Committees—Senators

Amy Klobuchar (D-MN) and Ted Cruz (R-TX) and Congressmen Raul Labrador (R-ID) and Cedric Richmond (D-LA).

For each member, I looked at the official government Facebook page; in the cases of Senators McConnell and Klobuchar, who had no official government page, I examined their campaign Facebook pages.[18] Nine of the thirteen members had a link from their House or Senate website to their official Facebook page. House Speaker Boehner had no link to his Facebook page on his website, and Congressman Cantor's Facebook link was to the House chamber page, though he did have his own official Facebook page. McConnell and Klobuchar had no Facebook link because members cannot use their official websites for campaign purposes, and their Facebook pages were campaign pages. Seven members had updated their pages that day, and four had done so within the past two days. Only two, Pelosi and Labrador, had not posted anything in more than two days.

Like Twitter, Facebook can be used for a variety of purposes, from re-election to policy. And Facebook offers multiple ways to communicate different messages. Members can post photos that highlight their connection to constituents and their states or districts (e.g., festivals or constituent meetings) or that emphasize their work in Washington (press conferences or committee hearings) or graphics and figures that highlight issues and policy outcomes. Members can list "likes" that provided links to other individuals or organizations on Facebook. These "likes" ranged from the political (other politicians) to policy (nonprofit organizations in the member's home state or policy proposals such as "the American Energy Initiative" on Boehner's page) to the personal (Harry Reid's choice of the music group The Killers and boxer Manny Pacquiao). And of course, the comments and links that members post can communicate a variety of events and issues—some geared toward re-election, others toward policy. With all of these aspects of the page taken into account, eight members' pages were predominantly oriented toward policy—posts that focused primarily on issues currently before Congress or in the media, members' media appearances or floor speeches on these issues, and photos or graphics highlighting national issues. Four members offered a fairly balanced mix of policy and re-election-oriented posts and photos. House Majority Leader Cantor's page was unique and somewhat surprising given what we know about party leaders' important role in party communications. Although his likes (all key Republican politicians) and his photos (graphics and photos with other politicians and a few with constituents) pointed mostly toward policy, his posts were nearly devoid of current policy issues or political commentary. Most were commemorating political events like the ratification of the Constitution and former President Ronald Reagan's speech at the Brandenburg Gate in Germany; none were focused on the hot topics others in Congress were addressing. Overall, however, regardless of their position in Congress or how long they have been there, most members seem to be using Facebook to weigh in on policy debates.

Members certainly address a broader range of issues on Facebook than they do in traditional media. Based on the three most recent posts on each member's Facebook page, the "other" category was the subject of nearly one-third of the posts. Immigration was a distant second at 13 percent. That issue was playing out in both the Senate and the House at the time, and it was especially significant to members of the Judiciary Committees, who were tasked with crafting the immigration legislation. The only other issue that was mentioned in at least three posts was civil liberties and rights, with Congressman Conyers commenting on the Supreme Court voting rights decision and Congresswoman Pelosi commenting on a Republican abortion bill and gun control on the six-month anniversary of the Sandy Hook elementary school shooting. The issues that were most often discussed in traditional media—budgets and taxes, government affairs, foreign policy, and national security—were mentioned no more than twice each, but most of eighteen specific issue categories were mentioned by at least one member. The environment, crime, and transportation issues were the only ones not mentioned at all.

Partisanship was evident on Facebook, though it did not dominate most members' messages. In fact, among the three most recent posts on each member's page, twenty were not blatantly partisan issues. In the remaining nineteen, Democrats posted comments on seven issues that favored Democrats or were explicitly critical of Republicans, and Republicans had twelve posts on issues favorable to them or framed in ways that opposed Democrats. Nine members directly attacked the opposing party or President Obama on at least one issue. All the Republicans except Cantor criticized President Obama and the Democrats, with two of the newer members of Congress, Congressman Labrador and Senator Cruz, being highly partisan in their opposition to Obama. For example, Cruz, in reaction to the Obama administration's decision to stop White House tours because of the budget sequester, commented on a photo of President Obama returning to the White House under a headline "Home Sweet Home" that had added "For Me Not for Thee." Regarding this photo, Cruz noted that the "people's house is STILL closed for tours." Labrador provided a link to a video of his questioning of the FBI director about what he called "Administration abuses." Only three of the six Democrats explicitly opposed Republicans in their three most recent posts. Pelosi criticized the GOP for trying to place more restrictions on abortion and for standing in the way of gun control efforts; Reid complained about the budget sequester, which he attributed to Republicans; and Conyers blamed Republican cuts to the food stamp program for his decision to vote against the farm bill.

Despite the partisanship in some Facebook posts, two members tackled issues that put them at odds with their own party or President Obama. Democratic Senator Leahy posted a link to his questioning of Obama's national security director in a committee hearing on recently disclosed domestic surveillance programs by the National Security Administration. Republican Senator Cruz chose to highlight his opposition to two issues—the Senate immigration bill and the Obama administration's announcement that it would consider arming Syrian rebels—both of which enjoyed support from a significant fraction of Republicans. It may be easier for members to oppose their parties on Facebook without serious repercussions because party leaders are not as likely to notice what is said on Facebook as in traditional media, and reporters may be less likely to notice Facebook than Twitter. Thus, members can appeal to their supporters on Facebook when they disagree with the party or their own president without the consequences that might accompany higher-profile intraparty disputes in traditional media.[19] Indeed, Cruz received strongly supportive comments from his Facebook followers for his position on immigration.

YouTube

Another new media platform that members have adopted is YouTube. In summer 2012, only nine House members and one senator did not have a YouTube channel. However, the extent to which members actively use YouTube varies dramatically, with some members uploading new video many times a week, while others have not added video in nearly a year or more. To get a sense of how members use this video-sharing platform, I looked at YouTube channels for ten senators and seven House members.[20] I chose both leaders and rank-and-file members. Among the rank and file, I selected members who are often on television and those who are not, those whose committee assignments or interests connected them to current events and those who were not obviously tied in to recent issues, and those who had been in Congress for years as well as those who were new to Congress.

DOING THEIR OWN THING

Focusing primarily on the twelve most recently uploaded videos, I found significant variation in the members' use of YouTube. There were big differences between the parties, with Republicans updating their videos more frequently. All eight Republicans in the sample had uploaded all of their most recent videos within the previous month, several of them within the past three weeks. Only four of the nine Democrats had uploaded that many videos within the previous month, and two Democrats had not uploaded anything more recently than ten months before. Within each party, there was little difference between the rank-and-file members and the party leaders. There were no significant differences between minority and majority party members. There was evidence that more junior members of Congress are more frequent users of YouTube. Of the seven members elected in 2006 or later, all but one had posted twelve or more videos within the last month. Three of the ten more senior members of Congress had four or fewer videos posted within the last month.

The kinds of videos members chose to upload fell into three main categories. Most frequent were work-related video of members speaking on the House or Senate floor, in committee hearings, or at Capitol Hill press conferences; all members included at least some of these. The second kind of video were media appearances. Thirteen of the members highlighted their television or radio appearances, much as they did with Twitter and Facebook. Interestingly, the party leaders rarely posted their television appearances. Among the four leaders, only Senate Minority Leader Mitch McConnell included a media appearance. In contrast, junior Republican House members Jason Chaffetz and Trey Gowdy posted eight and seven appearances, respectively, while second-term Republican Senator Lindsey Graham led all members with nine television appearances. Perhaps most interesting is that seventeen of the combined twenty-four national television interviews with these three members were on Fox News, and all had occurred within the previous month, reiterating that cable television provides more opportunities for members to go public, and YouTube and other social media become a way to extend the reach of these media appearances. Finally, some members produced their own videos. These included John Boehner answering constituent questions on camera from his office, Jason Chaffetz and Elizabeth Warren commenting directly to the camera on current events, and House Minority Leader Nancy Pelosi using videos produced by her staff to criticize the Republican Party or key Republicans, like Congressman Paul Ryan, the chair of the House Budget Committee. For example, one video highlighted dissension within the GOP over tactics on the 2013 budget by mashing up clips from various news shows of Republican members criticizing their own party.

Like all social media, YouTube can be used for a variety of purposes from re-election to policymaking, and the members I studied incorporated all the possibilities. Senator Harry Reid, despite being majority leader, appeared to be intent on connecting to his home state, focusing mostly on issues of interest to his Nevada constituents—local wildfires, a local grant, clean energy, and immigration. House Minority Leader

Nancy Pelosi, perhaps with partisan electoral outcomes in mind, drew attention to the differences between Democrats and Republicans and was particularly critical of Republicans for not trying to solve major issues like the budget and immigration. However, the vast majority of videos seemed aimed at influencing policy debates, though some no doubt did double duty in serving the members' electoral interests as they highlighted policy positions that played well with constituents. Senator Jeff Sessions (R-AL) devoted ten of his twelve most recent videos to his opposition to the immigration reform bill working its way through the Senate. His opposition—explained in a combination of his own floor speeches, committee statements, one television appearance, and conservative television pundits offering arguments that supported Sessions's position on the issue—was popular with his Republican constituent base in Alabama, but his arguments also provided support for Republican House members who opposed what the Senate had passed; thus, the comments had the potential to influence the continuing debate.

The issues members addressed on YouTube were more focused on national issues than local ones. Based on the three most prominent issues for each of the fifteen members in my sample who had uploaded videos within the last three months, members were talking about the issues that were in the news at the time. Six addressed immigration, some many times, while five mentioned national security issues, particularly the leaks about the National Security Agency's domestic surveillance programs. Four reacted to recent Supreme Court rulings on civil rights—the Voting Rights Act decision and the decisions on gay marriage. Only four members had videos that involved the "other" issues category devoted mostly to local matters, an important contrast to Facebook and Twitter, where local concerns were prominent.

Different from Other Social Media

To get a better sense of how the issues on YouTube compared to other social media, I looked at the three most recent videos and tweets for thirty-six members of the House and Senate Judiciary Committees within a one-week period (July 9–17, 2013).[21] One-third of the YouTube videos were about immigration, compared to only 11 percent of tweets. Sixteen percent of videos were on civil rights, 11 percent for Twitter. The "other" issues category, which mostly encompassed local concerns, was only 10 percent of the YouTube videos but 44 percent of the tweets. On the remaining issues the differences were small. The overall picture that emerges is that members who take the time to upload to YouTube focus primarily on national issues and events taking place currently in Congress or the broader political environment rather than local concerns.

If members are using YouTube to try to influence policy debates, does YouTube also reflect the partisan polarization we have found in members' public strategies in other types of media? The answer is a resounding yes. In fact, YouTube appears to have more overt partisanship than other social media. In the sample of seventeen congressional members I examined, there were at least some direct attacks on the opposing party or president from most of the members. The Republicans launched particularly partisan attacks on President Obama and his initiatives. The Republican House members focused much of their ire on the White House and State Department's handling of the attack on the American consulate in Benghazi, Libya, in 2012 and the Internal Revenue Service's extra scrutiny of conservative groups seeking tax-exempt status. In addition, most Republicans had at least one video, often more, criticizing Obamacare, the Affordable Health Care Act, and attempting to stop its implementation. Senator Mike Lee (R-UT) had five videos attacking Obamacare. Senate Minority Leader Mitch McConnell also had five videos attacking Obamacare or other Obama initiatives. Even in the midst of his battle with members of his own party over immigration, Senator Jeff Sessions (R-AL) included one video entitled the "White House's 'stealth' role in crafting immigration bill." Although Republicans embraced the partisan battles most enthusiastically, Democrats also chose to focus on partisan differences. Several House members included videos criticizing Republicans for wanting to cut the food stamp program in the 2013 Farm Bill. As already noted, Minority Leader Pelosi devoted many of her recent uploads to attacking Republicans on specific issues, notably the budget, or more generally on getting nothing done on key issues.

There were some exceptions to the partisan tone. Surprisingly, one of the least partisan YouTube channels was Senate Majority Leader Harry Reid. And as on Twitter, some members used YouTube to express their opposition to their own party or president. A few Democrats publicized their comments against the National Security Agency's domestic surveillance programs on YouTube, and Republicans used YouTube to draw attention to their internal battles over immigration reform. In general, however, members of both parties and those in and out of the leadership chose YouTube to emphasize their opposition to the president and often the other party while offering their arguments for or against issues making their way through Congress or being discussed in the current media environment. They used it in ways that could shape the national debate on policies.

CONCLUSIONS

Television and new media clearly provide members with additional means of going public to influence policy, and the patterns of usage we see in these media platforms reinforce much of what we have seen in print media. Those with less formal power in Congress have turned to the media to move beyond the limits of their institutional power to influence policy, and television and new media have in many cases provided more hospitable venues for these public strategies. Minority party members, especially in the Senate, were often guests on *Meet the Press*, and minority members in both houses of Congress have made frequent use of social media. Junior members of Congress have found expanded opportunities to join the television debates through cable news channels. Congressional members without leadership positions and those who are most junior in Congress have typically been more frequent users of the new media, uploading video more regularly to YouTube and posting the majority of comments on Twitter and adding regular updates to Facebook.

The content of the messages in these different types of media have revealed key differences between traditional and new media. Members' opportunity to use television hinges, as it did with newspaper, on the ability to fit the media's news values. The issues members addressed on television were similar to those they discussed in the print news, and members who had power in Congress or who were unpredictable in some way or were willing to use strong partisan rhetoric often had an advantage over members who did not possess these traits. However, such things did not matter for new media, where the unknown members had the same opportunities as leaders, and the boring could have their say along with the partisan fire-breathers (though probably to a smaller audience, but that is a topic for another day). Indeed, the issues members addressed on social media were substantially more varied than what they found possible via traditional media.

The trend toward partisan polarization we saw in print media was evident on television and social media. In both, opposition to the president almost always came from the opposing party, and what support there was for the president almost always came from his own party. The same was generally true for opposition or support for each party and the issues associated with a particular party. One important deviation from this was evidence of intraparty conflict on both Facebook and YouTube among a small number of members.

The last three chapters have established that members of Congress can and do use media to go beyond their institutional powers. We have seen that the political context and increased political polarization have had an impact on when and how public strategies have been employed and when they are most likely to attract coverage. In the next three chapters, we turn to three case studies to provide further understanding of how public strategies have adapted to changes in Congress and when and why members use them. We also begin to consider their effectiveness in shaping policy outcomes and accomplishing members' goals.

Congress Responds
to the President

The Case of Social Security Reform

COAUTHORED WITH MEGAN S. REMMEL ■

In May of 1977, Democratic President Jimmy Carter announced to Congress his plans for saving Social Security, including an increased payroll tax for employers and workers and partial funding of the program from the general tax revenues. While the article in the *New York Times* reporting Carter's detailed proposal mentioned that a "long and vigorous debate [was] expected in Congress," the article devoted only five paragraphs out of forty to congressional reaction, and those were only muted responses.[1] Two Democratic leaders offered an alternative proposal without expressly criticizing the Carter's plan. The Republican leader of the Senate said the plan was "pretty well conceived."[2] Only two other articles elaborated on congressional reaction during the remainder of the month.

The scene was quite different in 2005, when Republican President George W. Bush provided broad guidelines for Social Security reform in his State of the Union address. Congressional Democrats began attacking the president's ideas *before* the speech, accusing the administration of manufacturing a crisis in Social Security. Senator Edward Kennedy (D-MA) expressed the opinion of many Democrats when he said, "The biggest threat to Social Security today is not the retirement of the baby boomers—it's George Bush and the Republican Party."[3] Although few outside the Republican Party leadership wholeheartedly jumped on board the administration's bandwagon, many expressed optimism toward the plan. In the week following the speech, entire articles were devoted to Democratic and Republican congressional reaction to the president's suggestions, most of it negative and most of it not accompanied by alternative solutions.

In both of these cases, presidents publicly announced major reform proposals, and Congress responded in the press. This pattern is one we have become accustomed to in American politics, particularly since 1981, when President Ronald Reagan's public strategies helped him pass his budget and tax plans through a Democratic House, and flummoxed Democratic leaders were left vowing never to concede the media to the president again.[4] But as we have seen in earlier chapters, there is a growing sense that congressional reaction to the president and his proposals has changed over time, becoming not only more public but also more partisan. Also in keeping with what we have learned from preceding chapters, dealing with the president is one situation for which congressional members' institutional powers alone may be inadequate, making media strategies an attractive option for members to improve their position with respect to the president.

To gain a better understanding of how members of Congress use the media to react to the president, this chapter looks at congressional members' public reactions to presidential efforts to reform Social Security in 1977, 1981, and 2005. These three examples illustrate how members of Congress have increasingly used the media to compete on a more level footing with the president to shape major policy debates. Through them, we can also see the growing importance of party leaders in responding to the president and the impact of increasing partisan polarization on members' public reactions to the president.

Social Security reform provides a good case study because it has been addressed by multiple presidents, and although it is important to both parties and to politicians across the country, the complexity of the problems and potential solutions are not easily sorted into partisan divisions and do not generate predictably recurring partisan reactions. All three cases that are the focus of this chapter began with presidential proposals to reform Social Security. Conveniently, 1977, 1981, and 2005 provide substantial variance in party control of the government, with both Democratic and Republican presidents and united and divided party government, allowing us to consider the role political context plays in public strategies and how the media cover them. Additionally, the cases resulted in different outcomes, permitting us to consider for the first time in this book the possible effects of public strategies.

For each of these efforts to reform Social Security, we examined several media sources: the *New York Times*, the *Washington Post*, ABC News, CBS News, NBC News, and the PBS *NewsHour with Jim Lehrer*.[5] We searched each source for stories using the terms "social security" and "senator" or "representative" in the month following the formal announcement of Social Security reform by the president. Using criteria similar to those employed in the data sets discussed in Chapters 2 and 3, we analyzed all stories that included direct quotes or paraphrased statements from members of Congress reacting to the president's Social Security reform proposal. For each member quoted or paraphrased in a story, we recorded the political party, house of Congress, position in Congress, including party or committee leadership, and response to the president's reform proposal.

In addition to the detailed analysis of the month following the president's announcement, we looked more superficially at the coverage for the month preceding the announcement and the remainder of the year following each announcement. We examined the quantity and overall tone of coverage heading into the formal announcement and how quickly the controversy died down in the months following the announcement.

RESPONDING TO PRESIDENTS

As we look at these three cases, we are struck with how going public in response to the president appeared to grow over time. We found a total of 268 cases of congressional members reacting to the president in the one-month period following each of the Social Security proposals. In 1977, there were only 26 cases of members reacting to President Carter's proposal. In 1981, we found 83 cases, three times the number in 1977. By 2005, there were 159 cases, almost twice as many as 1981 and six times as many as 1977, reporting congressional reaction to the president's proposed Social Security reforms. These trends appear to reflect the reality of what was actually taking place in Congress, as coverage of Social Security in *Congressional Quarterly Weekly Reports* during the same time periods provided a similar pattern: one article in 1977, seven in 1981, and thirty-seven in 2005. Likewise, according to data from the Policy Agendas Project, there were six congressional hearings related to Social Security reform in the four months following the president's announcement in 1977, fifteen in a similar period in 1981, and sixteen in 2005.

In both 1977 and 1981, almost no statements concerning Social Security reform came from members of Congress before the president's announcement, perhaps because the White House simply did not leak its plans.[6] However, in 2005, when President Bush began talking about possible reforms shortly after the 2004 election, reactions from members of Congress came weeks before the official announcement, and they received coverage in more than forty news stories. The large volume of comments concerning Social Security also lasted longer after the announcement in 2005 than in either 1977 or 1981.

Congressional responses appeared to correlate with the level of presidential activity on the issue. In 1977 the White House had Vice President Walter Mondale announce the proposal while President Carter was out of the country. Therefore, the president did little going public on the issue immediately. That decision, combined with the fact that Social Security was just one of many priorities Carter had given to Congress, made it less likely congressional members would go public on Social Security. Reagan employed his Secretary of Health and Human Services, Richard Schweiker, to make the formal proposal, and initially the president did little going public. But within ten days, he responded to members of Congress himself. Bush made the most effort to use public strategies to push his Social Security plan, leaking parts of the plan well in advance of the announcement and mounting a full-blown campaign including a tour of "60 stops in 60 days" after the announcement.[7] His public strategy put more pressure on members of Congress, especially the Democratic minority, to counter with their own public campaign. Thus it appears that while going public to respond to the president has increased in Congress over time, the decision to use this strategy depends on additional factors, including the president's own strategies and the political environment.

Who Responds?

In Chapter 3 we found that party leaders played a greater role in reacting to the president than they did in going public more generally, and their coverage in comparison to other congressional members who responded publicly to the president grew over time. The congressional responses to presidential Social Security reforms corroborate those findings: party leaders received a growing share of coverage in 1981 and 2001 compared to 1977 (see Figure 5.1). The leaders' coverage appeared to come at the expense of coverage of committee leaders' reactions. In 1977 committee leaders were covered more than twice as often as other members of Congress in response to President Carter's Social Security plan, accounting for 69 percent of the cases, while party leaders made up only 12 percent of the reaction. Committee leaders dropped to 40 percent of the cases in 1981 at the same time party leaders rose to nearly 27 percent of the cases. In 2005 party leaders dominated committee leaders in responding to the president, 32 to 16 percent. Rank-and-file members also gained more attention for going public over time, moving from just under one-fifth of the cases in 1977 to a third in 1981 and jumping to more than half in 2005. And mirroring the trends we saw in Chapter 2, although the congressional majority received more attention than the minority in every year, minority responses did increase, especially in 2005 (19 percent of the cases in 1977, 29 percent in 1981, and 47 percent in 2005).

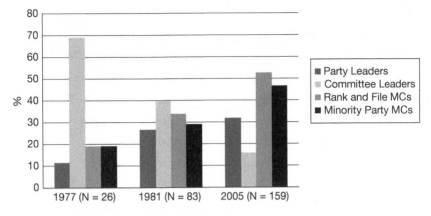

Figure 5.1 Who Went Public on Social Security

Opposing or Supporting the President

It is clear members of Congress use the media in reacting to the president, especially on major proposals like Social Security reform. But *how* do they react? Is going public an option primarily for opposing the president, or can members use the press to support the president or offer mixed assessments? Do reactions reflect the growing polarization in Congress? To learn more about the nature of these reactions, we coded each case as opposed to the president, mixed, supportive, or neutral. To be labeled opposed, a member of Congress had to state complete opposition to or rejection of the plan or say only negative things about it. For example, Senator Max Baucus (D-MT) claimed the idea of privatization had "nothing to do with the solvency of the Social Security trust fund. In fact, it makes the solvency of the Social Security trust fund much worse. Much worse."[8] Statements classified as mixed often came from members of Congress who supported one aspect of a plan but not another. These comments contained words like "caution" or "compromise," indicating an openness to work with the president to find a solution. For example, Congressman Jim McCrery (R-LA) said he thought Bush's plan would be a tough sell but that "we ought to shop it around."[9] Statements coded as supportive indicated a member of Congress completely supported the plan or made only positive comments about it. Finally, to be labeled neutral, a member of Congress had to express absolutely no opinion concerning the reform, such as Congressman Michael Fitzpatrick's (R-PA) comment that he could not "take a position on the president's plan until he saw the details."[10]

In all three Social Security cases, members of Congress largely did not support presidential reform proposals. Opposition accounted for 70 to 82 percent of responses in each case. However, the people opposing the president in 1977 differed substantially from those opposing him in 2005, as party played an increasingly important role in determining support or opposition to the president over time. Figure 5.2 reports how members of the president's party and those in the opposing party reacted to each president's proposal

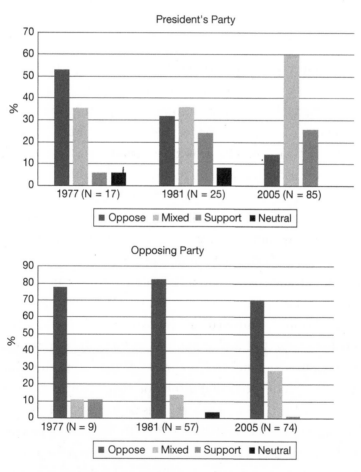

Figure 5.2 Support and Opposition by Party

to reform Social Security. In 1977, being in the president's party did not necessarily indicate whether a member of Congress would support or oppose
Carter's plan. About 11 percent of Republican comments openly supported
the proposal, and 53 percent of Democrats' statements openly opposed it. In
1981 party was still an imperfect predictor of support or opposition. While
we found no instances of Democratic support for Reagan's plan in 1981, with
the overwhelming majority of Democrats (83 percent) opposing it and the
remainder having mixed feelings, Republicans did not align themselves in
any coherent pattern. They divided among opposition (32 percent), support
(24 percent), and mixed feelings (36 percent).

In 2005, party was clearly important. Democrats almost uniformly
opposed President Bush. Out of seventy-four instances of members not
in the president's party, 70 percent expressed opposition, while only one
voiced open support.[11] The remainder (28 percent) had mixed feelings
towards the president's plan, most of them saying they would support the
aspects of the president's plan not involving personal retirement accounts.
Only 13 percent of Republicans responding in the coverage openly dismissed Bush's plan, and those expressing opposition tended to be well-
established members of Congress with long tenure or positions of power,
such as Majority Leader Tom DeLay, who objected to the president's
consideration of subjecting more earnings to payroll taxes.[12] However,
most members of the president's own party did not *fully* support the proposal either; 61 percent of Republicans expressed mixed feelings toward
the plan. Republicans who did not support the proposal often tempered
their expressions of doubt by stating their hope for a bipartisan solution.
Congressman E. Clay Shaw Jr. (R-FL) said the political center would hold a
bipartisan solution,[13] while Senator Charles Grassley (R-IO), chairman of
the Finance Committee, said, "[N]othing gets done that's not bipartisan."[14]

Growing Partisanship

To determine whether this apparent increasing partisanship was significant, we turn to multivariate analysis. To simplify the analysis, we dropped

the small number of neutral cases and looked just at opposition, mixed reactions, and support. With reaction to the president as our dependent variable, we used multinomial logistic regression to examine the relationship between members' positions in Congress (party leader, committee leader, minority party, or president's party) and the year on how they reacted to the president (see the column labeled "Model 1" in Table 5.1). Mixed reactions and support for the president were both more likely than opposition from members of his own party. Party leaders appeared

Table 5.1 REACTION TO THE PRESIDENT ON SOCIAL SECURITY

Independent Variables	Model 1 Coefficient	Change in Likelihood	Model 2 Coefficient	Change in Likelihood
Mixed Reaction				
Year	.070****a	.073	.046*	.047
Party Leader	−.895**	−.591	−2.100***	−.878
Committee Leader	.660	.934	.878**	1.406
Minority Party	−.493	−.389	.130	.139
President's Party	1.665****	4.286	−72.394	−1.000
Year × President's Party			.037	.038
Leader × President's Party			2.174**	7.791
Intercept	−140.700****		−91.997*	
Support				
Year	.066***	.068	−.030	−.029
Party Leader	−.243	−.216	.607	.835
Committee Leader	.489	.631	.884	1.419
Minority Party	.153	.165	1.064	1.898
President's Party	4.049****	56.349	−237.199*	−1.000
Year × President's Party			.121*	.129
Leader × President's Party			−.287	−.249
Intercept	−134.901***		54.336	
	N = 261		N = 261	
	R^2 =.419		R^2 =.449	

a Significant at ****p<.001, *** p<.01, **p<.05, *p<.10.

significantly less likely to offer mixed reactions than total opposition to the president, though we saw no significant difference in party leaders supporting or opposing the president. Coverage of mixed reactions and support for the president also increased over time compared to opposition.

These findings raise a few questions. First, did all party leaders behave the same way, or were there differences between those in the president's party and the opposing party? Second, did all members contribute to the increase in supportive reactions in the later years compared to opposition? Growing polarization would suggest that over time those in the president's party and those who were not would behave differently, and the difference would be strongest among party leaders. Therefore, we need to look at subsets within these various categories of members. To do this, we added two interactive terms to the model—the president's party with party leaders and with the year.[15] The results are reported in Table 5.1 under "Model 2."

First, we find that even as polarization increased, committee leaders were typically more moderate in their responses than party leaders. Compared to other members, committee leaders were 141 percent more likely to offer mixed reactions than outright opposition, while party leaders were 88 percent more likely than other members to oppose than offer mixed reactions. Indeed, party leaders expressed outright opposition to the president in 65 percent of the cases in which they responded; only 41 percent of the committee leaders' reactions were completely opposed. This divergence did not mean committee leaders were more supportive of the president; they were nearly equal to party leaders in their support (11 and 12 percent, respectively). But committee leaders offered mixed evaluations of the presidential proposals much more often than did party leaders (44 to 23 percent), suggesting committee leaders were more interested in reaching solutions than in scoring partisan points.

Model 2 also shows the impact of growing polarization. Most obviously, we see that support for the president within his own party increased 12.9 percent over time. And when we control for that interaction, the independent impact of the president's party on members' reactions to him becomes much less significant than we saw in Model 1 and is in fact substantially less likely to be connected to support for the president than opposition. Additionally, we see that mixed positions increased somewhat over time in comparison to opposition, though this did not depend on whether members were in the president's party. One possible explanation for this shift is that members in the president's party feel more pressure in the era of polarization not to offer outright opposition to their president, so they couch their concerns in more complex mixed responses that also offer support to the president. Similarly, members of the opposite party who support the president may feel compelled to offer mixed reactions to avoid the ire of their own party leaders.

PARTISAN RESPONSES AND FRAMING

Clearly responses to the president have become more partisan over time, but numbers can tell us little about the intensity of congressional reactions. For that kind of insight, we turn to a more qualitative look at the coverage of the Social Security reforms and see that the rhetoric has indeed intensified. In 1977 Carter's plan was controversial and met immediate and widespread bipartisan resistance, but the criticism was measured and focused on substantive concerns with the president's proposal. For example, Congressman James Burke (D-MA), described as reacting "coolly" to the plan, said, "Well, we're going to look it over very carefully. . . . We have to give them a chance to present their case."[16] And Republican Congressman Bill Archer of Texas declared his opposition to the plan because it would "raise the amount of workers' income on which employers must pay the Social Security payroll tax."[17] Those who disagreed with the administration's plan frequently offered proposals of their own or compromises. For example, Russell B. Long (D-LA), chairman of the Senate Finance Committee, said while the Senate "will vote to do much of what the President is recommending," Long had some ideas of his own to modify the proposal.[18] One might be tempted to argue the lack of harsh criticism or strong partisan rhetoric was a byproduct of a large Democratic majority enjoying its first taste of unified government in eight years. But in 1981, when Republicans regained the White House and the Senate, despite some harsh partisan rhetoric, we still saw some bipartisanship and substantive debate.

President Reagan's proposal to reduce benefits created an immediate backlash in Congress. Congressman Claude Pepper (D-FL) called the plan "nothing more than a wholesale assault on the economic security of America's elderly population."[19] House Speaker Tip O'Neill (D-MA) used words like "despicable," "breach of faith," and "stone-hearted."[20] But other Democrats were more measured in their responses. Congressman J. J. Pickle (D-TX) called Reagan's proposal a "sincere package."[21] Republicans were not as harsh as many Democrats in their responses, but they were skeptical of the president's plan, and the Republican-controlled Senate voted unanimously to oppose part of the proposal.[22] Within days, Reagan expressed a willingness to compromise with Congress, and from that point on, much of the opposition turned partisan, with Speaker O'Neill, Senator Daniel Patrick Moynihan (D-NY), and other Democrats maintaining their attacks through the summer.[23]

Interestingly, Democrats disagreed among themselves as to how bitter their opposition to the president should become. Within the first week of the announcement, O'Neill said, "I will be fighting this [Reagan's proposal] every inch of the way, and I hope that will be the position on [sic] every member of my party."[24] In the same article, Congressman Pickle, the chairman of the Social Security Subcommittee in the House Ways and Means Committee, said he wanted Democrats to "reserve [their] gunpowder." Their difference of opinion continued into the summer. After some Democrats held a press conference in July to criticize the president's efforts to reform Social Security, Pickle said, "The attacks by our leadership, the response by the president, these things are constantly painting us into a partisanship role which I hope will not go deeper."[25] Pickle made it clear he was working on a bipartisan compromise and had support for his efforts in his committee. Thus, in 1981, we see more partisan attacks on the president's plan than in 1977, but there were still members of both parties offering alternatives and searching for compromises.

In 2005 there was much more reaction to the president than in either of the other two years, but it did not elevate the political discourse. There was no bipartisanship, and the rhetoric was harsh. For example, Congressman Rahm Emanuel (D-IL) said, "The real face of the Republicans' Social Security 'reform' agenda: First, scare. Second, cut. Third, privatize. Now that's a reform agenda."[26] This effort to attach Bush's plan to the Republicans and attack the entire party was in contrast to 1981, where members opposed to Reagan's plan were more apt to attack the president himself than members of the other party. Unlike previous years, when many of the president's opponents offered alternative ideas, Democrats did not put forth their own plan in 2005. House Minority Leader Nancy Pelosi said Democrats had no alternative because they claimed there was no crisis in Social Security.[27] Congressman Harold Ford Jr. (D-TN) called out his own party for its lack of initiative, saying, "the Democrats are going to have to get a better message on Social Security. . . . Our only response cannot be to say, 'No.'"[28] Yet no Democratic proposal emerged. On the Republican side, Senator Lindsey Graham (R-SC) attempted to work with President Bush on compromises to his initial proposal, but those efforts proved insufficient to win support.

In addition to the increased intensity of the rhetoric and partisanship over time, we also found members became more effective in challenging the president's framing of the debate. In 1977, no one questioned the president's definition of the problem, and there was only one line of concern that might have reframed his solution. Congressman Al Ullman (D-OR), chairman of the House Ways and Means Committee, and Republican Bill Archer warned that Carter's reform might transform Social Security from an insurance program to a welfare program, but this did not appear to be a concerted or widespread effort to change the framing of the debate, and it certainly did not catch on in the press.[29] In the 1981 Social Security reform battle, most members of Congress accepted Reagan's framing of the situation as a crisis, though Majority Leader Jim Wright (D-TX) did suggest action on Social Security could be delayed until later in the year because it was "not in imminent danger of collapse."[30] And as partisan tensions rose during the summer, some Democrats claimed Reagan was exaggerating the problem.[31] But again, there was little coordinated effort to reframe the debate as all sides agreed some sort of reform was needed in the relatively near future.

However, by 2005 a highly polarized Congress focused much attention on framing the debate. First, there were different ideas concerning the definition of "crisis." President Bush told a gathering of supporters in Pennsylvania that his "first mission is to travel our country making it clear to people of all political parties, all demographics, we've got a problem. And you can define it 'crisis,' 'big problem,' whatever you want to define it."[32] Democrats, led enthusiastically by Senate Minority Leader Harry Reid of Nevada, centered their response on the claim no crisis existed in Social Security. Reid stated, "We have no crisis. For the next 50 years people on social security if we do nothing will draw 100 percent of their benefits. Even after 50 years if we decide to do nothing congressionally, they can still draw 80 percent of their benefits. That's not a crisis."[33]

In response to the plan itself, Democratic members of Congress reframed one crucial term: "personal retirement accounts" became "privatization." Senator Reid said, "We're going to use the word 'privatization' every chance we get."[34] Once they witnessed the public backlash against "privatization," many Republicans turned tail and also started to use the term, undermining the president's efforts; Senator Chuck Hagel (R-NE) said, "I don't think the solution is just private accounts."[35] In 1977 and 1981 the media adopted the White House frame, but in 2005 the media questioned the administration's claim of an imminent crisis and generally adopted the Democratic terminology of "privatization," allowing Democrats to win that battle. It appears that congressional responses to the president have become more partisan and potentially even more effective as members figure out what the media will cover and gain practice in communicating through the media.

IMPACT OF THE POLITICAL CONTEXT

One question set aside until now is the impact of the political context, particularly presidential approval ratings, on congressional members' public responses to the president. Certainly the more vocal and intense opposition to President Bush's Social Security plan in 2005 may have been in part a result of his low approval ratings. Bush was at 50 percent compared to Carter's 71 percent in 1977 and Reagan's 55 percent in 1981.[36] To get a better sense of the impact approval and other political factors might have on congressional reaction to the president, we conducted a content analysis similar to the Social Security study that looked at the two weeks of coverage in the *New York Times* and on NBC News following each announcement of the president's budget from 1977 to 2007. For each case, we recorded the percent of people approving of the president in the Gallup Poll immediately preceding the budget announcement. Using congressional members' reactions to the president's budget as the dependent variable, we analyzed the impact of whether members were in the president's party, part of the leadership, or in the minority and several aspects of the political context, including the year, whether it was an election year, and the president's approval rating.

The results in Table 5.2 provide additional insight into what we found in the Social Security cases. Looking first at the independent effects of the members' positions and the political context (Model 1), we found that being in the president's party was significantly associated with a higher likelihood of mixed or supportive reactions than opposition to the president. Being a party or committee leader was also connected to higher support than opposition, though it had no effect on mixed reactions. And members of the minority were more likely to offer opposition than mixed reviews of the president's proposal. The context variables were extremely important, with higher levels of presidential approval more likely to increase mixed reactions or support than opposition. In contrast, election years meant more outright opposition, as mixed reactions and supportive responses were less likely then. The independent effects of increasing polarization (as measured by the year) were not evident.

Model 2 in Table 5.2 adds interactive variables to see whether being in the president's party mediates the effects of a member's position in Congress, election years, presidential approval, or changes in polarization as measured by the year. As we saw with the cases of Social Security reform, this interplay is important. Although holding a leadership position seemed to have no significant effect on mixed reactions in our first

Table 5.2 REACTION TO THE PRESIDENT'S BUDGET:
EFFECTS OF PRESIDENTIAL APPROVAL

Independent Variables	Model 1 Coefficient	Change in Likelihood[a]	Model 2 Coefficient	Change in Likelihood
Mixed Reaction				
Party/Committee Leader	.032	.033	−.990**[b]	−.628
President's Party	2.049****	6.758	−169.303**	−1.000
Minority Party	−1.080***	−.660	−1.213**	−.703
Year	.010	.010	−.024	−.024
Presidential Approval	.033**	.033	.019	.019
Election Year	−.718**	−.512	−1.014**	−.637
Year × President's Party			.083**	.087
Leader × President's Party			2.842****	16.150
Approval × President's Party			.061*	.063
Election Year × President's Party			1.055	1.873
Constant	−21.532		46.949	
Support				
Party/Committee Leader	1.476**	3.375	−1.135	−.678
President's Party	4.546****	93.273	−441.543	−1.000
Minority Party	−.779	−.541	−.971	−.621
Year	.001	.001	−.181	−.166
Presidential Approval	.078***	.081	.154**	.167
Election Year	−.987*	−.627	−.305	−.263
Year × President's Party			.225*	.252

(continued)

Table 5.2 CONTINUED

Independent Variables	Model 1 Coefficient	Change in Likelihood[a]	Model 2 Coefficient	Change in Likelihood
Leader × President's Party			4.178***	64.220
Approval × President's Party			–.048	–.047
Election Year × President's Party			–.197	–.179
Constant	–10.396		347.684	
	N = 262		N = 262	
	R² =.433		R² =.511	

[a] Likelihood change in the dependent variable given a change in the independent variable, holding all other variables constant.

[b] Significant at ****p<.001, *** p<.01, **p<.05, *p<.10.

model, we found that once we separated leaders in the president's party from those who were not, leaders generally were more likely to oppose the president than offer mixed reactions, but those in the president's party were significantly more likely to offer mixed reactions or support than opposition. Evidence also suggests that growing polarization has affected the budget debates: the president's copartisans were more likely to offer mixed reactions and support over time than opposition, and the independent effects of the president's party moved in the opposition direction or disappeared when we controlled for polarization. Interestingly, we found that higher approval ratings were only somewhat significant for holding down outright opposition to the president among his copartisans. The independent effects of presidential approval on mixed reactions disappeared when the interactive variable was added. However, high approval continued to be significantly associated with a higher likelihood of support than opposition, regardless of the member's party. Minority party members were still more likely to oppose the president than offer mixed reactions. And in election years, members were more likely to offer outright opposition than mixed reactions. Context clearly matters in congressional members' reactions to the president.

CONCLUSIONS

Congressional response to the president in news coverage is not new, but in the last decade it has become more intense and more partisan, especially among party leaders, as members of Congress have turned to public strategies to augment their power with respect to the president. Responses to the president seem to have increased over time on high-priority issues like Social Security reform and budget proposals.[37] In part, this appears to be a reaction to presidents' greater use of the media. Although members have the same powers to use the legislative process to shape or even stop the president's proposals, they have to rely on the media to help them win the battle for public opinion. Along the way, party leaders have received more coverage for taking an active role in reacting to the president. Perhaps most importantly, we have seen a consistent increase in partisanship: Congress has gone public to respond to presidents, with members of the president's own party, especially the leaders, being more likely to support than oppose him publicly in recent years, while those in the other party almost never offer outright support.

These developments help explain why presidents are finding less success in going public today than they once did.[38] Members of Congress are going public to counter the president more often, or at least they are more successful in getting coverage for it. But why? As *New Republic* writer Michelle Cottle explains, getting covered is a challenge: "For members of Congress, it's always a struggle to avoid vanishing into the shadow of the White House"; compared to the president, the "average House member ... is one of 435 charisma-challenged, comparatively powerless dweebs."[39] But congressional members' counterstrategies appear to be becoming more sophisticated and better coordinated over time, as the Democrats' victories in framing the 2005 Social Security discussion illustrate. The more distinct partisan divisions seen in the coverage of the budgets and in the thirty-nine-year period covering a wide range of issues that we saw in Chapter 3 suggest the president has less of an advantage in shaping the public debate in recent years because members of Congress are reacting to his proposals not merely as individuals but as part of a larger partisan entity competing on more equal footing with the president in the eyes of the media. Members who are not in the president's party have certainly found the media useful in augmenting their formal congressional powers to oppose the president.

So if members of Congress can use the media to counter the president's efforts to go public, what impact might this have on policymaking? The Social Security cases raise concerns on this point. In 1977 and 1981, at least some members in both parties publicly suggested alternatives to the president's plans and advocated compromise. Agreements were reached in both cases. The 1977 legislation was scaled down but included some of President Carter's initial proposals, passing in the House by a 412–10 vote and the Senate by 96–0. In 1981 the result was more complicated, as Congress passed a short-term measure and agreed with the president to appoint a bipartisan commission to recommend a long-term solution and postpone action on that until 1983. The plan was passed in 1983 on a bipartisan vote of 243 to 102 in the House and 58 to 14 in the Senate. But in 2005, where congressional reaction was most intense and most partisan, nothing passed. While the problems facing Social Security were not as imminent in 2005, the congressional reaction against the president made no pretense of trying to find a solution even to the future problems everyone agreed the system would face. This trend towards partisan and coordinated reaction to the president and the increasingly effective public strategies of congressional members may portend ominously for the policymaking process as members' tactics appear to be aimed more at stopping legislation than moving it toward a compromise. We revisit this issue in the concluding chapter.

Overcoming Institutional Weakness

The Congressional Black Caucus Goes Public

In 1979 at a news conference, the Congressional Black Caucus (CBC) called President Jimmy Carter's proposed budget "immoral and unjust" and accused the president of being "out of step with the majority of the people" in the United States.[1] Even after meeting with Carter a month later, the CBC was unsatisfied. At a press conference following the meeting, CBC chairwoman Cardiss Collins told reporters, "We're going to go out and mobilize our troops[.] . . . We've laid down the gauntlet, so to speak. We're not going to sit back and take these budget cuts."[2]

Thirty years later, in December 2009, the CBC made it clear that just because President Barack Obama was a Democrat and an African American did not mean he would be spared from public criticism by the caucus. As reported by *Politico*, "The long-simmering family feud between the Congressional Black Caucus and the first African-American president burst into the open on Wednesday, with members boycotting a financial overhaul vote as a warning shot" at the president.[3] The article reported that Congresswoman Maxine Waters voiced the CBC's frustrations with the Obama administration during a press conference and left no doubt CBC members would vote against Democratic bills if Obama and his staff did not address the CBC's concerns on unemployment and home foreclosures.

The Congressional Black Caucus has a long history of resorting to the media to gain the attention of presidents, fellow congressional members, and the public. This chapter looks at how the CBC's use of the media has developed over time as the CBC's own formal powers have evolved and how the group's success in getting coverage has been affected by different political contexts. It will allow us to gain a better understanding of the strategic considerations that come into play in going public. We begin by examining why the CBC adopted public strategies early in its history.

THE CBC'S EARLY EMBRACE OF PUBLIC STRATEGIES

We have seen already in this book that members of Congress use public strategies to move beyond their own institutional weaknesses. They turn to the media to help them do what they cannot accomplish through their formal powers. This is manifested in a variety of situations members may face. Sometimes they find themselves with no institutional platform to initiate or influence policy because they are not on the right committee or do not hold a place in the party leadership structure. Coverage on an issue can be a way to bypass the leadership and the formal process to put issues on the legislative agenda and force members who do have power to take action.[4] For congressional members who find themselves losing the debate in Congress or even within their own party, going public is a way to gain influence by bringing others into the discussion or expanding the scope of conflict. And although it may be difficult for members of Congress to change minds, they can reframe an issue and shift attention to new dimensions of the conflict to bring in people and groups who were not previously interested in the issue.[5] They may also adopt public strategies to compete with the president in educating the public, forcing the president to address issues they consider a priority that might not be on his agenda, or gaining leverage to bargain with the president.[6] And when all else fails, they go public to oppose the president.

Of all the groups and individuals in Congress, the Congressional Black Caucus may have the most experience over time in working from a position of institutional weakness, and the media have been a key tool for CBC members who wanted to influence policymaking. The CBC has historically been at an institutional disadvantage in Congress. Treated as second-class citizens even by their fellow Democrats in the late 1960s and early 1970s, African American members turned to the media to get around the institutional constraints.[7] African American Congressman Adam Clayton Powell frequently took his ideas and issues to the media and found that his public strategies gained him "popularity within the mainstream press [that] expanded his influence within the House chamber."[8]

Even after the formation of the Congressional Black Caucus, through which African American members of Congress attempted to coordinate their efforts to enhance their influence, the CBC remained a minority faction within the Democratic Party and found that the institutions and structure of Congress limited the CBC's policymaking effectiveness.[9] In part, the CBC members were in a weak position in the early 1970s because they had junior status in Congress and did not possess the traditional sources of institutional power, like committee or subcommittee chairmanships or party leadership positions. To compensate for its lack of formal power, the CBC turned to public strategies to raise its profile. Extra-congressional activities—conferences, hearings, and protests—became an important way for the CBC to get media attention.[10] Following in the tradition of the civil rights movement and appealing to the media's interest in drama and conflict, the CBC was adept at using unconventional action to generate media attention to its concerns. Particularly in the area of foreign policy, members employed dramatic protests and threats to boycott meetings to call press attention to issues.[11] In one example from 1984, the CBC joined with other organizations outside of Congress to stage protests every day for more than a week at the South African embassy in Washington and at businesses that did business with South Africa, with some congressional members getting arrested, to call attention to the country's apartheid policies and pressure the US government to take stronger action against the South African government.[12]

Indeed the CBC discovered the value of going public and developed effective media strategies earlier than most groups and individuals in

Congress, including the party leaders. In 1977, at a time when many members of Congress still did not have a designated press secretary and party leaders were still chosen primarily because they knew parliamentary procedure, with little thought to their ability to interact with the media, the CBC had media-related strategies in place. It publicly released a biennial legislative agenda, published a monthly newsletter, and set up an action-alert communications network to mobilize African Americans at the grassroots level.[13] In the 1980s, following frustration with the budgets submitted by presidents of both parties and its own party in Congress, the CBC began to introduce publicly and push for a vote on its own budget each year, often receiving press coverage of its efforts. The caucus also routinely wrote letters to executive officials to push its agenda and concerns and made the letters available to the press.[14] In publicizing such letters, the CBC raised public awareness of the issue and with it the cost of inaction for the president or officials on the receiving end of the letter.

As they have gained seniority, moved into leadership positions, and increased in number, CBC members have found themselves better able to employ a legislative strategy in lieu of going public.[15] However, they have continued to use public strategies in conjunction with more traditional inside efforts to influence policy. In a 2008 interview with the author, CBC Communications Director Keiana Barrett described a well-developed communications strategy that attempted to coordinate the efforts of communications directors in all the CBC members' offices through frequent meetings. CBC communications staff posted a media guide on the CBC's website to provide reporters with information about CBC members and their areas of legislative expertise and interest. Additionally, communications staff worked to cultivate ongoing relationships with reporters—not just in the mainstream media but also in the new media, especially bloggers. Staff identified reporters who specialized in reporting on issues the CBC was concerned about and fed those reporters information so that when these issues came up in the press, the reporters were more likely to seek out the CBC for comments and reactions.

Given its long history of going public, the CBC provides an interesting case study for us to understand more about how members of Congress, and particularly groups within Congress, have used public strategies to influence policy. The remainder of this chapter looks at how different political contexts and media interest appear to influence the CBC's public responses and messages or at least which ones are likely to be covered. It examines the CBC's coverage in the *New York Times* from 1977 to 2009. From all articles that mentioned the CBC during that time period, 289 were selected for analysis.[16] They included all articles that quoted or paraphrased a CBC member speaking on behalf of the caucus. For example, one article stated, "Members of the Congressional Black Caucus ... have angrily denounced assertions that the lawyer is a sympathizer of Mr. Castro. 'We have to appeal to the Clinton Administration to explain to us why this guy is not acceptable,' Congressman Charles Rangel said."[17] The article explicitly states the CBC position and includes a quote from one of its members. The analysis also incorporated articles that contained information that made clear the CBC's position on an issue or event related to its work in Congress. For example, one article explained that the "Republican leadership rejected ... a Congressional Black Caucus alternative budget that would have sharply reduced spending cuts in many social programs and raised taxes to pay for deficit reduction."[18] Although the article includes no direct quotes, it does provide information about the CBC's public position on the issue. Articles that discussed the CBC's position on presidential candidates or events that were not relevant to the legislative or oversight responsibilities of Congress were not included because we are primarily interested in how the CBC uses the media to influence national policy rather than elections or state or local issues.

WHEN THE CBC GOES PUBLIC

Congressional members can use the media to influence policymaking only if they can get media coverage. Therefore, the CBC's ability to go public successfully—that is, get media coverage for its activities and statements—depends in part on how newsworthy it is on the particular issue in question. And that newsworthiness is as likely to result from the

CBC's own institutional strengths or weaknesses, which vary according to the political context, as from its actual message. Thus, which party is in control of Congress and/or the White House may be as important for determining when the CBC can use public strategies as anything that the group can control itself.

The Importance of Political Context

We have learned in earlier chapters that members of Congress who find themselves in the minority have limited powers with which to influence policy, making media strategies an attractive means to oppose the majority in these situations. So, at first glance, we might expect the CBC to be more interested in pursuing a public strategy when Republicans constitute the majority in Congress. However, the minority party's lack of power in such situations might give the CBC an incentive to suppress its own inclination to go public against a Republican majority and instead to cooperate in the strategies of Democratic Party leaders to enable minority Democrats to present a united front in the press. Similarly, if Democrats are facing a Republican president, the CBC may defer to the party leaders' strategies to counter the White House. In such situations, even if the CBC is not satisfied with the Democratic caucus's positions, there may not be much point in going public against a Republican majority or a Republican president because it is unlikely that the Republicans will need CBC support to pass policies on most issues, and thus, the media may not care what the CBC does.

The CBC may actually find it easier to use public strategies when Democrats control the White House or at least part of Congress. In those circumstances, the CBC would be more newsworthy for two reasons. First, the CBC's votes might be more necessary for passing legislation advanced by a Democratic majority than a Republican majority. Therefore, the CBC's actions could actually affect outcomes, something that would not usually be the case with a Republican majority. The media are typically more interested in those who have power in Congress. Second, intraparty opposition is newsworthy, especially if it might deprive the president or the majority party of the votes it needs to pass legislation.

But members of Congress do not go public just because they can. It is a means to an end. Would the CBC have any reason to go public with Democrats controlling Congress or the White House? Indeed it might. Although opposition between parties is often intended to stop policy from passing, intraparty opposition may be a way for members to attract media coverage to "compete to define the party message" to bring it in line with a member's own position or that of her constituents.[19] Likewise, a group may go public to critique a president of its own party or offer alternatives to his policies in an effort to change them before they are actually voted on in Congress. Given that the CBC is a faction within the Democratic Party, until recently a small faction at that, the CBC may lack sufficient formal power to influence its own party or president through regular legislative or oversight processes, leaving it to employ public strategies to influence Democratic policies and presidents. For these reasons, the CBC might decide to go public more when there is a Democratic president or a Democratic majority in Congress than when Republicans control the White House or the Congress.

So what does the *New York Times* coverage reveal? It is immediately evident that going public has been an important strategy for the CBC throughout the last forty years. Figure 6.1 shows the number of articles in which we see the CBC going public for each year. It ranges from a high of twenty-two articles in 1994 to just one in 2007, with an average of nearly nine articles a year. Dividing the time period into thirds, we find that the average number of cases declines over time from 10 per year from 1977 to 1987, down to just under 9 per year from 1988 to 1998, and finally to 7.4 cases annually from 1999 to 2009. Although this might be a result of declining coverage of Congress generally over time, this may also suggest that the CBC has become less reliant on public strategies as it has gained members and seniority that allow it to influence policy within the legislative process. CBC member Congressman John Lewis (D-GA) confirmed that CBC members do have more options to influence policy today than they once

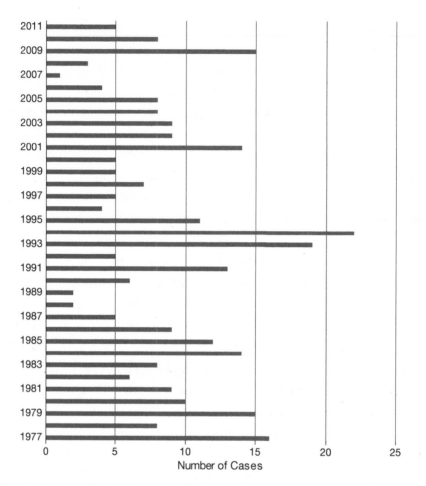

Figure 6.1 Cases of the CBC Going Public per Year

did. Because they now have leadership positions, they can go through parties and committees more easily. "Media aren't the only option."[20]

The CBC during Democratic Control

Looking deeper into the coverage, we find that the CBC does appear to go public more, or at least it gets covered more, when there is a Democrat in the White House than when there is a Republican. There were on average nearly eleven cases a year under Democratic presidents, three and a half

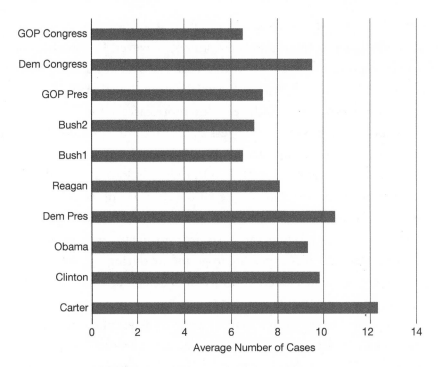

Figure 6.2 Average CBC Cases per Year by President and Party

more per year than under Republican presidents. Figure 6.2 shows the average cases per year for each president during the time period, and we can see that the averages are higher for all the Democratic presidents than for any of the Republican presidents. Similarly, we find that the CBC gets more coverage when Democrats control all or at least part of Congress. When the Republicans controlled both houses of Congress, there were 7.4 cases of the CBC going public per year. That number rose to 9.1 when control of Congress was split and to 9.5 cases per year under unified Democratic control.

It appears then that the political context may be linked to the CBC's ability to get coverage for its public strategies or perhaps even its decision to go public in the first place. Indeed the correlations between the number of times the *New York Times* covered the CBC's public statements each year and different aspects of the political environment indicate significant connections. During divided government, the CBC seems least likely to be able to use public strategies. The congressional context also is important. Interestingly, however, Democratic control of Congress seems less important than the overall number of seats Democrats hold in the House. There is a strong relationship between higher numbers of Democratic seats and more cases of the CBC's public statements being covered. A little less significant is the president's party, with somewhat more coverage of the CBC's public statements during Democratic administrations. Table 6.1 provides a look at how all these factors fit together to influence the CBC's coverage of its public statements, and it confirms that CBC members may find it easier to go public or get coverage when Democrats have larger majorities in the House and find it substantially less appealing to go public during times of divided government, when Democratic unity and deference to party leaders might be more effective.

It is not possible from this analysis alone to determine whether these results are a consequence of when the media are interested in covering the CBC or a change in strategy by the CBC, but Congressman Lewis offered his impression of what is going on. According to him, the CBC champions the same issues and speaks out about them regardless of which party controls Congress or the White House. However, he suggested that the media may be more interested in the CBC when Democrats are in control because the CBC has more influence in those situations. If that is the case,

Table 6.1 FACTORS AFFECTING THE CONGRESSIONAL
BLACK CAUCUS GOING PUBLIC

Independent Variables[a]	Coefficients	Standard Error	t-value
President's Party	1.958	1.429	1.371
Democratic Seats in House	.050*[b]	.023	2.145
Divided Government	−4.243**	1.498	−2.833
Election Year	−2.063	1.379	−1.495
Constant	−.491	5.935	−.083

[a] Dependent variable = Cases per year. N=35, R^2 = .41.

[b] Significant at **$p< .01$ *$p<.05$.

then these findings offer important insight into when public strategies may be most effective. Congressional members must first convince the media they are newsworthy if they wish to go public.

CBC ISSUES

On top of the political context affecting the CBC's news value and reasons for going public, the issues on which the CBC decides to go public would reasonably be shaped by what is possible. The media are not interested in all issues, and the CBC is not united on all issues. We saw in Chapter 1 that party leaders look for issues the party owns, those on which the caucus has a consensus that differs from that of the opposing party, in making decisions about when to go public. Extrapolating this to the CBC, we would expect the CBC to go public on issues that are related in some way to race. While this certainly includes the obvious issue of civil rights, it might also include broader issues, such as the economy and foreign policy, to the extent that those issues can be linked to blacks in the United States or abroad. Not only might the CBC be more united on these issues, but the press will be interested in hearing what African Americans in government have to say about race-related issues, making it easier for the CBC to obtain coverage.

Connections to Race

From the CBC's news coverage, we find that 76 percent of the articles focus on only five issues. Foreign policy, including immigration policy, makes up just over a quarter of the cases. The budget and economic policy are the subject of 16 percent, followed by government affairs (congressional rules, reforms in campaign finance and lobbying, and government ethics and scandals) at 12 percent, and at 11 percent each, civil rights issues (such as affirmative action, civil rights legislation, and discrimination in hiring, housing, education, and business) and presidential appointments to the executive branch and to the courts. A closer look at the specific topics within each issue category reveals that the CBC does focus on issues it owns—those that are linked to race in some way.

Although it is evident that the CBC's focus on civil rights is related to race, the other issues require a bit more explanation. In nearly three out of four articles on foreign policy, the CBC discussed issues affecting blacks in other parts of the world, primarily in Africa and Haiti. Concern about apartheid in South Africa during the late 1970s through the 1980s by itself accounted for a quarter of the cases related to foreign policy. The CBC's concerns about the budget and the economy often made explicit connections to poverty and social programs that significantly affected African Americans; thus there was an implicit connection to race. In conjunction with the president's nominees to the executive or judicial branches, the CBC often raised concerns about the nominee's record on civil rights. For example, the CBC's public accusations that President Carter's Labor nominee John Dunlop had opposed "federal efforts to promote equal employment opportunities for women and members of minorities" led to the withdrawal of his nomination.[21] Even many of the stories on government affairs issues had some connection to race. For example, some of the ethics cases involved members of the CBC, including the investigations of Congressman Harold Ford in 1987 and Congressman Charles Rangel in 2009. The CBC went public on election reform, often in response to alleged efforts to suppress black votes, as in 2001. And there were also cases in which the CBC took positions on redistricting issues that would affect representation of African Americans. The CBC focused heavily on issues with some connection to race even beyond the obvious category of civil rights.

Connections to Context

If we look more carefully at the issues the CBC addressed broken down by presidential administrations and party, we see an additional connection between the political context and the substance of the CBC's public statements. There are some important differences in the issues the CBC received coverage on during Democratic administrations compared to

Republican administrations. Although foreign policy was the top issue under presidents from both parties, it made up a greater percentage of the cases when Republicans were in the White House. In part, this may be a reflection of Republican presidents' placing a higher priority on foreign policy. Or perhaps it is simply the area where the CBC felt it had a chance of persuading a Republican president. On the other hand, budget and economic issues were mentioned much more frequently when Democrats controlled the presidency. The budget and economy accounted for nearly 21 percent of the cases under Democratic presidents but only 12 percent under Republicans. It makes sense that the CBC would feel freer to push fellow Democrats on domestic issues because the gap between the Democrats' position and the CBC would likely be smaller than that between the CBC and Republicans. Furthermore, the CBC might have a more realistic chance of using public pressure to move a Democratic president closer to its position than it would a Republican president because the CBC and the Democratic president have overlapping constituencies.

In addition to the differences we see in the issues that come up under presidents of different parties, there are some interesting changes over time. Cases of going public on civil rights declined regardless of which party was in the White House. This drop may be a result of the progress made in this area; civil rights–related issues of today are perhaps more wrapped up in economic inequalities, or they have become a part of larger issues. Two issues increased in proportion to other issues over time. Government affairs was not particularly prominent as a subject of the CBC's public strategies until the Clinton years. During the tenure of the first three presidents in our time period, it ranked last among the top five issues. But it was among the most frequent topics under Clinton and subsequent presidents. Likewise, the CBC appears to have become more outspoken on presidential nominees over time, though primarily during Republican administrations. Appointments made up fewer than 10 percent of the cases of going public during the Carter and Reagan years, but that jumped dramatically to 27 percent in the first Bush administration and 16 percent in the second Bush administration. During the Clinton years, it was higher than it had been under the first two presidents in the study but not as high as it was for either Bush. The increased attention to government affairs and political appointments may also reflect the changing interest of the media. Reporters have devoted more coverage to these often controversial issues in search of more conflict and drama in their stories.

A key component of public strategies is communicating on issues the media cares about. The CBC has willingly linked a variety of important and controversial issues to race, making it more likely the media will pay attention to the CBC's public statements.

REACTING TO THE PRESIDENT

Finally, we turn our attention to how the CBC goes public in reaction to presidents. I have discussed in earlier chapters that it is easier to get media attention for negative messages—that is, opposition—than positive ones, but with the rise of polarization and partisanship in Congress, members have also faced more pressure in recent years to adhere to the party line, which would mean publicly opposing the other party and keeping their opposition to their own party out of the media. If the CBC is subject to these forces, most of the coverage of the CBC's reactions to the president will occur when the CBC opposes the president, but polarization may lead the CBC to reduce its public opposition to and increase its support for Democratic presidents over time.

About 54 percent of the articles I analyzed involved the CBC going public in response to the president. More than two-thirds of those expressed opposition to the president—for example, the CBC "chastised [President Bush] on a foreign policy they deemed 'intransigent' . . . ."[22] Twelve percent of the cases were in support of the president, including an article that reported that the only support that President Clinton had in Congress for his policy on Haiti came from the CBC; that article quoted two CBC members explaining their support for the president.[23] The remaining 18 percent included mixed reactions to the president.

The breakdown by presidents and party is interesting, as Figure 6.3 shows. We do notice the CBC going public more often against Republican

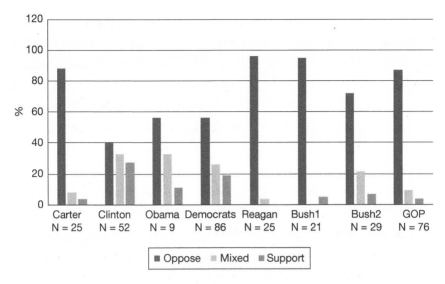

Figure 6.3 CBC Reaction to the President

presidents than Democratic presidents and reserving most of their support for Democratic presidents. However, the differences across presidents are striking. Democratic President Jimmy Carter received more public criticism from the CBC in four years than George W. Bush did in eight years both in percentages and absolute numbers. The sources of the CBC's frustrations with Carter were many, but they boiled down to the belief that he was not sufficiently attentive to poor Americans and minorities and that some of his policies and budgets made the conditions of minorities and the poor worse. Indicative of the exasperation is a comment by CBC member Cardiss Collins following Carter's announcement of his oil policy in 1979:

> The Administration has once again demonstrated that its priorities are the opposite of those who elected it—the minorities, low income families, the elderly and Democrats supporting the historic principles of the party.[24]

In contrast, the CBC's reaction to Democratic President Bill Clinton was by far the most supportive among the presidents. Only 40 percent of

CBC comments aimed at Clinton were exclusively oppositional. Nearly a third included support along with the criticism, and just over a fourth were completely supportive of Clinton. The CBC's reactions to Obama are notable in part because there were so few, even taking into account that the analysis includes only the first three years of the Obama presidency. Only nine cases involve the CBC reacting to Obama, most coming in the first year. Just over half were negative, and only one was completely supportive. The others were mixed.

The CBC's reaction to the Republican presidents was a little more uniform. There was little difference between the CBC's treatment of Ronald Reagan and George H. W. Bush. More than 90 percent of the CBC's reactions were in opposition to each of those administrations, though the CBC went public in response to Bush almost as much in four years as it did to Reagan in eight years. The relatively high percentage of mixed reviews of George W. Bush is a little surprising given the Democrats' overall disdain for the younger Bush and his low approval ratings in the last four years of his presidency. However, most of the mixed or supportive reactions to Bush occurred in the first two years of his presidency in the wake of the September 11 attacks, when his approval ratings were relatively high.

Given the number of factors that may affect how the CBC reacts to presidents and the countervailing influences some of these might have, statistical analysis allows us to see better the impact of the president's party and the political context on the CBC's opposition to and support for the president. Using a three-point measure of reaction to the president (opposition, mixed reaction, and support) as the dependent variable, I created a regression model that helps us see the impact of the president's party, changes over time (as measured by the year), the point during the president's tenure (first, second, third, or fourth year of his term), and whether there was divided government. The results are reported in Table 6.2 in the column labeled Model 1. It shows that as expected, the president's party was very significant, with reaction being more supportive for Democratic presidents than Republican presidents. We also see that mixed and supportive reactions are covered more over time. Although this appears to be mostly the

Table 6.2 CBC SUPPORT FOR AND OPPOSITION TO THE PRESIDENT

Independent Variables	Reaction to President Model 1 (OLS)	Opposition to President Model 2 (Logistic)	Support for President Model 3 (Logistic)
President's Party	.700****a	−2.433****	2.617****
	(.116)b	(.526)	(.764)
Year	.019****	−.072***	.033
	(.005)	(.024)	(.033)
Year of President's	−.102**	.454**	−.587*
Term	(.047)	(.233)	(.306)
Divided	.410****	−1.161**	1.747***
Government	(.117)	(.526)	(.659)
Constant	−36.472****	144.686***	−68.944
	(10.652)	(48.244)	(68.518)
N = 161	R^2 = .259	R^2 = .344	R^2 = .253

[a] Significant at ****$p < .001$, ***$p < .01$, **$p < .05$, *$p < .10$.

[b] The top number in each cell is the coefficient, and the standard error appears in parentheses.

result of increased positive reactions to Democratic presidents, as the literature on polarization would predict, George W. Bush also received more mixed and supportive reactions from the CBC than the earlier Republican presidents, which is somewhat unexpected. In addition, we see that the CBC's opposition to presidents increases as their term wears on. Finally, we find that support for presidents appears more often in times of divided government, probably the result of the CBC supporting Democratic presidents during times where Republicans controlled Congress.

Because the bulk of the CBC's reaction to presidents has been opposition, I also conducted logistic regression using dummy variables for opposition to the president and support for the president in Models 2 and 3, respectively. They mostly mirror what is going on in Model 1. We see the CBC consistently more likely to oppose Republican presidents and more likely to support Democratic presidents, and we see support declining as the president's term progresses but increasing during times of divided government.

DOES GOING PUBLIC WORK?

One final question to consider is the effectiveness of going public. Does it get results? While it would certainly be difficult to determine whether the CBC's public strategies are the cause of particular outcomes, we can observe potential correlations, which is a step in the right direction. The CBC has enjoyed some notable outright victories in going public. Its sustained public pressure to raise awareness of apartheid in South Africa and push for US sanctions on the South African government eventually helped force the Reagan administration to change its policies toward the country. Sometimes victory was not as evident, but the CBC was invited into the process, as in cases where its public comments led to meetings with the president or congressional leadership. In other cases, the CBC's public strategies appeared to have no effect—presidential budgets did not reflect CBC priorities, and CBC budgets did not win congressional approval. But even when the group appeared to fail in its goal, the fact that it made news often raised the profile of an issue or a vote, thus increasing the traceability of the actions of others in Congress or the president, which makes it easier for those who supported the CBC to hold their elected officials accountable.

The CBC's record on presidential appointments is a microcosm of its overall efforts to go public. Its public opposition to some presidential nominations, particularly under Democratic presidents, helped lead to withdrawals of some nominations. In other situations, the CBC won the immediate battle by delaying the nomination and forcing the nominee to answer additional questions, but the nominee was ultimately confirmed. And in Republican administrations, the CBC's opposition to nominees did little to influence outcomes, though it enjoyed some short-term victories as its opposition encouraged Senate filibusters of a few judicial nominations during the George W. Bush administration. However, most of these nominees were eventually appointed by the president during Senate recesses or were confirmed as part of a bipartisan agreement to get judicial nominations moving during the 2005 legislative session.

CONCLUSIONS

Overall, the CBC's coverage is consistent with most of our expectations and earlier findings that the political context affects public strategies. Attempting to use the media to compensate for its institutional disadvantages, the CBC has most often been able to use public strategies when Democrats controlled the White House and when Democrats controlled at least one house of Congress. It has been able to go public primarily on issues owned by the CBC—that is, those with some connection to race—though the range of issues the CBC has linked to race is quite broad. And we see that the CBC tends to use public strategies to oppose presidents in both parties, though it has shown some support for the most recent Democratic presidents.

We are, however, left with an important question: is the news coverage of the CBC a reflection of the group's strategies, or is it more of an indication of the media's interest and definitions of what is newsworthy? Congressman Lewis's insights suggest the media's own interests are an important consideration in when public strategies are likely to achieve news coverage. Not only does he indicate that the media may be more interested in the CBC when Democrats control the House or White House because the CBC has more influence in those situations, but he also admits that it is easier to get coverage on issues the press is already paying attention to. Recognizing the media's preferences, the CBC readily provides public comments on issues, like civil rights, that are obviously race-related. And in the interest of serving its own broader agenda, the CBC has learned to tie a variety of issues to race to help pique the media's interest in the issue and to capitalize on its own credibility on race to get the media interested in its comments on these larger issues. In this way, the CBC has learned to play the hand the media have dealt it to serve its own purposes. Of course, that hand is not without limits. There is little the CBC can do to make the media give it more coverage during periods of Republican control of government.

Although it seems likely that the coverage we have seen is in important ways a reflection of media interest, there is also evidence that coverage reflects the CBC's strategies in at least one major respect. The CBC tends to initiate public strategies when it is in a disadvantaged position. Congressman Lewis explains that the CBC tends to go to the media when its members want to mobilize people and gather support. Such situations are usually in reaction to events or actions taken by other political actors, and the fact that the CBC needs to mobilize support would indicate it is not already in the majority. Thus, the fact that we most often see the CBC opposing presidents or others in the press appears to be the reality and not merely the media's interest in conflict. Further support for this can be found in other research that has shown that the media are interested in the unexpected in politics. In an era of increasing polarization, members of one party praising members of the opposing party would certainly qualify as unexpected and be newsworthy.[25] Therefore, the fact that we see little coverage of the CBC supporting Republicans is probably a good indication that it rarely happens.

In a final piece of evidence that the CBC understands that success in going public requires an understanding of the media's ability to define what is news, the CBC's public strategies have demonstrated members' recognition of their own place in Congress, which has had an effect on what the group does to gain public attention. In the early days of the CBC, its members were few, and even with Democrats in control of Congress, the group had little formal power. It recognized that unconventional tactics were often the only way to receive news coverage. So CBC members boycotted meetings and got arrested at protests at the South African embassy. As their numbers have grown, such dramatic actions have been replaced by press conferences and legislative proposals.

But whatever the tactics, the group has always relied heavily on its unity to make the case that it is worthy of media attention. It is striking how often the CBC's position is publicized without connection to a specific member of Congress; 41 percent of the cases of the CBC going public in the news coverage do not mention a specific member of the caucus. Congressman Lewis noted that although the CBC does not have to be unanimous to seek coverage on an issue, members tend to go public on issues on which there is a majority or consensus position. As previous research on parties has shown, unity is an important factor in being able to attract media attention. The CBC is often able to maintain remarkable cohesion, but other groups in Congress that may not be as cohesive as the CBC may find this to be a real barrier to using public strategies.

What can we take away from our look at the public strategies of the CBC? For small groups within Congress to use public strategies effectively, they have to convince the media they are newsworthy through their unity, tactics that will appeal to the media's news values, their ability to influence the legislative process, and their ability to establish their credibility to speak on issues the media find important. If they can do that, this cursory look at the effects of the CBC's public strategies raises the possibility that going public can be an effective tool for those who lack formal power in Congress.

A Tale of Two Senators

Adapting Public Strategies to Different Goals

In the summer of 2009, South Carolina Senator Lindsey Graham made national headlines first with his questioning of judicial nominee Sonia Sotomayor and then with his decision to support her despite his disagreement with her ideology. Described as "[o]ne of the toughest questioners [on the Senate Judiciary Committee], Sen. Lindsey Graham (S.C.), raised the question of whether Sotomayor is 'a bully' who has 'a temperament problem.'"[1] But before the end of the month, Graham became the subject of numerous news articles and editorials when he announced that he would vote for Sotomayor, explaining that it was time to stop politicizing judicial nominations.[2] At the same time, South Carolina's other senator, Jim DeMint, was also making national headlines with his very public efforts to defeat President Obama's health care reform proposal. In a call to conservative activists, DeMint said that "if Republicans are able to stop Barack Obama on health care, 'it will be his Waterloo, it will break him.'"[3] The comment was widely reported, and it launched DeMint into the middle of the health care debate, elevating him as a national spokesperson for conservatism.

Although DeMint has since left the Senate, Graham and DeMint had much in common during their time in the Senate. In 2009 both were relative newcomers to the Senate. Graham was just beginning his second term, having been elected first in 2002, and DeMint was still in his first term, elected in 2004. Both men replaced long-serving senators who had spent more than three decades in the Senate and risen to the rank of committee chairs. Both men served in the House prior to moving to the Senate. Graham had a somewhat higher national profile than DeMint because he had been one of the House managers during the impeachment trial of President Bill Clinton in 1999. Perhaps the most important similarity was the constituency they shared as Republican senators from the conservative state of South Carolina.

After Graham and DeMint were elected to the Senate only two years apart, local reporters wondered how South Carolina would fare with the loss of seniority and power of the state's previous senators—Strom Thurmond and Ernest "Fritz" Hollings.[4] But as the events of the summer of 2009 indicate, Graham and DeMint made their presence known in the Senate. And while they did this in very different ways and for different ends, both men quite intentionally turned to the national press to compensate for their lack of seniority and formal power, and both enjoyed success with the strategy.

As a first-term senator, Graham used extensive national press coverage and seats on two important committees—Armed Services and Judiciary— to become a major player on key issues in the Senate, including the treatment of detainees from the wars in Afghanistan and Iraq, the Iraq war, and domestic issues from immigration and Social Security reform to Supreme Court appointments. Graham's media image as a maverick in the Republican Party enhanced his bipartisan reputation in the Senate and enabled him to participate in negotiations to shape legislation and processes in the Senate.

Initially, DeMint maintained a fairly low profile in the Senate, but after the Republicans lost their majority in 2006, he became an outspoken advocate for conservative ideology, prodding his own party to take a more conservative turn, especially on fiscal policy, and criticizing the Democratic majority and its president for pursuing liberal policies and government intervention in the economy and health care—an approach that perhaps foreshadowed his eventual departure from the Senate to take a position at the Heritage Foundation, where he has continued on this path, though with considerably more resources.

This chapter looks at how both senators used the national media to communicate, what they tried to accomplish by going public, and the extent to which they were effective. It also examines why they chose going public over other strategies. The study of these two senators is based primarily on their comments in the national press—the *Washington Post*, evening television news from ABC, NBC, CBS, CNN, and Fox News, and the Sunday morning talk shows from each of these networks—from the start of their first term in the Senate through the end of 2009. I included all news stories that quoted or paraphrased Senator Graham or Senator DeMint commenting on any issue, event, or action relevant to the senator's legislative or oversight functions. I omitted their comments that focused exclusively on elections. Thus, quite a few articles from 2008 quoting Graham were left out because they were only about his support of Senator John McCain's presidential bid. Because the interviews on Sunday talk shows often covered multiple issues, rather than code the interview as just one case, the senators' comments on separate issues were recorded as separate cases. I supplemented the content analysis with a telephone interview with each senator.

GRAHAM: PRAGMATIST AND (RELATIVELY) POLITE CRITIC

When he entered the Senate in 2003, Lindsey Graham had already enjoyed a turn in the media spotlight, most prominently for his role as one of the House managers during President Bill Clinton's impeachment trial in the Senate. During the impeachment proceedings, the press had found Graham accessible and highly quotable.[5] And throughout his tenure in the House, he was reliably conservative but quite willing to part ways with his party's establishment when he believed they were wrong. He had been part of the Republican freshmen who challenged Speaker Newt Gingrich on several occasions in 1995, and he had been among those who considered a coup against the Speaker in 1996.[6] He was an early supporter of Senator John McCain's presidential aspirations, campaigning openly for McCain against George W. Bush in the 2000 South Carolina presidential primary. His quotability in conjunction with his maverick tendencies within his own party made him potentially interesting to the media.

Graham's potential newsworthiness was enhanced by his committee assignments. He landed spots on the Armed Services Committee and the Judiciary Committee. Each had jurisdiction relevant to some of the most important issues on the public agenda, including the war in Iraq, the war on terror and all its concomitant questions about detainee rights and domestic surveillance, judicial nominations, and immigration reform. Graham's presence on these committees, combined with his own expertise as a military lawyer, insured that he would be a participant on many of the issues the media found most interesting.

Looking at Graham's coverage during his first seven years in the Senate (see Figure 7.1), we can see these factors certainly afforded Graham more coverage than most first-term senators would expect to obtain. In his first year, he was quoted in the news 21 times, and he peaked in 2005 (his third year) with 102 stories or interviews in which he was quoted. He averaged

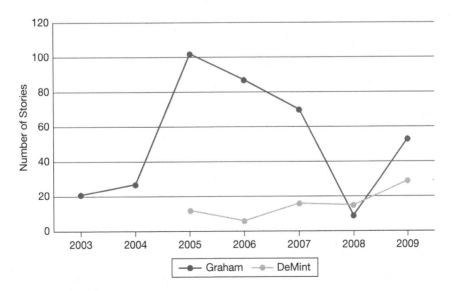

Figure 7.1 Making News

53 stories per year. And if we leave out 2008, where much of Graham's coverage was omitted from this study because it pertained to his campaign efforts on behalf of McCain's presidential race, his average climbs to 60 per year.

Two interesting patterns emerge in the types of media through which Graham has been able to communicate. First, in all three venues—newspaper, television news, and Sunday television talk shows—Graham's coverage jumped considerably after his second year in the Senate and stayed fairly high. Again, we must factor out 2008 because of the campaign coverage. Second, Graham found increasing success in obtaining television coverage. In an era where congressional news has declined, Graham consistently made the evening news more than once every two weeks and appeared on a Sunday morning talk show more than one-fourth of the weeks in each year from 2006 through 2009.

Graham explains that he has sought press attention over the years, but he also points out that reporters, especially on the Sunday morning talk shows, seek him out because he is active on the issues they want to cover.[7] "If you're active when the media want to talk about these issues, they'll call you," he says. He admits that it helps that he says things that "aren't doctrinaire," which makes him interesting to the shows. And it appears that these things feed on each other. His initial efforts to get media coverage and his accessibility to the press on key issues put him on the reporters' radar, and now they call him "because [he's] in the rolodex." Whether the product of direct efforts to attract media attention or the media's interest in him, which he has cultivated, Graham's frequent coverage has put him in an excellent position to use the national media to communicate and influence policymaking and events.

What Graham Communicates and How

Most of Graham's statements in the press through 2009 centered on six major issues. Nearly half of his comments came on military and national security issues—most prominently the wars in Iraq and Afghanistan and issues stemming from the war on terrorism, including the treatment and rights of detainees in Iraq and at Guantánamo Bay, and domestic surveillance. Judicial appointments and the confirmation process accounted for 14 percent of Graham's remarks. Foreign policy issues received Graham's attention in 7 percent of the stories—particularly trade issues with China and concerns about Iran. Finally, Graham devoted extensive public comments to fiscal issues such as budget matters and economic stimulus bills (7 percent), immigration reform (6 percent), and Social Security reform (4 percent). Although most of these issues were relevant to Graham's committee assignments, the foreign policy issues, Social Security reform, and fiscal issues were not in his committees' bailiwicks, making it more necessary for him to seek media coverage to exercise influence on them.

REACTIONS TO THE PRESIDENT

What did Graham communicate on these issues? Did he use public strategies in opposition to or support of the president, his own party, or the Democratic Party? Many of Graham's public comments simply conveyed and explained his policy preferences. For example, on the war with Iraq, Graham often defended the war, and earlier than most public officials, including the president, he argued in favor of a surge of troops to Iraq.[8] In 41 percent of the stories or interviews, Graham offered his own views on events or policy without any commentary—favorable or unfavorable—on the president, Democrats, or Republicans. The remaining 59 percent, as reported in Figure 7.2, included at least some position or comment in support of or opposition to the president or at least one of the parties.

Nearly 44 percent of Graham's public comments supported or opposed the president or his administration. About 22 percent of the time, Graham made statements favorable to the president. In some cases his praise was explicit. For example, when President George W. Bush began to push for Social Security reform, Graham "applauded Bush's willingness to take a stand in the intraparty argument ... [saying] the President 'dramatically shaped the debate within the Republican world by embracing index changes and rescheduling benefits.'"[9] In other situations Graham defended the president's actions or policy preferences, sometimes without

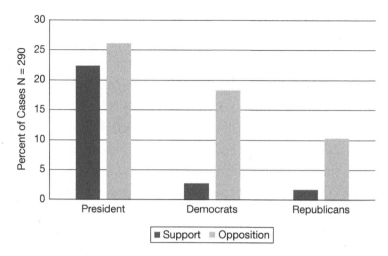

Figure 7.2 Graham's Support for / Opposition to the President and Parties

mentioning the president explicitly. He defended Bush's Supreme Court nominees from attacks, including at least initially Harriet Miers, whose nomination was ultimately withdrawn amid criticisms from Republicans. In the early days of the Miers nomination, Graham claimed that the president "has made a solid pick for the Supreme Court."[10] He consistently supported the president's decision to send more troops to Iraq and pleaded publicly for Congress and the public to give General David Petraeus the time to make it work.[11]

Just over one-fourth of Graham's remarks included opposition to or criticism of the president. Many of these were policy disagreements. Graham opposed the Bush White House on the tactics used to interrogate detainees from the war on terror and the Iraq war and disagreed with the warrantless wiretaps approved by the administration.[12] He was also critical of some of President Obama's early policies to improve the economy.[13] In addition to disagreements over policy, Graham from time to time leveled criticism at the presidents for the way they handled an issue, the way they responded to Congress, or the process they used in crafting legislation. In one case where Graham and a group of senators were trying to amend legislation to fund the Iraq war to convert some of the direct aid to Iraq to loans, President Bush threatened to veto the bill if it included the loan.[14] Noting that the party leadership in Congress agreed with the president and would probably remove the loan during the conference process, Graham criticized the president's veto threat as unnecessary. Following the mostly partisan vote on President Obama's first stimulus bill after Obama had promised more bipartisanship, Graham complained on one Sunday morning talk show, using part of Obama's campaign theme in his comments, "if this is going to be bipartisanship, the country is screwed. . . . There's nothing about this process that's been bipartisan. This is not change we can believe in."[15]

REACTIONS TO DEMOCRATS

Twenty-one percent of Graham's public comments involved reaction to Democrats. Not surprisingly given that Graham is a Republican, 88 percent of the comments aimed at Democrats were critical, but 12 percent were supportive. As we saw in Graham's comments toward the president, some of his opposition to Democrats stemmed from policy disagreements, particularly relating to the war in Iraq. On CNN's *Late Edition with Wolf Blitzer*, for example, Graham, without naming Democrats specifically, said, "those who want to set deadlines and timelines and benchmarks with consequences are the authors of a greater war, and I'm not going to be part of that crowd" (May 13, 2007). In the same interview, Graham accused Senate Majority Leader Harry Reid (D-NV) of declaring the war lost. Throughout debates over the war in Iraq, Graham criticized Democrats for micromanaging the war and wanting to withdraw precipitously.

In many circumstances Graham criticized Democrats for their rhetoric, partisanship, and tactics. At the outset of the Abu Ghraib prison scandal, Graham was critical of what went on, but he chastised some Democrats for immediately demanding Defense Secretary Donald Rumsfeld's resignation.[16] On Iraq, he took Democrats to task for complaining about the Bush administration's strategy in Iraq without offering a "viable alternative."[17] Graham called Democratic efforts to block President Bush's appointment of John Bolton as UN ambassador "ridiculous."[18] Charging them with politicizing the judicial confirmation process, particularly during the Alito nomination, Graham criticized Democrats for opposing Alito based on ideology and accused them of wanting "to make 'a campaign issue of the decisions on the court.'"[19]

Despite his disagreements and criticisms of Democrats, Graham did praise them on occasion, particularly when paired with a congressional Democrat on a Sunday morning talk show. Most often he found common ground with the other party on issues where he found himself at odds with the Bush White House. He agreed with Democratic Senator Patrick Leahy that Congress needed to verify how the Bush administration was pursuing domestic surveillance, and he agreed with Democrats that the interrogation techniques approved under the Bush administration were problematic even as he disagreed with them about making the techniques public.[20]

REACTIONS TO HIS OWN PARTY

Finally, 12 percent of Graham's comments expressed opinions of his own party. Eighty-eight percent of the comments reacting to Republicans were critical, while 15 percent included some positive message. Most of Graham's criticism of Republicans was directed at their unwillingness to solve difficult problems. For example, when members of the GOP insisted that Bush must provide a detailed plan to reform Social Security and do most of the selling of the plan before they would sign on to it, Graham accused them of "acting like a bunch of children hiding behind their father," and he insisted that Congress, rather than the president, needed to write the legislation.[21] On the issue of the federal deficit, Graham directly contradicted House Republican Majority Leader Tom DeLay when he said Republicans were "failing when it comes to controlling spending."[22] Graham was particularly frustrated with his party's inability to pass immigration legislation. In a rather prescient moment in 2006, he reminded Republicans of the electoral consequences of inaction: "If it is perceived by the public that the Republican Party—which owns the House, the Senate, and the White House—cannot solve hard problems working with Democrats, then we will lose our majorities."[23]

Another line of criticism that Graham directed at his own party was about how Republicans responded to public concerns and tried to sell their policies to the public. For example, Graham critiqued his party's efforts to protect American jobs from moving overseas, claiming Republicans had "an academic response to emotional issues, and that never serves you in politics."[24] And Graham said Republicans had "made a strategic mistake" in focusing on private accounts in Social Security—something Graham called a "sideshow"—rather than talking about what they would do to keep Social Security solvent.[25]

Avoiding Partisan Food Fights

The picture that emerges from Graham's comments about and reactions to the president and the two parties is that Graham has used the media to push his own views but also to offer critiques of the substance of the policies of public officials in both parties as well as *how* they push their policies—that is, the process, strategies, and tone of the debates. Before we turn to the question of what exactly Graham hopes to accomplish by going public, we should look at how he delivers his messages, especially the criticism, and the tone he often uses in his public remarks.

Graham tends to be a relatively polite critic, often avoiding partisan rhetoric and complimenting those with whom he disagrees or pointing out where he agrees with them.[26] A May 23, 2004, interview with Chris Wallace on *Fox News Sunday* illustrates Graham's approach. Asked to respond to comments by Democratic Party Leader Nancy Pelosi that President Bush was an "incompetent leader" in Iraq, Graham said simply, "It's not going to do us any good to say that." But he continued by giving Pelosi the benefit of the doubt by saying he thought she was trying to say "We have made some mistakes," a point on which Graham agreed with her. In the same interview, Graham was asked about Bush's opposition to legislation Graham was supporting that would give military reservists the same health benefits as active-duty soldiers. Before explaining his own support for the legislation, Graham proclaimed his support for Bush's policies in Iraq. He concluded his comments by saying, "I love the people in the Pentagon most of the time, but I disagree with them over this." In a battle over language in legislation regarding how suspected terrorists could be treated or interrogated, Graham discussed his disagreement with Vice President Dick Cheney, explaining, "The vice president believes in certain circumstances the government can't be bound by the language McCain is pushing. I believe that out of bounds of that language, we do harm to the U.S. image. It doesn't mean he's bad or I'm good; it just means we see it differently."[27] And in a joint appearance with Senator Patrick Leahy (D-VT) on CNN's *Late Edition with Wolf Blitzer* on January 21, 2007, although Graham disagreed with Leahy's support for cutting off funding to the war in Iraq, Graham said, "I really do respect Senator Leahy, because he is acting on his convictions. He believes this is another Vietnam," and if that were true, cutting funding and leaving the country would be the right thing to do.

Acknowledging that the media "don't call me to get in a food fight," Graham explains that he tends to be polite when going public because he is not really comfortable criticizing people's motives. He says he can disagree with people on policy, but he never plans to question their motives or their patriotism—advice he received from former Senators Strom Thurmond (R-SC) and Joe Biden (D-DE). Besides, he says, "I usually like the people I'm on TV with." He often finds agreement with them, and he believes that approach is more effective because it allows him to find answers and solutions: "The more reasonable you are, the more people will work with you."

Occasional Bluster

There were exceptions to Graham's typically polite tone. In the wake of congressional opposition to a White House plan to turn over operation of several US ports to a company in Dubai, Graham called the president and White House "non-responsive and arrogant."[28] Near the end of the health care reform battle in the Senate in 2009, Graham pulled no punches, accusing the Democratic "Senate leadership and the administration of 'backroom deals that amount to bribes' and 'seedy Chicago politics.'"[29] He notes that when he criticizes the president or one of the parties in harsh terms, people pay attention "because I don't use [that tactic] all the time"; those situations become a way of starting debate.

Occasionally, Graham's emotions do come into play. On NBC's *Meet the Press* on July 15, 2007, moderator Tim Russert looked on silently when a heated exchange between Graham and Senator Jim Webb (D-VA) escalated into a shouting match as the two senators first interrupted and then talked over each other in an attempt to explain their views on the surge in Iraq. Graham admits the dust-up was evidence of "genuine feeling" on both their parts, but it reflected the debates going on around the country.

Graham's maverick reputation has been enhanced by his willingness to go public on issues on which he is working across party lines. One-fifth of Graham's comments were related to his bipartisan actions across a variety of issues. He used press appearances to push for legislation he and then Senator Hillary Clinton (D-NY) sponsored to improve health care for military reservists. He received extensive coverage for his work with Democrats to avert filibusters of judicial nominees and to pass immigration reform. And he made numerous press statements with Senator Charles Schumer (D-NY) on US policy toward China.

Graham's reputation for bipartisanship does not mean Graham's public comments were unaffected by partisanship. He has been more negative toward Obama than he was toward Bush. In 2009 Graham had twenty-nine public comments in the news that were negative toward Obama. Although he did have twenty-six unfavorable comments about Bush in 2006, he averaged fewer than fifteen negative comments a year about Bush from 2003 through 2008. However, his praise of the two presidents was nearly equal, with Bush receiving on average twelve positive comments from Graham per year and Obama receiving ten favorable comments from Graham during 2009.

Graham's Audience and Goals

The picture of Graham that emerges from the news coverage and his own comments is a pragmatic policymaker who wants to be a player in the legislative process. He is someone who wants to solve problems, and he is definitely no ideologue. Graham's apparent target audience and goals support this view of him as a pragmatic policymaker.[30]

INFLUENCING ELITES

Forty-eight percent of his comments were directed toward public officials or parties (see Figure 7.3). Just over one-fifth of his comments were aimed at the president. We can see this in 2006; as Congress began to consider immigration reform, Graham said in an interview, "the president has provided great leadership on the tenor of the debate, the tone of debate. Now it's time for him to provide more leadership on the substantive outcome."[31]

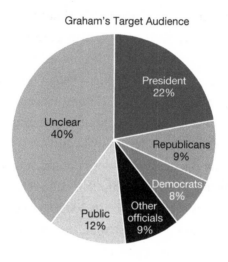

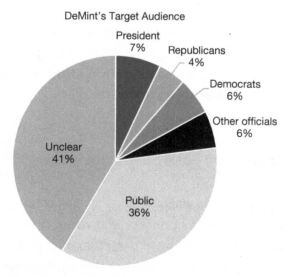

Figure 7.3 Target Audience

In 9 percent of the cases, Graham's comments were intended for his own party. Often these were warnings of potential problems or consequences the party might face if it continued on its current course. For example, he raised the specter of possible electoral consequences if Republicans failed to pass immigration reform.[32]

Graham spoke to Democrats through the press nearly as often as he did his own party (8 percent of cases). In some instances, he was merely criticizing their policies or pushing them to offer alternatives instead of just criticizing GOP policies. On other occasions, his comments to them were an effort to further debate or make clear his own negotiating positions. During debate over a funding bill for the wars in Iraq and Afghanistan, when House Democrats considered removing a provision to ban public release of government photos showing detainee abuse that had passed in the Senate version of the bill, Graham publicly stated that "he would look to block the bill in the Senate if the ban was not included."[33]

Only 12 percent of Graham's comments were obviously aimed at the public. Most of these were efforts to frame the debate to encourage support of Graham's position, as when he told viewers of *Face the Nation* on CBS that the Iraq surge was working (March 23, 2008).

While the intended audience for 40 percent of Graham's comments was unclear, the fact that almost half of his statements in the press were clearly directed to others in government indicates Graham's interest in using the media to influence political elites to help make Graham a player in the policymaking process.

In his conversation with me, Graham confirmed that his intended audience did match the patterns apparent in the coverage. He said that sometimes he aims his comments at the public—usually sound bites that will get people talking. He offered as an example his description of the health care reform process 2009 as "sleazy Chicago politics," which he hoped would get the public to start debating the issue. But he estimated that at least 70 percent of his public comments are directed toward opinion makers (other members of Congress, congressional staff, the president, or the media).

BEING A PLAYER IN THE PROCESS

Graham's apparent goals in going public offer additional evidence of his desire to be directly involved in the policy process. Sixteen percent of his comments were efforts to pass policy—for example, issuing an "impassioned plea" to pass the immigration bill, Graham said on a talk show, "To my Republican colleagues, this is the best deal we're ever going to get."[34] Only 4 percent of Graham's comments were clearly intended to stop policy or block some action. When Democrats attempted to pass legislation that included withdrawal deadlines and imposed guidelines on how quickly troops could be redeployed to combat areas, Graham explicitly said he would fight these bills, and when President Obama announced plans to bail out the auto industry in 2009, Graham openly declared it a bad idea.[35]

The remaining 80 percent of the cases of Graham going public encompassed a wide range of goals, mostly aimed at influencing policy or process. At times, Graham explicitly tried to frame the debate on an issue (9 percent of cases). This was particularly evident in his discussions of the surge in Iraq: Graham persistently maintained that the surge was working, even if slowly, and he equated failure in Iraq with losing the war on terror.[36] Sometimes his purpose appeared to be an explicit effort to influence policy or process (15 percent of cases). For example, on Social Security, Graham insisted that the process had to be bipartisan: "The Republican party cannot fix this by themselves. Ideology will not fix this. This is going to take give-and-take, and sacrifice by both parties will be essential."[37] Nearly 10 percent of his comments overtly attempted to influence the actions of the president or members of one or both parties. Prior to one nomination of a Supreme Court justice, Graham publicly floated names of judges he would be willing to support.[38] On another occasion, Graham publicly called on the White House to explain its domestic surveillance program.[39]

Graham frequently used his comments to the press to defend or support certain policies or actions (8 percent of cases) or to criticize or oppose other policies (5 percent). Some of these cases were aimed at influencing public opinion, as was true of his frequent defense of the surge in Iraq. But others were intended to pressure those in government, as was the case when he chastised conservatives who tried to defend Republican committee staffers' who had unethically gained access to Democrats' committee files and leaked them to the press.[40]

In about 18 percent of the cases, Graham merely offered an opinion or assessment of an issue or event, often at the prompting of a reporter or talk show host. In some circumstances, Graham's assessment or opinion was sought because of his expertise on the issue, such as detainee rights, or because of his firsthand experience, as in the case of his updates and opinions on the situation in Iraq following his visits to the country. Although Graham may have simply been responding to reporters' queries, these statements of opinion and his evaluation of a situation or process in Congress contributed to the public debate on the issue, regardless of whether Graham intended his comments to have an impact.

Why Graham Goes Public

Graham is very intentional about using the media, and he has a strong sense of what he can accomplish by going public. He talks frequently about wanting to "solve problems" or "get the debate moving." How does a public strategy help him with this? He explains that he uses media to "set markers and send signals—I'm ready to compromise or I'm ready to fight." He believes that it lets people see him as "a guy they can do business with." He offers the example of what the government should do about detainees held at Guantánamo Bay. The Obama White House conferred with him on this issue because his public statements indicated that although he believed that some detainees should not be given civilian trials, he did acknowledge that there was a place for such trials. Obama administration officials saw him as someone they could work with on the issue to enhance their own credibility.

Graham notes that this strategy is particularly important when he is in the minority party. Through the media, he has built his reputation as someone the other party can work with, and he uses the media to let the president or members of the other party know "you're in the ballpark, or that's too far." And it is in these situations where his reputation for civility is especially important. When he praises the Democratic president, it makes news, and when he criticizes the president or Democrats, it has more of an impact than it might coming from other Republicans because he uses criticism judiciously.

Graham also points out that going public is a way to force policymakers and opinion leaders to pay attention. He explains that opinion makers are often affected by how much coverage an issue gets: "You say something to them in a private conversation, and they say, 'whatever.' You say the same thing on the news, and they call you to talk about it." Media coverage "gives more weight to the private conversation."

Graham's Success

So has Graham found success as a result of going public? To the extent that his efforts have been covered by the press, Graham has been extraordinarily successful. Few members of the Senate who hold no committee or party leadership position have gained the national exposure Graham has been able to command. For that matter, not even the party leaders have been able to keep up with him in Sunday morning talk show appearances. The Senate Republican leader (Bill Frist from 2003 to 2006 and Mitch McConnell from 2007 to 2009) had more appearances than Graham only in 2003, Graham's first year in the Senate. The most appearances by a Republican leader during Graham's tenure in the Senate were by the then Minority Leader McConnell, who had fifteen appearances in 2009; Graham was on thirty-five Sunday talk shows that year. Democratic majority leader Harry Reid averaged only three appearances per year from 2007 to 2009, nowhere close to Graham's double-digit bookings. Even New York Democratic Senator Charles Schumer, widely known for his affinity for television coverage, has been unable to match Graham on Sunday talk shows. Schumer's peak years were 2005 and 2006, when he had twelve appearances in each year. Graham had thirty-one and twenty-two appearances, respectively, in those years.

But Graham's success has not been limited to just being covered. His coverage has appeared to translate into genuine influence in the Senate.

Despite his lack of leadership positions and seniority, he has participated in many major policy negotiations in Congress and between Congress and the White House. He was involved in trying to craft an immigration bill during the Bush presidency and participated in the Senate's successful bipartisan immigration bill in 2013. He has been an important participant in discussions on detainee policy and the wars in Iraq and Afghanistan. And although he found himself in the minority in the Senate after 2006, Graham's bipartisan image and willingness to break with his party on occasion have led key Democrats to seek him out as a partner to craft important legislation. Senator John Kerry (D-MA) worked closely with Graham for months to try to craft an energy policy that would address climate change, although the legislation ultimately fell victim to partisan politics. Midway through 2010, Graham had attended meetings at the White House nineteen times during the Obama presidency, more than any other Republican senator.[41] In just the first eighteen months of Obama's presidency, Graham had been asked to work with the administration or Democrats in Congress on Afghanistan, closing the prison at Guantánamo Bay, climate change, and immigration reform. Although Graham's public strategies have not necessarily led to passage of legislation, they have allowed him to participate in the behind-the-scenes negotiations and influence executive decisions. They have certainly allowed him to be a player in the process.

In 2015 Graham launched a presidential campaign bid for the Republican nomination. Because of his relationship with the national media, Graham continued appearing on the Sunday talk shows and cable news channels despite never hitting 2 percent in national polls. Though he was never in jeopardy of winning, he continued to be a player in the national conversation and forced some of his GOP rivals to address national security issues they might otherwise would have ignored.

JIM DEMINT: CONSERVATIVE ADVOCATE

Senator Jim DeMint was relatively quiet during his first two years in the Senate while his party enjoyed majority status, but his media appearances increased significantly when Republicans lost their majority in the 2006 elections (see Figure 7.1). DeMint had about nine mentions per year while in the majority, all but two of those coming in the *Washington Post* (the other two on network evening news). After the 2006 elections left Republicans in the minority, DeMint's press coverage jumped to at least fifteen stories per year with increasing television news attention. In 2009 his media presence exploded to twenty-nine stories, including four Sunday talk show appearances.

DeMint's public remarks focused on six main issues. Just under a third of his statements pertained to fiscal issues: the economy (particularly the stimulus and bailout legislation at the end of the Bush administration and beginning of the Obama presidency) and budget and tax issues, including the excessive number of earmarks in appropriations bills. These issues were staples of DeMint's public comments throughout his time in the Senate. The next most frequent subjects of DeMint's comments were related to specific bills going through Congress: immigration bills during 2006 and 2007 and health care reform in 2009 (15 percent each), all bills he opposed. Just behind these two issues were foreign policy and defense issues (11 percent combined). Most of his discussion in this area focused on the war in Iraq and a 2009 coup in Honduras. The final two topics addressed most frequently by DeMint related to the internal workings of government: appointments to the executive branch and the courts and government affairs (including the response to Hurricane Katrina and earmark reform). The focus of DeMint's public comments, unlike Graham's, was often not related to his committee assignments.

What DeMint Communicated and How

Half of DeMint's comments in the news merely offered his opinions on an issue or legislation without explicitly mentioning the president or a particular party. Most often DeMint's positions and comments reflected his conservative ideology, with the recurring themes of less government and free market solutions being applied to a host of issues. For example, in a Senate hearing on Internet privacy, DeMint, not wanting to inhibit free enterprise, suggested that regulation might not be necessary because consumers would opt not to do business with companies that did not provide adequate privacy protections.[42] Some of DeMint's public comments were calls for reform, particularly reforms of the tax code to reduce taxes on both corporations and individuals.[43] Many, however, were demands for changes in legislation, calls to block legislation, or efforts to raise concerns about an issue, bill, or nomination—all of which contained implicit criticism or opposition to one or both parties or the president. Contrary to many even in his own party who seemed determined to have Tim Geithner confirmed as Treasury Secretary, DeMint joined Senator Jeff Sessions (R-AL) to criticize Geithner's failure to pay all his taxes and claim the error was intentional rather than an oversight, as many were suggesting.[44] At one point during the debate over immigration reform, DeMint criticized the bill without naming parties or the president, saying, "The longer this bill hangs out there, the more opposition grows . . . and more senators realize this is not the right immigration bill for America. It cannot be adequately fixed, and it must be stopped."[45]

When DeMint did explicitly evaluate either party or the president, he was usually critical. Only five times in the years studied did DeMint receive coverage for positive comments toward his own party or President Bush. He offered no public praise of President Obama and only one positive comment toward Democrats in the articles and media appearances included in this analysis. Perhaps most interesting is that DeMint's public criticism of his own party and President Bush was practically nonexistent until after 2006, when Republicans lost their majority in Congress (see Figure 7.4). And in 2009, when Democrats controlled both the White House and Congress, DeMint's attention turned exclusively to criticism of the majority party and its president.

Intensifying DeMint's negative comments toward both parties and presidents was the tone of his comments. In contrast to Graham, whose critiques were often polite and combined with praise for those he was opposing, DeMint did not soft-pedal his attacks. His comments were often blunt and highly ideological. During the immigration debates,

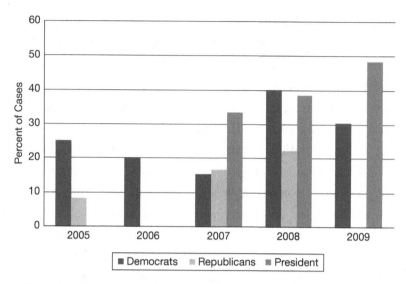

Figure 7.4 DeMint's Criticism of the President and Parties

which pitted DeMint not only against Democrats but also some Republicans, DeMint publicly touted his desire to kill the legislation and unabashedly admitted his tactics to accomplish his goals. After voting for an amendment that spelled disaster for the overall bill and weakened a provision DeMint had originally supported, he explained, "If it hurts the bill, I'm for it."[46] When the bill was killed, DeMint claimed, "They tried to railroad this through today, but we derailed the train."[47] In other cases, DeMint used inflammatory language to frame the debate. He described the Bush administration's plan to bail out mortgage companies as "socialism,"[48] and during debate over economic stimulus measures in early 2009, DeMint called President Obama "the world's best salesman of socialism."[49] And perhaps most famously, DeMint said that defeating health care would be Obama's Waterloo. His strident tone was often reflected in reporters' descriptions of DeMint's actions. Reports described him as "crowing" about and "exulting" over the defeat of immigration[50] and as "accusing" President Bush of "abandoning" conservative principles.[51]

The picture of DeMint that emerged from his public communication was of a conservative senator determined to advocate for conservative policies and call out members of either party who deviated from conservatism. His ideological commitment was further corroborated by the fact that there was only one case in the coverage of DeMint commenting on bipartisan action he had taken—that was an effort to pass legislation to cut inappropriate travel costs in Congress.[52]

DeMint's Audience and Purpose

Who was the target and what was the purpose of DeMint's communication? In contrast to Graham, whose comments were largely aimed at those in government, DeMint's audience was more often the public, as Figure 7.3 shows. More than a third of DeMint's comments were clearly directed toward the public. For example, he encouraged people "to take to the streets to stop America's slide into socialism."[53] In his first year in the Senate, he teamed up with the Heritage Foundation to introduce an "index of dependency" to educate the public on how much Americans rely on government.[54] In addition, DeMint wrote op-ed pieces to explain his ideas to the public. The audience for just over 40 percent of his public efforts was unclear, but DeMint confirmed in an interview that he usually directed his message to the public and grassroots activists in hopes they would put pressure on members of Congress.[55]

Only 23 percent of his comments were aimed at the president, DeMint's own party, Democrats, or others in government. Most of DeMint's comments directed toward the president were explanations for why DeMint had placed a hold on the president's nominee to some position in the executive branch or had taken action against the president's position. For example, he held up the nomination of the Transportation Security Administration head because he was concerned that the Obama administration intended to allow TSA workers to unionize.[56] And in particularly pointed comments following the defeat of immigration reform in 2007, DeMint said, "The first step as we leave here today is to make sure the administration got the clear message from this vote."[57] The comments DeMint aimed toward his own party were typically complaints about deficit spending.[58] His statements directed at Democrats varied over time from admonitions for Democrats not to be obstructionist when they were in the minority[59] to warnings of his own willingness to use obstructionist tactics when he was in the minority.[60]

DeMint's goals were aimed at pushing conservative policies and stopping policies and actions that were not conservative, but given the amount of time he was in the minority party during his tenure in the Senate, blocking policy was the primary goal. Forty percent of his public comments made clear his desire to block legislation or nominations, as the examples of his comments on immigration and health care reform illustrate. Only 13 percent of the cases of DeMint going public were efforts to pass policy, and nearly half of those pertained to earmark reform. The others were efforts to pass personal savings accounts in Social Security reform, tax cuts, and other conservative ideas. The impact of being in the minority is evident when we consider changes in DeMint's goals over time. Although DeMint's public efforts to pass policy were consistent, albeit limited, over time, the focus on stopping legislation increased when Republicans became the minority party in 2007, and it intensified when they were faced with unified Democratic government in 2009.

In the remaining cases, DeMint tried to accomplish a wide range of goals. Many of these were attempts to push a conservative agenda. In some cases, he encouraged specific changes to legislation; for example, threatening to delay passage of a bill to stabilize the housing market in 2008 in an effort to add an amendment to the bill that would prohibit mortgage firms Fannie Mae and Freddie Mac from lobbying Congress if they became "indebted to the federal government."[61] And during the early months of the Obama administration, he went public to express concerns about nominees. He also used the press to try to reframe debates, especially after he moved into the minority. In one instance he tried to reframe the idea of economic stimulus as tax cuts that allowed the public to spend as opposed to the government spending being advocated by the president.[62]

Why DeMint Went Public

DeMint's use of public strategies fits perfectly the theory that members of Congress use the media to compensate for institutional weaknesses. As a first-term senator whose party had lost its majority in only his second year in the Senate, DeMint was in no position institutionally to make much of a difference. But he explains that his frustration actually reached farther back than Republicans' loss of the majority in 2006. DeMint says that he tried to work through the Republican caucus during his time in the House, but "you had to get too many people on your side" just to be heard in the House caucus. And in 1999, his first year in the House, the options for going public were limited to the occasional op-ed in the local press. That left him with little influence, even within his own party. When he arrived in the Senate, he says he "tried to be a team player the first few years" and work within the caucus, but after the 2006 elections, DeMint consciously decided it was time to change tactics. Instead of trying to convince the party to change direction from the inside, he opted to go outside with a public strategy to raise voters' awareness and create pressure from the public that would move the party in a more conservative direction. It was a classic case of deciding to expand the scope of conflict to try to bring into the debate more people who would support his ideas and goals.

The expanded media environment of the twenty-first century made a public strategy more feasible for DeMint. Often DeMint started a public campaign by commenting online via blogs, websites, Twitter, and social media. Then he moved to interviews on conservative talk radio shows, and from there he could begin to attract the attention of television, usually starting with Fox News. He notes that "you have to hit a certain noise threshold" to get the attention of the nonconservative news outlets, but if "you can stir things up enough," the other networks and newspapers would pick up the story and call him for his comments.

That need to get loud enough to pique the interest of the mainstream media is the reason that DeMint often employed partisanship and harsh rhetoric in his public statements. For those who know DeMint away from the spotlight, he is mild mannered and almost reserved, so the tough comments were often quite jarring and a bit of a surprise. DeMint admits his own discomfort with the tone, explaining, "You hate to be contentious," especially within your own party, but "mild-mannered didn't work. You have to get to a certain level" to be heard.

DeMint's Success

DeMint's decision to adopt a public strategy paid off quickly, as he succeeded in his first concerted effort to go public to stop a specific bill. As Bush administration officials worked with Democrats and some Republicans to craft an immigration reform bill in 2007 and get it through the Senate, DeMint recognized that the president and Democratic leaders would want to move the bill quickly. He prepared public comments even before the final bill was released. Knowing that the legislation would include some sort of pathway to citizenship for those who were already in the United States illegally, DeMint condemned the legislation as amnesty for illegals. As parts of the bill were released, DeMint made them available online and began to post blogs and do interviews on talk radio and eventually Fox News, criticizing the legislation and vowing to stop it. The public reaction that DeMint's public campaign elicited made enough senators nervous, and the legislation died on the Senate floor. DeMint also enjoyed some success in pushing earmark reform via a public campaign in 2007.

Although DeMint was not able to stop health care reform from passing in 2010, his public campaign against President Obama's plan did cause major headaches for the president and Democrats in Congress. With DeMint and others publicly characterizing the plan as a major step toward socialism, the public insurance option that many Democrats wanted in the legislation was ultimately left out of the final bill. And the negative publicity generated by DeMint and others helped make the legislation unpopular with nearly half the country by the time it was passed, which left Democrats in a precarious position heading into the 2010 midterm elections, as Republicans used the controversial vote against vulnerable incumbents to retake the majority in the House.

Because of the harsh rhetoric DeMint employed at times, his public strategy came with the risk of a backlash from his Senate colleagues, members of the press, and the public. DeMint admits that there were some strains with other senators. There were some stories in the national press that suggested that DeMint's tactics left him with few friends in the Senate. One such report in *Politico* said, "Many GOP senators privately scoff at DeMint as a showboating opportunist."[63] DeMint, however, downplays the tension, saying that he received encouragement from his colleagues and gained their respect. He explains that his willingness to take the public hits for his tough tactics made other members of Congress more willing to work with him. He also says that reporters were often willing to cover what he said if they thought he had stumbled by being too outrageous or offending those in his own party. He points to the coverage of his Waterloo comments received as evidence that the press covered what they think were his mistakes. Stories like the one in *Politico* provide additional support for DeMint's theory.

However, such coverage seems to have done little to damage his reputation beyond Congress. DeMint became a de facto spokesman for conservative ideas and a favorite of the Tea Party movement. His willingness to endorse Republican candidates in primaries who were not the preferred choice of the party establishment—including Rand Paul in Kentucky and Marco Rubio in Florida—combined with his outspokenness on policy raised DeMint's public profile well beyond what most first-term senators would expect. During the health care debate in 2009, the president of the Heritage Foundation, a conservative think tank, introduced DeMint by saying, he "may be the junior senator from South Carolina, but here we call him the senior senator from the Heritage Foundation."[64] Ultimately, DeMint left the Senate in 2013 to become the president of Heritage, where he has continued to criticize the Left and push his fellow Republicans to the right, using many of the same media tactics he employed in the Senate. While DeMint may have found it difficult to influence his party through the Republican caucus in the Senate, he certainly helped shape the debate once he began employing a public strategy as a first-term senator.

CONCLUSIONS

The stories of Lindsey Graham and Jim DeMint are instructive about the use and effectiveness of public strategies as a tool to influence policymaking. Media attention is certainly a source of power in the Senate, and it is available to even the most junior senators. As Graham puts it, "The days of where you wait two years to say hello in the Senate are over because of the media." Senators no longer have to wait to be relevant if they can devise a successful press strategy.

And there are different routes available to attract attention. Graham made himself newsworthy by being active on issues the press was interested in and providing interesting sound bites. DeMint accomplished the same thing by raising a ruckus. They also illustrate how different types of media provide more opportunities for members of Congress. Graham has typically relied on more traditional media—television and newspapers. To attract these organizations, a senator may still need to have some of the traditional trappings of power or credibility—in Graham's case, he is on committees relevant to many of the issues he has tried to influence. But DeMint focused on new media—creating his own conservative network of blogs, websites, and social media—that allowed him to start a discussion and generate controversy that eventually spilled over into mainstream media.

Furthermore, we see from the two senators that going public is adaptable to different goals. Graham used the press to create an image as someone who would cross party lines to solve problems, an image that cannot be attributed to a moderate voting record or ideology, as he has

consistently received high scores from a variety of conservative interest groups and has supported his party in more than 90 percent of the
votes he has cast in the Senate.[65] The perception of Graham as someone
who can work with all sides has allowed him to be involved in numerous important policy discussions and negotiations that his junior status
and lack of leadership positions might normally have precluded. In short,
he used the media to become a player inside Congress and in national
debates. In contrast, DeMint used the media to expand the scope of conflict and generate public pressure on elected officials. He tried to make
himself a credible spokesperson for conservatism and move the country
and the Republican Party in a more conservative direction. He became
a sought-after endorsement for conservative congressional candidates,
leading him to be introduced on ABC's *This Week* Sunday talk show as
"South Carolina's powerful senator" (September 4, 2011). Both Graham
and DeMint have been effective in enhancing their power in the Senate
and even around the country through the media.

Effectiveness in their policy goals has been more mixed, and it is in this
area where the limitations of going public are clear. Although both men
can point to some examples of how public strategies have been accompanied by successful passage or defeat of legislation, they have also experi-
enced major failures on policy despite going public. Graham could not get
immigration reform passed (in part because of DeMint's successful public
strategy), and DeMint was unable to accomplish much of his proposed
dramatic tax and government-spending reform. Where going public
appears to hold the most potential for policy goals is in killing legislation
or altering it by extracting concessions on provisions that were publicly
unpopular. Public strategies appear more limited in persuading the public
or members of Congress to support passage of controversial or unpopular
policies.

Whatever the limitations of going public, it is becoming an important
tool for members of Congress and one that offers the promise of results.
As Graham explains, he and DeMint have been effective in using the
media "to gain influence beyond [their] years" in the Senate, and a host

of junior senators—most notably Rand Paul (R-KY), Ted Cruz (R-TX), Marco Rubio (R-FL), and Elizabeth Warren (D-MA)—seem determined to follow in their footsteps. Clearly the media can be used to compensate for institutional weaknesses that come with lack of seniority and leadership positions.

The Possibilities and Limits
of Going Public in Congress

Forty years ago, many members of Congress did not have a press secretary. Today, media relations is an integral part of the policymaking process in Congress. In this book, I have examined the communication of members of Congress through traditional print and broadcast media over the last forty years and new media more recently in an effort to understand the evolution of the use of public strategies in Congress and how the political environment may affect congressional members' decisions to use the media and their ability to do so successfully to move beyond their institutional powers to influence policymaking. The results confirm that members do routinely utilize public strategies in ways that supplement their formal powers or compensate for lack of power in Congress, but they also suggest that members face some constraints imposed by the media and the political context on who can use the media and when, what they can communicate, and how can they communicate. The findings also offer some insight into the potential effectiveness of going public and its limitations. In this chapter I review the important findings, assess what we have learned about the effects of going public, and consider the implications.

INFLUENCES ON GOING PUBLIC IN CONGRESS

A variety of factors determine who in Congress needs or wants to go public, on what issues and for what purposes they will do so, and importantly, when they are likely to be successful in gaining media attention for their efforts. The analyses and case studies in this book have paid particular attention to four considerations or developments that interact to influence going public in Congress: the individual member's position or power in Congress, the media's determination of what is newsworthy, the political context, and increasing political polarization in Congress.

Position in Congress

Congressional members' institutional position or the power that they hold often determines whether or not they go public. Party and committee leaders certainly have an interest in extending their institutional power by influencing the public debate and shaping media coverage of issues or events to favor their party or position. For party leaders especially, being active in communicating the party's message has become an expected part of the job. We saw earlier that party and committee leaders make up an outsized proportion of those whose public comments attract media attention, at least compared to their absolute numbers in Congress. Individuals who received the most attention in both print and television were leaders rather than rank-and-file members. In transition years, party leaders increased their share of the coverage over time, and Republican Party leaders particularly made up an increasing share of the Republican members who successfully went public over time.

Although leaders have embraced media strategies to communicate and influence policymaking, the minority party in Congress may have the most incentive for going public as it has the least institutional power. The analysis of the *New York Times* indicated that most members of Congress were more interested in trying to pass policy than in trying to stop it, but minority party members and especially minority leaders were more likely to be focused on stopping policy, often because it was their only option. Additionally, we clearly see the importance of public strategies to minority factions and minority party members in the case studies of the Congressional Black Caucus and Senators Graham and DeMint. Both the CBC and former Senator DeMint used coverage to pressure their own parties and leaders to try to gain influence within their caucuses. Senator Graham often used the media when his party was in the minority or when he was in a minority within his own party to signal his willingness to reach across the aisle and work with Democrats in ways that allowed him to continue to be part of the political discussion even when his formal powers were limited. Over time, we see increased use of public strategies, or at least greater success in getting covered, by minority party members. Although minority party members still find traditional news coverage a challenge, they made up a growing percentage of the cases of going public over time in both print media and broadcast media.

A congressional member's position in Congress not only affects the member's incentive to go public but also affects the media's interest in that member, which brings us to a second important factor that influences public strategies in Congress.

Media Interest

Coverage of congressional members' public strategies depends significantly on what the media think is newsworthy. Some aspects of newsworthiness are beyond members' control. Certain members and groups in Congress are inherently more newsworthy than others. Specifically, those with power—party or committee leaders or key factions within a party—are most attractive to journalists. But in other ways, members can affect the newsworthiness of their message by catering to media news values. We have seen evidence of members trying to fit into existing news values in both the substance and style or framing of their public messages.

The issues members have gone public on have changed little in traditional media over time. Budgets and taxes, government affairs, foreign policy, executive and judicial appointments, national security, health care, and social policy issues like Social Security have consistently dominated members' public comments in the press. These issues affect many people and are debated regularly, so they meet the media's definitions of what is newsworthy. When members have addressed other issues in the press, their comments have often been driven by events the media were already covering; for example, discussing energy policy when gas prices rise or shortages occur or focusing on gun control in the wake of a school shooting. And some members or groups have found the media amenable to covering their messages when they are willing to address issues the press is already interested in on which the member or group has expertise or experience. So the Congressional Black Caucus can get coverage if its members are willing to discuss issues in the context of race, and Senator Lindsey Graham has been able to capitalize on the media's consistent interest in the controversial issues over which his Judiciary and Armed Services Committees have jurisdiction and on which he has expertise as a result of his legal and military background.

Not only have members tried to fit the substance of their messages to what the media want to cover, but they have also adopted styles or frames that highlight conflict, generate controversy, or depict themselves as unpredictable, making it more likely they will receive coverage of their public strategies. Conflict occurs naturally in Congress, and members call attention to it in their opposition to the president and to the other party or other house of Congress. We have seen in the analysis of newspaper and television coverage that public statements of opposition have increased over time. The case studies provide additional evidence that members and groups recognize the importance of conflict in piquing the media's interest. The Congressional Black Caucus has often succeeded in gaining attention when it resorted to unconventional activities such as participation in protests and even getting arrested to make the news in its early days and opposition to presidents of its own party in more recent years. And former Senator DeMint admitted to using heightened partisan rhetoric intentionally in new media to generate controversy that would be noticed by more traditional news organizations. Resorting to harsh rhetoric and trying to generate conflict through opposition and obstructionism have been especially important to members who lack power, particularly those in the minority party.

More recently, we have seen junior members of Congress combine obstructionist tactics with media campaigns not only to try to stop the majority party but also to pressure their own party leaders to join in their obstruction. Freshman Senator Ted Cruz (R-TX) provides a notable example. Beginning in the August recess before the expected fall 2013 budget battle in Congress, Cruz went to the media to rally conservative congressional members to demand that defunding Obamacare be required for their support for a budget deal that would keep the government operating beyond September 30. He threatened to filibuster any agreement that did not cut Obamacare funding. Once the House passed a budget deal that defunded Obamacare, Majority Leader Harry Reid used some careful parliamentary maneuvers, with the help of Republicans who were not in agreement with Cruz, to avoid the promised filibuster. Cruz and ally Mike Lee (R-UT) managed to delay the vote on the House resolution a couple of days with their objection to a procedural rule before the inevitable debate and vote were to take place. During the delay, Cruz spoke for twenty-one hours against Obamacare.[1] Although the Senate was able to pass a clean budget resolution without defunding Obamacare, the House refused to cooperate, in part because conservatives were energized by Cruz's talkathon.[2] During the ensuing government shutdown, Cruz and his allies continued to air their views in the press. It is hard to imagine a freshman senator providing public cover for a government shutdown forty years ago.

An additional challenge for congressional members who want to use public strategies is the apparent waning interest of the traditional media in Congress generally. Reporters appear to spend less time sitting in on committee hearings and floor debates today than they did in the late 1970s or early 1980s. Therefore, congressional members may need to be more intentional in contacting reporters directly and creating events especially for them in order to get coverage today.

New media give members opportunities that do not require them to comply with traditional news values. Through social media, members can pursue their own more varied issue agendas, those that mix national and local concerns. They can communicate for a wider range of purposes, including more cooperative, bipartisan endeavors, not just those that high-light conflict. Although social media seem ideal for re-election-oriented communication, the fact that the majority of the messages I studied in all three new media platforms focused on policy suggests that members appreciate the freedom of communication social media afford.

Political Context

The political context is an important factor in shaping public strategies in Congress. Which party controls each house of Congress and the White House certainly influences which members of Congress are considered newsworthy. As the earlier analysis showed, all members seem to have more opportunity to go public during divided government than unified government. Part of this is likely because both parties are relevant in the policymaking process during divided government and because there is increased likelihood that at least one house of Congress will not be content to defer to presidential leadership, and therefore, to some extent people in both parties have a modicum of power. In particular, party and commit-tee leaders appear best able to get coverage (and are perhaps most in need of it) when control of Congress is split or one party controls Congress and the other the White House. For the minority party, however, unified government—when the party is at its weakest institutionally, controlling neither house of Congress nor the executive branch—is when the media seem to be most interested in minority members because they can be the voice of opposition to the majority party.

Another aspect of the political environment that appears to affect public strategies and coverage of them is the party of the president. Over time, we saw that the president's party was less likely to receive attention for going public. Over the last forty years, the media have become more focused on the president, often at the expense of Congress. Individual members of the president's party do not appear to be able to compete effectively with him for media coverage, thus limiting their ability to go public. Members of the president's party might find it easier to gain coverage for messages that oppose the president, but increasing partisan polarization in Congress creates pressure on members not to go public with their internal disagreements (this is discussed in the next section).

The case study of the Congressional Black Caucus demonstrates the way the party of the president and the partisan balance in Congress can affect the newsworthiness and power of a faction in Congress. The CBC had more coverage of its comments when Democrats controlled Congress and during Democratic presidential administrations, situations in which the CBC members would have had more power to influence outcomes as their own party needed their votes and a president of their own party would have been more likely to listen to their concerns.

The analysis revealed one other aspect of the political environment that has a consistent impact on members' public strategies over time: the election cycle. In election years, especially presidential elections, members appear to have less interest in and less opportunity for making national news. The members are often more focused on local media and spend fewer days in Washington, and the campaign news consumes much of the news space available for political coverage. The election cycle also seems to affect the goals members have in going public. During the first part of a president's term, his own party is more focused on trying to pass policy. But in the later years of his term, his party becomes more defensive, as the opposing party, usually having picked up seats in the midterm election, becomes more active in trying to pass policy.

Political Polarization

The increasing partisan polarization in Congress, evident in members' statements in response to the president, has changed going public over time. When members react to the president, the analysis and case studies have shown that it is most often to oppose him. But we also see that the responses to the president have become more partisan and more intense over time. Members from the president's own party have become more supportive publicly, while those in the opposition party have become increasingly negative toward the president over time. The case study of congressional responses to presidential proposals to reform Social Security reveals that in recent years, even when members of the president's party oppose him, they are more likely to do so with mixed evaluations that include some positive reaction rather than exclusively negative reactions, even though more decisively negative comments would almost certainly be considered more newsworthy.

A few brave or brazen members do violate the norm and criticize their own party or praise the opposition, but such tactics, while likely to attract coverage, are not without serious risks. Senator Graham's public criticisms of his own party and occasional positive comments toward the other party have left him open to attacks from his conservative constituency, including charges that he is a RINO (Republican in name only). Meanwhile, Senator Cruz's public comments criticizing members of his own party for being too quick to compromise or cave in to Democrats have not endeared him to his Republican colleagues, who have been open in their negative assessments of him. Members who dare cross their party leaders or elders too often may risk loss of committee positions or cooperation and support from their colleagues. These members must calculate whether such risks are worth the potential benefits of publicly going against their party in an era of partisan polarization.

Somewhat surprisingly, the effects of polarization, though evident in new media, have not consumed members' communications via new media. Members do take swipes at the other party and the president, especially if he is from the other party, but new media, without the need to be concerned about what is newsworthy, provide room for nonpartisan communications as well. Somewhat removed from scrutiny of party leaders, some new media, particularly Facebook, also offer members a safer venue for intraparty dissent. They can "confide" their frustrations with party positions to their followers, who may put pressure on party leaders or other members, but the mainstream media are less likely to notice a member's comments and bring them to the attention of party leaders, who would no doubt be displeased with the member and might exact retribution for the decision to break with the party line or at least give the member a stern talking to.

EFFECTIVENESS OF GOING PUBLIC IN CONGRESS

This book's primary focus has been on understanding what affects congressional members' ability and decisions to go public to influence policymaking. Throughout, the book has shown evidence that members do indeed turn to the media to supplement their formal powers or compensate for their lack of power. But is going public effective? Do members actually accomplish their goals by going public? Admittedly, this question has not been at the center of the analysis and case studies, but they do offer insights into what members hope to accomplish through going public and the extent to which they are able to do so. The data suggest, not surprisingly, that public strategies can lead to success but that they also encounter serious limitations. Before we consider what this research tells us about the effectiveness of going public, I want to acknowledge several challenges in determining whether going public has been effective.

Defining and Measuring Effectiveness in Going Public

Figuring out whether a public strategy has been effective is not the straightforward empirical enterprise we would hope. Several major challenges arise in evaluating the outcomes of going public. First, effectiveness depends in part on what members are trying to accomplish with their strategy. Earlier chapters revealed a host of goals members might have in going public. Some goals, including passing policy or stopping policy, are linked to outcomes that are easily observed and measured. For other purposes, such as framing the debate, trying to influence those negotiating the legislation by generating public pressure to make changes in the bill, or enhancing the traceability of a vote, success is linked to outcomes that are not readily measured. In still other cases, the goal may simply be making the news.

Let's take as an example Senator Cruz's public opposition to the budget agreement and his public defense of shutting down the government in fall 2013. Although the senator did have some clear policy goals—notably to repeal or defund the Affordable Care Act (Obamacare) and to cut long-term spending—there was absolutely zero chance of these policies passing with a Democratic Senate and a Democratic president. So was going public a failure? Maybe not. It became apparent during the shutdown that there was no realistic alternative compromise proposal that the senator and his House allies wanted in place of their original demands. Thus, it appears that the primary objective of generating this conflict and pushing their message in the press may have been to get news coverage of their policy positions even if they had no chance of enacting them in the current political context. If that is what these members hoped to do, then we might safely say they succeeded because they certainly made the news.

It is also evident that the publicity Cruz generated put pressure on other Republicans to withhold support and pressured the GOP leadership to postpone putting a clean bill up for a vote, leading to the government shutdown. So if a shutdown was the goal, perhaps going public was a success. Then again, the coverage was largely negative, and public opinion polls showed a drop in approval for Republicans in Congress, who were already in a tenuous position with the public. Of course, the Democrats and the president suffered their own decline in favorable opinion, and at least some of these Republicans, particularly those, like Cruz, who were most vocal, probably gained favor with like-minded constituents back home. So they likely did view this as an effective strategy. The point for us, however, is that defining or measuring the effectiveness of going public is not necessarily easy, and it depends in part on the goals members have, which are not always obvious or measurable.

Even if we can agree on what constitutes effectiveness and find a way to measure it, we face a second challenge: isolating the impact of a particular public strategy from all the other factors affecting the observed outcomes. As presidential scholars have shown in their own debates about whether going public is a useful strategy for presidents, there are a multitude of confounding factors in the policymaking process.[3] In addition to the political environment, the nearness of the next election, and outside events, there are other policymakers' efforts to go public, which may also have an influence on outcomes. Figuring out in that milieu whether a particular public strategy was effective may be impossible. Complicating matters is our inability to know that we have accounted for all the public strategies that were employed in a particular case.

Effective Uses of Public Strategies

These obstacles might tempt us to throw up our hands in surrender and abandon any attempt at evaluating the effectiveness of going public in Congress. However, not being able to draw definitive conclusions about the impact of public strategies should not cause us to avoid these inquiries altogether. Despite the challenges, we can still glean insights from the analysis and case studies in this book about the kinds of conditions in which going public is likely to be effective and when its limitations are likely to be reached.

INFLUENCING THE LEGISLATIVE PROCESS

In the battle between passing policy and stopping it, the evidence suggests that going public is most effective in stopping policy. The preceding chapters include numerous examples of presidential nominations that were derailed as congressional members voiced opposition to the nominees and policies and fragile compromises that blew up in the face of concerted public opposition by members of Congress. In some of these situations, one might argue that the side in favor of the nomination or policy was not as committed as the opposition. For example, in Chapter 5, we saw those opposed to President Bush's plans to reform Social Security being much more vocal in their opposition than those who supported him. But in some cases both sides clearly made an effort to win the public debate, and the opposition was much more successful. The failure of immigration reform during the Bush administration provides a clear example. Senator Graham and others were on television and in the newspapers advocating for the bipartisan reform legislation, but it was Senator DeMint and his supporters, with their harsh rhetoric and well-timed public attacks on the legislation through mainstream and new media, that generated enough public reaction to pressure Republicans to walk away from the legislation. Particularly interesting in the research is that over time, opposition to the president seems to be aimed more at stopping policy than replacing it or compromising on it. This suggests that members have found that simple opposition can attract coverage and be effective where more complex or nuanced positions that partially oppose a bill or seek to find common ground may be harder to convey or even to get covered, and even if they do receive media attention, their impact on the public may be smaller than outright opposition.

Shaping the National Debate

Going public may also be effective for accomplishing more subtle goals. We have seen evidence that members of Congress can use public strategies to shape and encourage the public conversation in several ways. Members' public comments can help frame debates. Former Senator DeMint and other Republicans cast Obamacare as a government takeover of health care, and though they did not succeed in stopping the legislation, their framing certainly seems to have helped keep public support for the plan low throughout the early stages of implementation. Additionally, public strategies, particularly those that incorporate new media, can bring more people into the conversation, thus expanding the number of perspectives in the debate. More members of Congress can weigh in on public debates through Facebook and Twitter, and we see this in the considerable numbers of obscure rank-and-file House members who found their way into the sample of congressional tweets analyzed in Chapter 4. But members' communication via new media also invites their followers to join the discussion. Members' Facebook posts often prompted comments from both supporters and opponents of the members' position and even resulted in some substantive exchanges among these followers. It is not yet clear what impact this expanded discussion will have on legislative outcomes or whether some public strategies are more effective or successful in framing the public debate. But we do know that how debates are framed and who participates in them has an impact on outcomes, which suggests public strategies can be influential if they affect these things.

Public strategies hold promise for raising awareness of issues and votes in Congress. The Congressional Black Caucus enjoyed success in making people aware of its opposition to some presidential nominees. Though the CBC was not always successful in defeating the nominations, its opposition increased media interest in the votes on those nominations, which raised the traceability of those votes, making it easier for the public to know how their own members had voted on the nominee. In other cases, we have seen members who knew they did not have the votes to win on a policy go public to insure that voters would know where members stood on the issue. Again, the public strategies of Republicans during and after the debate on Obamacare are instructive. Even though they lost the vote, Republicans' very public opposition made it impossible for Democrats to hide from their votes, and many appear to have lost in the next two elections at least in part because of that vote.

Pursuing Personal Goals and Power

Beyond the institutional goals members have, going public can also be an effective way to advance members' personal goals. Public strategies can assist individual members who want to become players in the policy process or within an ideological community. Senators particularly have found success in this regard. As we saw with Senator Graham, his ability to make the news, despite having little formal power in the Senate, has given him credibility on a number of issues and signaled to members of both parties that he is a potential partner in crafting legislative compromises; it also led him to venture into presidential politics. Former Senator DeMint also found public strategies effective for raising his profile within conservative circles and trying to influence policy debates within his own party. Although DeMint's success in getting coverage did not always result in his party following his preferences, it did eventually open an alternative path for him to influence policy: he left the Senate to take over the Heritage Foundation think tank, where his public strategies have become even more overtly focused on influencing votes in Congress as he often reacts publicly to *possible* compromises and bills floated by Republican Party leaders. The public strategies of Senators Ted Cruz and Rand Paul (R-KY), among other newer members of Congress, seem to mirror those of DeMint as both men try to become influential within Republican circles to affect policy and run for higher office.

These areas where going public seems most likely to be effective offer good news to members of Congress who are in the minority or who otherwise lack power. In the best-case scenario, going public may give them an opportunity to weigh in on the discussion and even influence the framing of the debate and thus shape policies. In the worst, if members or groups do not have sufficient numbers to pass policy, they can at least resort to public strategies to compensate for that weakness and have a chance to stop the majority from accomplishing its goals, leaving the status quo in place until the next election changes the balance of power. Or they can raise awareness of the vote to make it easier for their supporters to hold members accountable for votes. Members may also benefit at an individual level by going public to establish themselves as players in Congress, either as someone who can work across party lines or as a force to be reckoned with in their own party. Thus, we see the potential for members to use public strategies effectively to go beyond their institutional powers or compensate for institutional weaknesses. But there are also considerable limits to the effectiveness of going public and potential risks in the strategy.

Limits of Public Strategies

Perhaps the most important constraint congressional members face in using the media to influence policy is the challenge of getting coverage and reaching a sufficiently large audience. Although the data presented in this book focused only on members of Congress who succeeded in getting coverage, the small number of congressional members analyzed here shows that many members do not get covered. Furthermore, except for a small handful of leaders, most of those that do are covered infrequently. Cable television news outlets have opened up more opportunities for some members, but these organizations seem primarily interested in members who are willing to embrace and inflame conflict and controversy, which is more conducive to stopping legislation and nominations than passing policy. Social media make it possible for all members to communicate directly with the public, but the audience for those media is often small and thus unlikely to have much impact on public opinion unless the member is able to use the new media to pique the interest of more traditional mass media outlets.

Part of the challenge members of Congress face in gaining coverage is the limited range of issues the media tend to be interested in. As the analysis in Chapter 2 showed, a relatively small number of issues dominate, and the other issues often require events to make them newsworthy. As a result, going public is unlikely to be an option for congressional members on many issues they may want to influence. Of course, members can address these on social media, and they do, but again, the audience for this is usually quite small.

The Challenge of Changing Minds

When members are able to get coverage, the limitations of going public that they encounter are similar to those that have been documented for presidents employing public strategies. Presidential scholars have recounted numerous examples of presidents using media strategies to try to increase public support for their policies only to see little movement in public opinion on the issue and the ultimate failure of their policy in Congress.[4] President George W. Bush ran into this problem when he pushed for Social Security reform in 2005, and President Obama hit the same wall in his efforts to generate support for Obamacare, both before and after its passage. In these cases, the presidents were quite successful in getting covered, but the coverage did not move public opinion or congressional members. For members of Congress, getting substantial coverage may be a challenge in itself, but even if they succeed, they face the same limits on the media's ability to rally public support. And as just discussed, it appears to be easier to use the media to spark opposition than to foster support for proposals. This finding is particularly troubling for those in the majority, especially leaders, and for those who are part of bipartisan coalitions who typically use the media more to try to pass policy than to stop it. Public strategies may be of little use if the policies being pushed are not already popular.

IMPEDIMENTS TO BARGAINING

As some scholars have claimed in relation to the president, going public may actually impede congressional members' ability to negotiate.[5] A few high-profile examples illustrate the problem. In July of 2009, Senator Charles Grassley (R-IA) was engaged in bipartisan talks on health care reform at the same time President Obama was pushing health care reform. On July 24, Senator Grassley told reporter Al Hunt that he thought the likelihood of passing reform was "very, very good." That same day, Senator Grassley tweeted, "PTL BluDogs Keep barkin Pelosie bill is Govt take-over of healthCare Breaks Obama promise 'keep what u hv' Puts Wash Burocrats in chrg MUSTSTOP" [sic].[6] Senator Grassley's tweet criticizing the Democrats was one of several that raised questions about how committed he really was to working with Democrats to find a compromise. As National Public Radio reporter Liz Halloran explained, "[A]s Grassley has pivoted from defending bipartisan work on a Senate bill to criticizing a competing House bill, he has increasingly sown confusion over just where he stands in negotiations to overhaul health care."[7] Halloran cited as further evidence doubting Grassley's sincerity about working toward reform a Twitter argument he had with Senator Specter over the alleged death panels in the Democrats' plan. Eventually, the bipartisan reform effort collapsed.

In another example where going public rendered negotiations moot, in January 2009 House Republicans let the media know that then Minority Leader John Boehner had asked members to vote against President Obama's stimulus bill *before* the president met with Republicans that same day to talk about the legislation in hopes of picking up Republican votes.[8] Although the president kept his appointment with House Republicans, incidents such as this certainly do not help to build trust among politicians and can have an impact on future negotiations.

THE DILEMMAS OF RAPID RESPONSE

There are other ways members can get themselves into trouble by going public. The current media environment, particularly Twitter and cable television, encourages members to react to events or the comments of others immediately and with charged rhetoric; once those comments get online, they can go viral before the congressional member has even had time to consider the consequences of his or her statement. For example, in July of 2013, as many congressional Republicans were trying to figure out how to reform immigration in an effort to make them more competitive with Hispanic voters, Congressman Steve King (R-IA) did an interview with a conservative website in which he took issue with those who wanted to provide a path to citizenship for undocumented students, "saying that for every valedictorian who's legalized, 'there's another 100 out there that weigh 130 pounds and they've got calves the size of cantaloupes because they're hauling 75 pounds of marijuana across the desert.'"[9] His comments drew strong rebukes from House Speaker John Boehner and Republican strategists, though Congressman King refused to back down. The episode generated unwanted scrutiny for Republicans who were supportive of a path to legalization and undermined the GOP's efforts to reach out to Hispanic voters.

In other cases, members of Congress have gone public with claims and stories that made for a compelling message only to have political fact checkers poke holes in their claims or expose inaccuracies in their stories. Congressman Darrell Issa (R-CA), chairman of the House Oversight Committee, became a serial offender as Glen Kessler's *Washington Post* "Fact Checker" column awarded him multiple Pinocchios (the rating system to determine the degree of false and misleading information) for a series of claims and statements he had made about multiple investigations he was conducting of the Obama administration, from Benghazi to the IRS scrutiny of conservative groups applying for tax-exempt status.[10] Although Issa's claims were designed to call attention to his committee's work and to cast doubt on the Obama administration, which they did, the questionable veracity and intentional repeated use of such tenuous claims left him open to charges that he was merely conducting a partisan witch hunt and diminished his credibility, raising questions about how effective he could really be in his oversight. Indeed, Congressman Issa is one of many congressmen who could have heeded the wisdom of Winnie-the-Pooh in their dealings with traditional and new media: "When ... you Think of Things, you find sometimes that a Thing which seemed very Thingish inside you is quite different when it gets out into the open and has other people looking at it."[11]

Therefore, although members of Congress believe there are benefits to going public and often devote substantial resources to it, there are potential pitfalls. The need to cater to media news values and to react quickly in a never-ending news cycle can push members to communicate harsh messages that make negotiations less likely or to go public with messages that have not been carefully considered or vetted for accuracy, leading to unexpected reactions or to scrutiny that distracts from or even undermines the member's message and purpose. Such problems are further compounded by the inevitability that members must deal with competing messages from their colleagues. Such challenges are particularly daunting for those who are trying to pass policy rather than block it.

IMPACT ON THE POLITICAL SYSTEM

It appears that public strategies offer both potential and hazard for members of Congress. On the one hand, going public can help members move beyond their institutional powers to influence policy and to build a reputation as someone who is serious about policymaking. On the other hand, the tactics members may need to use to gain public attention or any public comments they make without careful consideration of the consequences can cause friction with other members of Congress or other politicians, eroding trust or making it difficult for members to work together. While the effectiveness and costs of going public in Congress invite additional research, we can begin to consider the impact of public strategies and their evolution on the political system.

Benefits of Going Public

As is often the case when the media are involved, there is both promise and peril for the political system. Perhaps most promising is that going public allows more voices to join the debate, adding more perspectives to our public discussions. As congressional members have become more adept at making the news, they have kept the president from dominating public debate. And the ability of party leaders and individual members of Congress to comment on a range of issues in the press or on social media means that those not on the relevant congressional committees can weigh in on issues even before the issues get to the House or Senate floor, providing a wider variety of perspectives earlier in the legislative process. The adoption of new media by members has further extended the debate and brought in interested citizens beyond Congress to participate in the discussions as they comment on members' tweets and Facebook posts.

A second positive development for the political system, especially in light of the trends toward centralization of power in the parties and increasing partisan polarization, is that going public can serve as a check on the majority and those with power in Congress and thus be a useful tool for those whose lack of formal power leaves them at a disadvantage. As documented in the presidency literature, the ability of members of Congress to go public gives them leverage in dealing with the president. If Congress can effectively limit the president's ability to frame an issue, he is forced to work with at least some members to accomplish his goals. And particularly in areas where the president's formal powers are considerable, most notably foreign affairs and national security, congressional members can turn to the media to question the president's statements, actions, or inaction to try to influence his decisions. Given the expansive views of executive power embraced by the most recent presidential administrations, going public may be an important equalizer in the balance of power between the legislative and executive branches. Within Congress, the success of the minority party and more junior members of Congress in gaining media attention over time has insured that those with power inside Congress typically cannot just run roughshod over their colleagues who lack formal power, especially if these folks coordinate their efforts. Lack of power does not necessarily mean lack of influence in today's Congress.

Finally, going public can improve accountability at least on the issues that make the media's agenda. Not only can members' public strategies make it more difficult for members to hide their votes on controversial or unpopular legislation, but these strategies can also generate public reaction to issues leading up to votes that allow members to know more about their constituents' preferences in advance of the members' vote decision. The relatively recent practice of combining formal congressional actions with media campaigns, not just in filibusters but also congressional oversight hearings, has the potential to heighten the president's accountability as well. As committee members make themselves accessible to news outlets, particularly cable television, to discuss their concerns about executive agencies' activities, implementation of legislation, or presidential actions, they expand the audience that is aware of these concerns. The resulting bad publicity and negative public reaction for the president or executive branch may be an important factor in fixing the problems or stopping certain practices. This use of public strategies in the context of oversight and their impact on executive accountability are potentially a significant development ripe for further research.

Perils of Going Public

Alas, despite the potential benefits of members of Congress going public, the popularity of this strategy and the way members pursue it may also contribute to problems in the political system. Although certainly not a cause of partisan polarization, the use of partisan rhetoric and the emphasis on partisan conflict that members may employ to appeal to news values no doubt exacerbate partisan divisions and the decline of civility in Congress. The media reward members for outrageous behavior and rhetoric with coverage, as Senator DeMint noted. The open hostility between parties, sometimes even within them, can erode trust and make working together more difficult, which leads to a second peril for the political system.

Going public may also contribute to gridlock in government, which may make solving problems difficult. As the analyses and case studies in this book and in other research on congressional communication have shown, members who want to use public strategies, particularly those who want to coordinate with other members, have an incentive to oppose the majority party or the president or even a majority within their own party and not necessarily offer constructive solutions to make their public message clearer and to maintain the unity of their own coalition. The failure to offer alternatives or compromises leaves only two options—the policy on the table is stopped and the status quo prevails, or the majority and the president have sufficient support to pass their preferred policy in spite of the negative publicity. Given intransigent factions within the majority party in the House and the difficulty of gaining supermajorities in the Senate to avert filibusters, the more likely scenario in recent years seems to be the status quo, even when all sides agree that it is unacceptable.

Further increasing the likelihood of gridlock are the number and volume of additional voices that going public can add to the debate. While earlier we considered this a positive development for the political system, it can also complicate policymaking. Expanding the number of people involved in the debate can make finding common ground and acceptable solutions more challenging. And because many of these additional voices may not be as well informed on the issue as those who have gained expertise by serving on the relevant committees, inaccurate and incomplete information may create unnecessary conflict and opposition that derails the policy process.

One final way public strategies may contribute to gridlock is that publicity of congressional members' views may make it more difficult for those members to compromise. There was a reason the founding fathers

debated the Constitution in relative isolation from the press and public and
agreed not to discuss the deliberations publicly. Privacy offers room for
changing one's opinion. As James Madison explained in his defense of the
secrecy surrounding the deliberations at the Constitutional Convention,
"the minds of members were changing and much was to be gained by a
yielding and accommodating spirit. Had the members committed themselves publicly at first, they would have afterwards supposed consistency
required them to maintain their ground."[12] Public comments may lock
members into particular positions, and any moves away from those positions leave members open to accusations of waffling and become fodder
for campaign opponents in the next election.

A final peril of going public is that it may discourage deliberation, as
sustained attention to an issue is difficult and the new media environment
encourages rapid response. Deliberation takes time, and the media are
always looking for the next big issue or controversy. As we have seen, members will find it easier to go public if they are willing to talk about issues
the media are interested in. Most issues cannot be debated and solved in
the media's short time frame. Therefore, members may be able to use the
media to focus attention on an issue and encourage discussion of it for a
brief time, assuming the press finds the issue newsworthy, but sustained
attention is unlikely. And when the issue falls off the media's agenda, it
may fall off the congressional agenda as well, as members are encouraged
to shift their attention to whatever issue the media have moved on to. Also
creating obstacles for deliberation is the pressure to respond rapidly via
new media. Deliberation implies thoughtfulness. New media and twenty-
four-hour news stations encourage and reward rapid response to events
and issues. These quick reactions put members on the record often before
they have had a chance to think through the issue or their position on it; as
just noted, once made public, positions are hard to back away from. While
the media in theory provide a place for deliberation and debate, current
news media practices and the way members use social media do not seem
suited for the practice of deliberation. Of course, institutions change and
adapt, and there is no reason that members could not find ways to employ
social media and other online media for more deliberative purposes.

Much Left to Learn

In this book, I have endeavored to provide a foundation for understanding how members of Congress use mass communication to overcome institutional weakness or supplement institutional power to influence national policy and debate and how these communication efforts have changed over time and with regard to the political context. The evidence suggests that even as members' media strategies constantly evolve in response to changing political contexts and media environments, both traditional and new media provide avenues for members to move beyond the limits of their institutional power. But as this concluding chapter makes clear, this is merely the beginning of the work necessary to understand the impact of going public in Congress, not the end.

New York Times Analysis Methodology

The two data sets used in Chapters 2 and 3 come from the *New York Times*. For the full data set, I randomly selected three days that Congress was in session for each year from 1977 through 2015. For the transition-year data set, I selected January and May of each year that marked the first year of a new presidential administration (1977, 1981, 1989, 1993, and 2001) or that followed a shift in partisan control of either house of Congress (1987 and 1995) from 1977 through 2001. For both data sets, my research assistants and I searched the *New York Times* for the selected days and months, using the search term "Representative" or "Senator" or "Speaker" to identify any article that might include public comments of members of Congress. "Speaker" was necessary as a separate term because articles often referred to the Speaker of the House by his or her formal title rather than as Representative. That issue did not arise with Senate leaders. We eliminated articles that did not pertain to the US Congress. Of the remaining articles, we kept those that quoted or paraphrased a congressional member commenting on a public issue, policy, or event related to his or her job in Congress (as opposed to the district or a member's private life).

In each article, the unit of analysis was the member or coordinated group of members being quoted or paraphrased. Therefore, it was possible to code several cases for one article. Members were coded separately unless the article explicitly stated they were working together, as in the case of a joint statement to the press. This probably underestimates the extent of coordinated communication, but we found no consistently reliable way to divine which members were working in concert apart from the reporter mentioning it. We ended up with 3,713 cases in the transition-year data set and 921 in the full data set.

THE CONTENT CODE

For each case, we recorded the following information:

I. Date
II. Information about the congressional member who was speaking
   A. The specific person(s) speaking and the category the person(s) fit into
      1. Majority party leader
      2. Minority party leader
      3. Committee chair
      4. Ranking minority member of the committee
      5. Caucus (a formal caucus within Congress, such as the Congressional Black Caucus)
      6. Coalition (an informal group that comes together just for this specific issue at this time)
      7. Other majority party individual
      8. Other minority party individual
      9. Other (specify)
   B. The party the congressional member belonged to
   C. The house of Congress the congressional member belonged to
III. Information about the content and purpose of the congressional member's comments
   A. Issue: a two- or three-word description of the major issue and the category that best describes that issue
      1. Budget/taxes (includes deficits)
      2. Economy (includes recession, unemployment, jobs outlook, and any other references to the health of the economy)

3. Business (regulation or oversight of industries, finance, or banking issues unrelated to the economy or a specific issue category)

4. Foreign policy (treaties, trade agreements, relations with other countries)

5. Defense (includes military issues, war, national security)

6. Health care (includes Medicare, Medicaid)

7. Social policy (welfare, Social Security, and other safety-net programs)

8. Environment (all environmental issues, including conservation, pollution, nuclear waste cleanup, etc.)

9. Energy policy

10. Crime (includes law enforcement)

11. Agriculture

12. Education

13. Civil rights (civil rights and liberties, including abortion, gay rights, criminal rights, freedom of speech and religion, etc.)

14. Government affairs (includes congressional rules or procedures, ethics investigations and government scandal, and campaign finance)

15. Appointments (judicial or executive branch nominations, confirmation hearings, etc.)

16. Party politics (party fundraising, elections for party leadership, general party strategy that does not fit one of the other issues)

17. Immigration

18. Transportation

19. Other

B. Reaction: whether the effort to go public was in reaction to something else (such as an event or announcement) or was an attempt to initiate something new

C. Reaction to president: whether the congressional member was reacting to something the president had said or done,

and if so, whether the member was supportive of the
president or opposed to the president

D. Direct contact with the press: whether it appeared that the
congressional member had direct contact with the press in
going public: news conference, op-ed columns, interviews
with talk shows or quotes in the story that were made to
the reporter rather than during floor debate or committee
hearings

E. Work-related activity: whether comments were made in the
course of the congressional members' regular work activities,
including public hearings, filibusters, and floor debate

F. Goal: the apparent goal of the congressional member; this
may have been explicitly stated in the article. If not, we
attempted to discern the goal based on the political context.

1. Get the member's policy preference passed or enacted
2. Stop legislation or action from taking place
3. Other

Intercoder Reliability

In the early stages of the *New York Times* analysis, multiple coders analyzed
the same articles in the transition-year data set to help identify potential
problems with the content code. These early coding efforts led to some
revisions in the content code to improve reliability. Some of these changes
are detailed in the relevant chapters.

Ten percent of the articles in the full thirty-nine-year data set were analyzed by a second coder to measure intercoder reliability for the revised
content code used in both *New York Times* data sets and the television
analysis in Chapter 4. On the variables related to information about the
congressional member, reliability was nearly 100 percent, with discrepancies usually resulting from accidental data entry errors. Reliability on
the content of congressional members' messages was a little lower, but no
variable dropped below 80 percent agreement.

CHAPTER 1

1. Martin Tolchin, "The Troubles of Tip O'Neill," *New York Times*, August 16, 1981, sec. VI, 30.
2. Al Kamen, "In the Loop: Pumping Up the GOP," *Washington Post*, May 16, 2001, A21.
3. Mike Allen, "Democrats Turn Energy on Bush," *Washington Post*, May 20, 2001, A9.
4. Timothy Cook, *Making Laws and Making News: Media Strategies in the U.S. House of Representatives* (Washington, DC: Brookings Institution, 1989), 73.
5. Richard D. Lyons, "Howard Henry Baker Jr.," *New York Times*, January 5, 1977, 14.
6. David R. Mayhew, *America's Congress: Actions in the Public Sphere, James Madison through Newt Gingrich* (New Haven, CT: Yale University Press, 2000), 101.
7. See, e.g., Samuel Kernell, *Going Public: New Strategies of Presidential Leadership*, 4th ed. (Washington, DC: CQ Press, 2007), and George C. Edwards III, *Governing by Campaigning: The Politics of the Bush Presidency* (New York: Pearson Longman, 2007).
8. Kernell, *Going Public*, x.
9. Douglas Rivers and Nancy L. Rose, "Passing the President's Program: Public Opinion and Presidential Influence in Congress," *American Journal of Political Science* 29 (May 1985): 183–196.
10. C. Danielle Vinson, *Local Media Coverage of Congress and Its Members: Through Local Eyes* (Cresskill, NJ: Hampton Press, 2003), and R. Douglas Arnold, *Congress, the Press, and Political Accountability* (Princeton, NJ: Princeton University Press, 2013), do look at this aspect of congressional communication in their studies of local media coverage of Congress.
11. Plato, *Gorgias*, trans. James H. Nichols Jr. (Ithaca, NY: Cornell University Press, 1998), 33.
12. David R. Mayhew, *Congress: The Electoral Connection* (New Haven, CT: Yale University Press, 1974).
13. Karen M. Kedrowski, *Media Entrepreneurs and the Media Enterprise in the U.S. Congress* (Cresskill, NJ: Hampton Press, 1996), 169; Gary Lee Malecha and Daniel J. Reagan, *The Public Congress: Congressional Deliberation in a New Media Age* (New York: Routledge, 2012) .
14. Mayhew, *America's Congress*, 7.
15. Mayhew, *America's Congress*, 4.

16. Ronald Brownstein, *The Second Civil War: How Extreme Partisanship Has Paralyzed Washington and Polarized America* (New York: Penguin, 2007), 122.

17. Malecha and Reagan, *Public Congress*; Timothy Cook, *Governing with the News: The News Media as a Political Institution*, 2nd ed. (Chicago: University of Chicago Press, 2005); Barbara Sinclair, *Party Wars: Polarization and the Politics of National Policy Making* (Norman: University of Oklahoma Press, 2006).

18. C. Danielle Vinson, "Congress and the Media: Who Has the Upper Hand?," in *New Directions in Media and Politics*, ed. Travis Ridout (New York: Routledge, 2013).

19. Cook, *Governing*.

20. Paul S. Herrnson, *Congressional Elections: Campaigning at Home and in Washington* (Washington, DC: CQ Press, 2004); Martin P. Wattenberg, *The Decline of American Political Parties* (Cambridge, MA: Harvard University Press, 1984).

21. Robert D. Putnam, *Bowling Alone: The Collapse and Revival of American Community* (New York: Simon and Schuster, 2000).

22. Kedrowski, *Media Entrepreneurs*.

23. Malecha and Reagan, *Public Congress*, 24–25.

24. Cook, *Governing*; Kernell, *Going Public*.

25. Edwards, *Governing*.

26. Cook, *Governing*; Frank R. Baumgartner and Bryan D. Jones, "Positive and Negative Feedback in Politics," in *Policy Dynamics*, ed. Baumgartner and Jones (Chicago: University of Chicago Press, 2002); Shanto Iyengar and Donald R. Kinder, *News That Matters: Television and American Opinion* (Chicago: University of Chicago Press, 1987).

27. Paul M. Kellstedt, *The Mass Media and the Dynamics of American Racial Attitudes* (New York: Cambridge University Press, 2003); John Zaller, *The Nature and Origins of Mass Opinion* (New York: Cambridge University Press, 1992).

28. Iyengar and Kinder, *News That Matters*; Mayhew, *America's Congress*.

29. E.g.,Robert M. Entman, *Projections of Power: Framing News, Public Opinion, and U.S. Foreign Policy* (Chicago: University of Chicago Press, 2004);Shanto Iyengar, *Is Anyone Responsible? How Television Frames Political Issues* (Chicago: University of Chicago Press, 1991); Zaller, *Nature and Origins*.

30. George C. Edwards III, *The Strategic President: Persuasion and Opportunity in Presidential Leadership* (Princeton, NJ: Princeton University Press, 2009); Jeffrey E. Cohen, *Going Local: Presidential Leadership in the Post-Broadcast Age* (New York: Cambridge University Press, 2010). Edwards and Cohen raise doubts about how much of presidents' successes can be attributed to going public, and others have noted that this has become more difficult in today's fragmented media environment. Nevertheless, the perception that this can be beneficial persists.

31. Barbara Sinclair, "Hostile Partners: The President, Congress, and Lawmaking in the Partisan 1990s," in *Polarized Politics: Congress and the President in a Partisan Era*, ed. Jon R. Bond and Richard Fleisher (Washington, DC: CQ Press, 2000), 143.

32. William G. Howell and Douglas L. Kriner, "Congress, the President, and the Iraq War's Domestic Political Front," in *Congress Reconsidered*, 9th ed., ed. Lawrence C. Dodd and Bruce I. Oppenheimer (Washington, DC: CQ Press, 2009), 316–319.

33. Matthew A. Baum and Tim Groeling, "What Gets Covered? How Media Coverage of Elite Debate Drives the Rally-'Round-the-Flag Phenomenon: 1978-1998," in *In the Public Domain: Presidents and the Challenges of Public Leadership*, ed. Lori Cox Han and Diane J. Heith (Albany: State University of New York Press, 2005), 50.

34. Cook, *Governing*; Tim Groeling and Samuel Kernell, "Congress, the President, and Party Competition via Network News," in *Polarized Politics: Congress and the President in a Partisan Era*, ed. Jon R. Bond and Richard Fleisher (Washington, DC: CQ Press, 2000).

35. Mayhew, *America's Congress*, 115–116.

36. Groeling and Kernell, "Congress," 92; Tim Groeling, *When Politicians Attack! Party Cohesion in the Media* (New York: Cambridge University Press, 2010).

37. Sinclair, *Party Wars*.

38. Kernell, *Going Public*.

39. Cook, *Governing*, 162.

40. Kedrowski, *Media Entrepreneurs*, 124–125.

41. Kedrowski, *Media Entrepreneurs*, 138.

42. See Sinclair, *Party Wars*, and Brownstein, *Second Civil War*, for a detailed look at how and why polarization occurred.

43. Sinclair, "Hostile Partners," 144–145.

44. C. Lawrence. Evans, "Committees, Leaders, and Message Politics," in *Congress Reconsidered*, 7th ed., ed. Lawrence C. Dodd and Bruce I. Oppenheimer (Washington, DC: CQ Press, 2001).

45. Nicol C. Rae, "Republican Congressional Leadership in Historical Context," *Extensions* (Spring 2005); Barbara Sinclair, "The Senate Leadership Dilemma: Passing Bills and Pursuing Partisan Advantage in a Non-majoritarian Chamber," in *The Contentious Senate: Partisanship, Ideology, and the Myth of Cool Judgment*, ed. Colton C. Campbell and Nicol C. Rae (Lanham, MD.: Rowman and Littlefield, 2001).

46. Rae, "Republican," 8.

47. Juliet Eilperin, *Fight Club Politics: How Partisanship Is Poisoning the House of Representatives* (Lanham, MD: Rowman and Littlefield, 2006), 5.

48. Evans, "Committees," 239.

49. Lori Montgomery, "Debt Strategies Diverge as Talks Hit Another Wall," *Washington Post*, July 25, 2011, A1.

50. Eilperin, *Fight Club*, 129.

51. Kedrowski, *Media Entrepreneurs*.

52. Aldrich and Rohde, "Consequences."

53. Lawrence C. Dodd, "Re-envisioning Congress: Theoretical Perspectives on Congressional Change," in *Congress Reconsidered*, 7th ed., ed. Lawrence C. Dodd and Bruce I. Oppenheimer (Washington, DC: CQ Press, 2001), 396–397.

54. Groeling and Kernell, "Congress," 84; Groeling, *When Politicians Attack!*

55. Dodd, "Re-Envisioning Congress," 396.

56. Groeling and Kernell, "Congress," 95.
57. Groeling and Kernell, "Congress," 78.
58. Kedrowski, *Media Entrepreneurs*, 124.
59. Sinclair, "Hostile Partners," 147; Sinclair, *Party Wars*, 255–307.
60. E. E. Schattschneider, *The Semisovereign People: A Realist's View of Democracy in America* (Hinsdale, IL: Dryden Press, 1975).
61. Baumgartner and Jones, *Agendas and Instability in American Politics* (Chicago: University of Chicago Press, 1993), 4, 30.
62. MacLeod, "Logic," 56.
63. Baumgartner and Jones, *Agendas*, 4–5.
64. R. Douglas Arnold, *The Logic of Congressional Action* (New Haven, CT: Yale University Press, 1990).
65. Kedrowski, *Media Entrepreneurs*, 56.
66. Kedrowski, *Media Entrepreneurs*, 5.
67. Daniel Lipinski, "Navigating Congressional Policy Processes: The Inside Perspective on How Laws Are Made," in *Congress Reconsidered*, 9th ed., ed. Lawrence C. Dodd and Bruce I. Oppenheimer (Washington, DC: CQ Press, 2009), 353.
68. Kedrowski, *Media Entrepreneurs*, 63–64.
69. S. Robert Lichter and Daniel R. Amundson, "Less News Is Worse News: Television News Coverage of Congress, 1972–1992," in *Congress, the Press, and the Public*, ed. Thomas E. Mann and Norman J. Ornstein (Washington, DC: American Enterprise Institute and Brookings Institution, 1994); Mark J. Rozell, *In Contempt of Congress: Postwar Press Coverage on Capitol Hill* (Westport, CT: Praeger, 1996).
70. Rozell, *In Contempt*, 55.
71. Baum and Groeling, "What Gets Covered"; Cook, *Making Laws*; Stephen Hess, *The Ultimate Insiders: U.S. Senators in the National Media* (Washington, DC: Brookings Institution, 1986); Stephen Hess, *Live from Capitol Hill! Studies of Congress and the Media* (Washington, DC: Brookings Institution, 1991).
72. Hess, *Ultimate Insiders*.
73. Vinson, *Local Media Coverage of Congress*.
74. Rozell, *In Contempt*.
75. Lichter and Amundson, "Less News."
76. Rozell, *In Contempt*, 7–8.
77. Rozell, *In Contempt*, 72.
78. Rozell, *In Contempt*, 112.
79. MacLeod, "Logic," 59.
80. Sinclair, *Party Wars*, 288–306.
81. Baumgartner and Jones, "Positive"; Mayhew, *America's Congress*.
82. Evans, "Committees"; Malecha and Reagan, *Public Congress*.
83. Patrick J. Sellers, *Cycles of Spin: Strategic Communication in the U.S. Congress* (New York: Cambridge University Press, 2010).
84. For a detailed discussion of issue ownership, see John R. Petrocik, "Issue Ownership in Presidential Elections, with a 1980 Case Study," *American Journal of Political Science* 40 (August 1996): 825–850.

85. Evans, "Committees."

86. Sellers, *Cycles*; Evans, "Committees," 230–232.

87. See, e.g.,Daniel J. Palazzolo, *Done Deal? The Politics of the 1997 Budget Agreement* (New York: Chatham House, 1999); Sinclair, "Hostile Partners."

88. Steven S. Smith and Eric D. Lawrence, "Party Control of Committees in the Republican Congress," in *Congress Reconsidered*, 6th ed., ed. Lawrence C. Dodd and Bruce I. Oppenheimer (Washington, DC: CQ Press, 1997), 163–192.

89. Evans, "Committees," 219.

90. Evans, "Committees," 235.

91. Sarah A. Binder, "Elections and Congress's Governing Capacity," *Extensions* (Fall 2005): 10, 14.

92. Groeling and Kernell, "Congress," 95.

93. Sinclair, "Hostile Partners," 144.

94. C. Lawrence Dodd and Bruce I. Oppenheimer, "The Politics of the Contemporary House: From Gingrich to Pelosi," in *Congress Reconsidered*, 9th ed., ed. Dodd and Oppenheimer (Washington, DC: CQ Press, 2009), 26.

95. See, e.g., Cook, *Making Laws*; Evans, "Committees"; Kedrowski, *Media Entrepreneurs*; Malecha and Reagan, *Public Congress*; Mayhew, *America's Congress*; Sellers, *Cycles of Spin*; and Sinclair, *Party Wars*.

96. Baumgartner and Jones, "Positive," 23.

97. Kedrowski, *Media Entrepreneurs*, 201.

98. Kedrowski, *Media Entrepreneurs*, 202ff.

99. Baumgartner and Jones, "Positive," 5.

100. Mayhew, *America's Congress*, ix.

101. Success here is defined as making the news. This is distinct from the issue of whether members have achieved their goals in going public (passing, reshaping, or stopping legislation), which I'll refer to as effectiveness.

102. Complete transcripts of any Sunday talk shows dating back farther than 1990 were not available.

103. The combination of years and months does bias the data in at least one significant way: certain issues—most notably presidential appointments—are more prominent than they would be if we studied an entire presidential or legislative term. Similarly, other issues—such as appropriations bills—that come up later in a term appear less frequently. However, there is no reason to expect the choice of dates to skew who went public or their reasons for doing so, and the second data set should allow us to identify any biases in the issues.

104. Gadi Wolfsfeld, *Making Sense of Media and Politics: Five Principles in Political Communication* (New York: Routledge Press, 2011), 10–11.

105. Lawrence R. Jacobs and Robert Y. Shapiro, *Politicians Don't Pander: Political Manipulation and the Loss of Democratic Responsiveness* (Chicago: University of Chicago Press, 2000), 60.

106. Jacobs and Shapiro, *Politicians*, 60, 175.

107. Sellers, *Cycles*, 199.

108. Sellers, *Cycles*, 198.

CHAPTER 2

1. Martin Tolchin, "Cranston to End Press Briefings after Meeting in the White House," *New York Times*, May 11, 1977, 8.
2. Rozell, *In Contempt*.
3. There was no difference between committee chairs of different parties.
4. Brownstein, *The Second Civil War*; Thomas E. Mann and Norman J. Ornstein, *It's Even Worse Than It Looks: How the American Constitutional System Collided with the New Politics of Extremism* (New York: Basic Books, 2012); Mayhew, *America's Congress*, 84; Sinclair, *Party Wars*, 114.
5. Barbara Sinclair, *Unorthodox Lawmaking: New Legislative Processes in the U.S. Congress*, 4th ed. (Washington: Sage/CQ Press, 2012).
6. Aldrich and Rohde, "The Consequences of Party Organization."
7. Initially, I tried to separate these topics, but most of the time they were discussed in tandem, and intercoder reliability fell below acceptable standards when they were separate. Combined, the category posed no problems for intercoder reliability.
8. I used the Policy Agenda Project's data on congressional hearings that corresponded to the months and years of the *New York Times* transition-year data. The Policy Agenda Project data can be accessed at http://www.policyagendas.org/. The data used here were originally collected by Frank R. Baumgartner and Bryan D. Jones, with the support of National Science Foundation grants nos. SBR 9320922 and 0111611 and were distributed through the Department of Government at the University of Texas at Austin. Neither NSF nor the original collectors of the data bear any responsibility for the analysis reported here.
9. Roger H. Davidson, Walter J. Oleszek, and Frances E. Lee, *Congress and Its Members*, 13th ed. (Washington: CQ Press, 2012), 284–285.
10. Lance T. LeLoup and Steven A. Shull, *The President and Congress: Collaboration and Combat in National Policymaking* (Boston: Allyn and Bacon, 1999), 85.
11. Kernell, *Going Public*.
12. Malecha and Reagan, *The Public Congress*.
13. Statements were coded as work-related only if that was explicitly clear in the article. E.g., if the reporter mentioned the member's comments had come during floor debate or in a committee hearing.
14. A single case could use both methods, and 13 percent of the cases did use both.

CHAPTER 3

1. Carl Hulse and Kate Zernike, "House Passes Detainee Bill as It Clears Senate Hurdle," *New York Times*, September 28, 2006, A20.
2. Bill Vlasic and Nick Bunkley, "U.A.W. to Modify Contracts in Bid to Help Detroit," *New York Times*, December 4, 2008, A1.
3. In coding the news coverage, my research assistants and I tried to divide the "other" category into more specific goals, but the intercoder reliability was unacceptably low. These other goals were less clear than passing policy or stopping policy, and there was often overlap among them. Using three broad categories, coders agreed 85 percent of the time, and most of these remaining discrepancies involved whether something should be coded as passing policy or some other reason, such

as explaining an issue. For these reasons, we settled on using three categories for coding goals.

4. Brian F. Schaffner and Mary Layton Atkinson, "Taxing Death or Estates? When Frames Influence Citizens' Issue Beliefs," in *Winning with Words: The Origins and Impact of Political Framing*, ed. Brian F. Schaffner and Patrick J. Sellers (New York: Routledge, 2010).

5. Arnold, *The Logic of Congressional Action*.

6. Groeling, *When Politicians Attack!*

7. Michael Wines, "Democrats Strongly Attack GOP Budget Plan," *New York Times*, January, 7 1995, I.1.

8. Editorial, "The Dole Challenge," *New York Times*, January, 7 1995, I.22.

9. Cook, *Making Laws*; Vinson, *Local Media*.

10. Cook, *Governing with the News*; Jacobs and Shapiro, *Politicians Don't Pander*.

11. Gary C. Jacobson, *The Politics of Congressional Elections*, 7th ed. (New York: Pearson Longman, 2009), 159–160.

12. Jacobs and Shapiro, *Politicians*.

13. Groeling and Kernell, "Congress, the President, and Party Competition."

14. Robert Pear, "Moynihan Joins Welfare Debate with Bill of His Own," *New York Times*, May 14, 1995, A22.

15. Susan Crabtree and John Bresnahan, "Boehner Facing Plenty of Heat from Conservatives," *Roll Call*, May 3, 2001, accessed March 23, 2016, http://www.lexisnexis.com.libproxy.furman.edu/hottopics/lnacademic/?verb=srandcsi=259944andsr=SUBJECT%28SUPREME+COURTS%29+AND+DATE%3E=%25CURRDATE-14%25.

16. Groeling, *When Partisans*.

CHAPTER 4

1. Ben Smith, "Weiner, Chaffetz, Goat," *Politico*, June 10, 2010, accessed August 5, 2013, http://www.politico.com/blogs/bensmith/0610/Weiner_Chaffetz_goat.html.

2. Marin Cogan, "Mohair Subsidies Get Reps' Goats," *Politico*, June 10, 2010, accessed August 5, 2013, http://www.politico.com/news/stories/0610/38379.html.

3. Of course, the limits of going public are also apparent. Despite the widespread attention, six years later mohair subsidies are still with us.

4. Malecha and Reagan, *The Public Congress*, 22.

5. Cook, *Making Laws*, 60.

6. Hess, *The Ultimate Insiders*, 5.

7. Complete transcripts of any of the Sunday talk shows dating back farther than 1990 were not available. Interviews were included based on the same criteria used in the analysis of the *New York Times* data. Congressional members had to be discussing issues relevant to their work in Congress, which led to the exclusion of some interviews that were strictly about elections.

8. I coded the first three issues mentioned in each congressional interview, using the same issue categories used in the analysis of the *New York Times*.

9. Amber E. Boydstun, *Making the News: Politics, the Media, and Agenda Setting* (Chicago: Chicago University Press, 2013).

10. Malecha and Reagan, *The Public Congress*, 56–66.

11. Richard Davis, *Typing Politics: The Role of Blogs in American Politics* (New York: Oxford University Press, 2009), 94–95.

12. Robert Behre, "DeMint Taps into Power of Web," *Post and Courier*, March 23, 2008, accessed March 23, 2016, http://www.postandcourier.com/article/20080323/PC1602/303239916.

13. The House members were Collin Peterson (D-MN), Ed Pastor (D-AZ), and American Samoa Delegate Eni Faleomavaega. The lone senator was Thad Cochran (R-MS).

14. Matthew Eric Glassman, Jacob R. Straus, and Colleen J. Shogan, "Social Networking and Constituent Communication: Member Use of Twitter during a Two-Week Period in the 111th Congress," *Congressional Research Service Report* 7-5700 R40823 (February 3, 2010), https://www.fas.org/sgp/crs/misc/R43018.pdf.

15. *Tweet Congress*. August 7, 2013, accessed August 7, 2013, http://www.tweetcongress.org/tweets

16. Initially, there were some major discrepancies between coders on the issue categories. However, closer examination revealed that all of the disagreements stemmed from two sources. First, there was confusion about whether the Violence against Women Act should be categorized as a civil rights issue or crime. We decided that it fit more consistently with the other crime issues than civil rights. Second, one coder initially put all weather-related tweets in the environment category. However, most of these tweets were about weather events (major snowstorms and such) rather than environmental policy. We decided that weather events, unless explicitly connected to policy issues, should go to the "other" category. After resolving these differences, intercoder reliability was 100 percent.

17. Malecha and Reagan, *The Public Congress*; Vinson, "Congress and the Media."

18. My research assistant looked at the campaign or political pages for each of these senators and found that campaign sites still typically have significantly more followers and traffic than the official government pages for most members, but we found some were not updated as frequently if the member was not up for re-election or had little opposition.

19. Groeling, *When Partisans Attack!*; Sellers, *Cycles of Spin*.

20. The House members were John Boehner (R-OH), Nancy Pelosi (D-CA), Jason Chaffetz (R-UT), Jared Polis (D-CO), Trey Gowdy (R-SC), Marcia Fudge (D-OH), and Luis Gutierrez (D-IL). Senators included Harry Reid (D-NV), Mitch McConnell (R-KY), Chuck Schumer (D-NY), Lindsey Graham (R-SC), Carl Levin (D-MI), Jeff Sessions (R-AL), Claire McCaskill (D-MO), Mike Lee (R-UT), Elizabeth Warren (D-MA), and Ted Cruz (R-TX).

21. I wanted to look at all the members during the same time period to control for the emergence of different issues. The Twitter and YouTube channels of any individual member were examined on the same day, but time constraints made it impossible to look at all thirty-six members on the same day. The one-week time period was the next best thing. With no new issues or major events arising during that week, all members were operating in essentially the same political and media environment. They all faced the same basic issues and events.

CHAPTER 5

1. Edward Cowan, "Carter Asks Tax Rises, Funding Shift to Ease Social Security Drain," *New York Times*, May 10, 1977, 69.

2. Cowan, "Carter Asks Tax Rises."

3. Adam Nagourney, "Kennedy Warns Democrats Not to Be Republican Clones," *New York Times*, January 13, 2005, A24.

4. Sinclair, "Hostile Partners," 143.

5. We used LexisNexis Academic Universe, Vanderbilt Television News Archives, and ProQuest's *New York Times* Historical Full Image, and *Washington Post* Historical Full Image databases. Coverage from the *NewsHour with Jim Lehrer* was available only for 2005.

6. A search of the *New York Times* turns up no articles mentioning President Carter's plans for Social Security in the months prior to the announcement, and only small pieces of the Reagan plan appear to have found their way into news accounts before the announcement.

7. Edwards, *Governing by Campaigning*.

8. Robin Toner, "In Montana, Bush Faces a Tough Sell on Social Security," *New York Times*, February 6, 2005, A15.

9. Sheryl G. Stolberg, "In Eye of Social Security Storm, a Quiet Power Broker," *New York Times*, February 22, 2005, A12.

10. Robin Toner, "On Social Security, a Political Appeal to the Young Draws the Attention of Their Elders," *New York Times*, February 23, 2005, A16.

11. The one Democrat was Representative Allen Boyd of Florida, who cosponsored legislation that would create private accounts as Bush wanted to do.

12. Richard W. Stevenson and Robin Toner, "2 Top G.O.P. Lawmakers Buck Bush on Social Security," *New York Times*, February 18, 2005, A17.

13. Jonathan Weisman, "Competing Visions for Social Security," *Washington Post*, February 24, 2005, A1.

14. Todd S. Purdum, "Bold Goal, Risky Path," *New York Times*, February 3, 2005, A1.

15. There were too few cases to separate committee leaders or members of the minority by whether they were in the president's party.

16. Edward Cowan, "Carter Asks Tax Rises, Funding Shift to Ease Social Security Drain," *New York Times*, May 10, 1977, 69.

17. Mary Russell and William Chapman, "Carter's Bailout Plan For Social Security Is Opposed on Hill," *Washington Post*, May 10, 1977, A2.

18. Cowan, "Carter Asks Tax Rises," 69.

19. David Broder, "Reagan Proposes 10% Cut in Social Security Costs," *Washington Post*, May 13, 1981, A1.

20. Art Pine, "Democrats Vow to Fight on Social Security Cuts," *Washington Post*, May 14, 1981, A1; David Broder, "Republicans Issue Reassurance on Benefits Reagan Compromise Indicated," *Washington Post*, May 17, 1981, A1.

21. David Broder, "Reagan Proposes 10% Cut in Social Security Costs," *Washington Post*, May 13, 1981, A1.

22. Harrison Donnelly, "Senate Opposes Social Security Cuts," *Congressional Quarterly Weekly Reports*, May 23, 1981, 895–896.

23. Bill Keller, "Democrats Run with Social Security Issue," *Congressional Quarterly Weekly Reports*, August 1, 1981, 1379.

24. Warren Weaver Jr., "Coalition Plans Drive against Move to Trim Social Security Benefits," *New York Times*, May 14, 1981, B15.

25. Bill Keller. "Democrats Run with Social Security Issue," *Congressional Quarterly Weekly Reports*, August 1, 1981, 1379.

26. Jonathan Weisman and Jim VandeHei, "GOP Is Divided on Social Security Push," *Washington Post*, January 7, 2005, A4.

27. George Stephanopoulos, "Interview Nancy Pelosi," ABC News Transcripts, February 6, 2005.

28. Chuck Babington and Mike Allen, "Bush's Address Wins over Few, If Any, Democrats" *Washington Post*, February 3, 2005, A16.

29. Edward Cowan, "Califano Says Shift on Social Security Could Be Permanent," *New York Times*, May 11, 1977, 1.

30. Spencer Rich, "90 Organizations Join Up to Guard Social Security," *Washington Post*, May 28, 1981, A6.

31. Spencer Rich, "Plight of Social Security Is Being Exaggerated, Democrats Charge," *Washington Post*, July 8, 1981, A3.

32. Office of the Press Secretary, "President Participates in Social Security Conversation in Pennsylvania," February 10, 2005, accessed July 21, 2007, http://www.whitehouse.gov/news/releases/2005/02/20050210-16.html.

33. Kate Snow, "Political Hot Potato Bush Administration," ABC News Transcripts, January 16, 2005.

34. David E. Rosenbaum and Robin Toner, "To Social Security Debate, Add Variable: Immigration," *New York Times*, February 16, 2005, A18.

35. Sheryl G. Stolberg and Carl Hulse, "Cool Reception on Capitol Hill to Social Security Plan," *New York Times*, February 4, 2005, A14.

36. Roper Center for Public Opinion from Cornell University, accessed July 21, 2007, https://presidential.roper.center/.

37. In the thirty-one years of reactions to the presidents' budget proposals, we find that the average number of reactions per year in the most recent ten-year period (1998–2007) was 4.5 cases higher than the average over the previous twenty-one years.

38. Jeffrey E. Cohen, "Presidential Leadership in an Age of New Media," in *Presidential Leadership: The Vortex of Power*, ed. Bert A. Rockman and Richard W. Waterman (New York: Oxford University Press, 2008); George C. Edwards III, "Impediments to Presidential Leadership: The Limitations of the Permanent Campaign and Going Public Strategies," in *Presidential Leadership: The Vortex of Power*, ed. Bert A. Rockman and Richard W. Waterman (New York: Oxford University Press, 2008).

39. Michelle Cottle, "Pimp My Rep," *New Republic*. May 20, 2009, accessed June 25, 2010, http://www.tnr.com/story_print.html?id=913edc39-b09e-49a8-8c9e-c.

CHAPTER 6

1. Associated Press, "Black Caucus Opposes New Budget as 'Unjust,'" *New York Times*, January 26, 1979, A23.
2. Martin Tolchin, "Congressional Blacks Vow to Stir Campaign against Budget Trims," *New York Times*, March 1, 1979, D16.
3. Glenn Thrush, "Frustrated CBC plays W.H. Hardball," *Politico*, December 3, 2009, accessed July 1, 2010, http://www.politico.com/story/2009/12/frustrated-cbc-plays-wh-hardball-030150.
4. Kedrowski, *Media Entrepreneurs*, 56.
5. Baumgartner and Jones, *Agendas*, 4, 30.
6. Sinclair, *Party Wars*, 255.
7. Alvin B. Tillery Jr., "Foreign Policy Activism and Power in the House of Representatives: Black Members of Congress and South Africa, 1968–1986," *Studies in American Political Development* 20 (Spring 1986): 94.
8. Tillery, "Foreign Policy Activism," 95.
9. Robert Singh, *The Congressional Black Caucus* (Thousand Oaks, CA: Sage, 1998), 14.
10. Singh, *Congressional*, 75.
11. Raymond W. Copson, *Congressional Black Caucus and Foreign Policy (1971–2002)* (New York: Novinka Books, 2003), 9–10.
12. Barbara Gamarekian, "Apartheid Protest Takes Page from 60's History," *New York Times*, November 30, 1984, A13.
13. Singh, *Congressional*, 84.
14. Copson, *Congressional*, 11.
15. Singh, *Congressional*, 75.
16. A second coder analyzed thirty randomly-selected cases (just over 10 percent) from the Congressional Black Caucus coverage. Agreement between coders was over 90 percent across all categories—the issue, the reaction to the president, whether the CBC was unified or divided, and which member of the CBC was speaking.
17. Howard French, "Clinton Choice for Latin Post Stirs Feud between 2 Groups," *New York Times*, January 27, 1993, A2.
18. Michael Wines, "Battle over the Budget: The Overview," *New York Times*, May 19, 1995, A1.
19. Groeling and Kernell, "Congress, the President, and Party Competition," 78.
20. John Lewis, telephone interview with the author, December 16, 2010. All comments attributed to Representative Lewis are from this interview.
21. "Dunlop Backers Call Him Victim of Unfair Action," *New York Times*, January 26, 1977. 15.
22. Maureen Dowd, "Black Caucus, Back in the White House, Uses Straight Talk," *New York Times*, May 24, 1989, A29.
23. Katharine Q. Seelye, "Few Opinions, Pro or Con, Seem to Change in Congress," *New York Times*, September 16, 1994, A11.
24. Nathaniel Sheppard Jr. "Black Caucus Assails Carter Oil Policy," *New York Times*, April 12, 1979, B8.
25. Groeling, *When Politicians Attack!*

CHAPTER 7

1. Dana Milbank, "Grasping at Nunchucks in the Hearing Room," *Washington Post*, July 15, 2009, A7.

2. Manu Raju, "Graham Takes on Conservatives," *Politico.com*, July 24, 2009, accessed June 5, 2011, http://www.politico.com/story/2009/07/graham-takes-on-conservatives-025361.

3. Manu Raju, "GOP leaders Fear Anti-Obama Tone," *Politico.com*, July 23, 2009 accessed June 5, 2011, http://www.politico.com/story/2009/07/gop-leaders-fear-anti-obama-tone-025302.

4. As a political scientist who studies Congress and lives in South Carolina, I received phone calls from reporters across the state asking this question.

5. Richard F. Fenno Jr., *Congressional Travels: Places, Connections, and Authenticity* (New York: Pearson Longman, 2007), 267–270.

6. Fenno, *Congressional Travels*, 240–244.

7. Unless otherwise attributed, all comments from Senator Graham come from a telephone interview with the author on December 29, 2010.

8. See, e.g., Graham's appearance on *Fox News Sunday*, May 23, 2004.

9. John F. Harris and Jim VandeHei, "Doubts about Mandate for Bush, GOP," *Washington Post*, May 2, 2005, A1.

10. Charles Babington and Thomas B. Edsall, "Conservative Republicans Divided over Nominee," *Washington Post*, October 4, 2005, A11.

11. See, e.g., Graham's interview on *CNN: Late Edition with Wolf Blitzer*, January 21, 2007.

12. Tim Russert, "Interview: Madeleine Albright and Lindsey Graham discuss the war in Iraq," *NBC News: Meet the Press*, December 11, 2005; Hope Yen, "Probe Sought on NSA Surveillance; Members of Congress Question Legality of Bush's Authorization," *Washington Post*, December 19, 2005, A5.

13. George Stephanopoulos, "This Week Debate Is Bipartisanship Dead," *ABC News: This Week*, February 15, 2009.

14. Jonathan Weisman, "Bush Aides Threaten Veto of Iraqi Aid Measure," *Washington Post*, October 22, 2003, A6.

15. Stephanopoulos, "*This Week* Debate: Is Bipartisanship Dead," *ABC News: This Week*, February 15, 2009.

16. Bob Schieffer, *CBS News: Face the Nation*, May 16, 2004.

17. Bob Schieffer, *CBS News: Face the Nation*, June 18, 2006.

18. Jim VandeHei, "Bush to Keep Pressing for Bolton Vote; Frist Says His Role Has Been 'Exhausted' but Softens Position after Talk with President," *Washington Post*, June 22, 2005, A10.

19. Charles Babington, "Alito Seems Assured of a Seat on High Court; Panel Endorses Nominee; Floor Debate Starts Today," *Washington Post*, January 25, 2006, A3. Graham made the same complaints against his fellow partisans during the confirmation of Sonia Sotomayor to the Supreme Court during the first year of the Obama administration.

20. *CNN: Late Edition with Wolf Blitzer*, January 21, 2007; Chris Wallace, *Fox News Sunday*, April 19, 2009.

21. Jonathan Weisman and Jim VandeHei, "GOP Is Divided on Social Security Push," *Washington Post*, January 7, 2005, A4.

22. Chris Wallace, *Fox News Sunday*, September 18, 2005.

23. Charles Babington, "Immigration Bill Expected to Pass Senate This Week; Hastert May Block Version That Divides House GOP," *Washington Post*, May 23, 2006, A3.

24. Jonathan Weisman, "Hill GOP Seeks to Limit 'Offshoring' Fallout," *Washington Post*, April 1, 2004, A10.

25. Mike Allen, "Graham Says GOP Erred Focusing on Accounts," *Washington Post*, March 9, 2005, A8.

26. During the first year of President Obama's second term in office, as Graham's own re-election was getting closer, Graham's rhetoric heated up, but it still rarely reached the consistent levels of hostility of many of his colleagues.

27. Dana Priest and Robin Wright, "Cheney Fights for Detainee Policy; As Pressure Mounts to Limit Handling of Terror Suspects, He Holds Hard Line," *Washington Post*, November 7, 2005, A1.

28. Jim VandeHei, "GOP Irritation at Bush Was Long Brewing," *Washington Post*, March 17, 2006, A1.

29. Michael Gerson, "For Sale: One Senator (D-Neb.). No Principles, Low Price," *Washington Post*, December 23, 2009, A19.

30. I used the senator's comments and the context of the article to determine one of several possible target audiences for the senator's comments—the president, the senator's own party, the other party, the public, or other. If the audience was not explicitly stated or obvious from the context of the article, I labeled it "unclear." To corroborate the content analysis, I questioned each senator about the intended audience in my interviews.

31. Jonathan Weisman, "Pressure, Frustration Mount," *Washington Post*, April 11, 2006, A12.

32. Chris Wallace, *Fox News Sunday*, April 2, 2006.

33. Perry Bacon Jr., "Left, Right Press Obama on War Funds; Points of Contention Include Guantanamo Bay, Abuse Photos and Loan to IMF," *Washington Post*, June 10, 2009, A6.

34. "A Weekly Roundup of the Buzz from the Sunday Talk Shows," *Washington Post*, June 18, 2007, A2.

35. Tim Russert, "Interview: Senator Lindsey Graham, Republican from South Carolina," *NBC News: Meet the Press*, March 4, 2007; Chris Wallace, *Fox News Sunday*, November 30, 2008.

36. George Stephanopoulos, *ABC News: This Week*, April 6, 2008.

37. Bob Schieffer, *CBS News: Face the Nation*, February 20, 2005.

38. Peter Baker, "President to Name Nominee for Court; Allies on Right Are Consulted on Conservative Judges," *Washington Post*, October 31, 2005, A1.

39. *ABC Evening News*, December 18, 2005.

40. Helen Dewar, "Judiciary GOP Supports Probe; Senators Break with Activists on Computer Hacking Case," *Washington Post*, February 13, 2004, A5.

41. Robert Draper, "This Year's Maverick," *New York Times Magazine*, June 28, 2010.

42. Peter Whoriskey, "Senate Grapples with Web Privacy Issues; At Hearing, More Questions Than Answers," *Washington Post*, July 10, 2008. D3.

43. E.g., David Cho, "Efforts Grow to Waylay Blackstone Stock Sale," *Washington Post*, June 21, 2007, D1.

44. Dana Milbank, "The Nomination That's Too Big to Fail," *Washington Post*, January 15, 2009, A3.

45. Jonathan Weisman, "GOP Backers Offer Immigration Bill Change; Provision Would Require Illegal Residents to Return Home to Gain Legal Status," *Washington Post*, June 26, 2007, A3.

46. Shailagh Murray, "Careful Strategy Is Used to Derail Immigration Bill; 'Amnesty' Becomes Achilles' Heel," *Washington Post*, June 8, 2007, A4.

47. William Branigin and Jonathan Weisman, "Immigration Measure Appears Imperiled Again; Defeat of Amendments Briefly Raised Hopes," *Washington Post*, June 28, 2007. A6.

48. Lori Montgomery and Paul Kane, "Housing Bill Won't 'Perform Miracles'; Senate Approves Measure, but Critics Say Law Unlikely to Prevent Most Foreclosures," *Washington Post*, July 27, 2008, A1.

49. Billy Wharton, "Obama's No Socialist. I Should Know," *Washington Post*, March 15, 2009, B1.

50. Branigin and Weisman, "Immigration Measure,"A6.

51. Jonathan Weisman, "Senators Unmoved by Bush Bid to Save Immigration Bill," *Washington Post*, June 13, 2007, A3.

52. Stephen Barr, "Senators Want Federal Employees to Fly by the Rules," *Washington Post*, October 23, 2007, D4.

53. Wharton, "Obama's No Socialist," B1.

54. Dana Milbank, "An Administration's Amnesty Amnesia," *Washington Post*, June 5, 2005, A4.

55. Unless otherwise cited, all comments from DeMint come from a telephone interview with the author conducted November 4, 2009.

56. Margaret Talev, "Nomination for TSA chief Is Held Up by GOP Senator," *Washington Post*, December 29, 2009, A13.

57. Dana Milbank, "Jabs and All, the Ides of March Arrives Late," *Washington Post*, June 29, 2007, A2.

58. Jonathan Weisman, "Revenue Surge Shrinks Deficit; Tax Cuts 'Working,' President Says, but Some Voice Caution," *Washington Post*, July 14, 2005, A1.

59. Mike Allen and Jonathan Weisman, "GOP Sounded the Alarm but Didn't Respond to It; Thomas Bill Does Not Address Social Security Solvency," *Washington Post*, June 24, 2005, A8.

60. *CBS Evening News with Katie Couric*, December 16, 2009.

61. Lori Montgomery, "Huge Housing Bill Set to Become Law; Bush Drops Veto Threat on Measure," *Washington Post*, July 24, 2008, A1.

62. George Stephanopoulos, *ABC News This Week*, February 1, 2009.

63. Jonathan Martin and Manu Raju, "DeMint Courts Tea Party, Irks GOP," Politico.com, March 12, 2010, accessed June 1, 2011, http://www.politico.com/story/2010/03/demint-courts-tea-party-irks-gop-034296.

64. Philip Rucker, "S.C. Senator Is a Voice of Reform Opposition; DeMint a Champion of Conservatives," *Washington Post*, July 28, 2009, A1.

65. Project Vote Smart, "Special Interest Group Ratings for Senator Lindsey O. Graham," accessed June 22, 2012, http://votesmart.org/candidate/evaluations/21992/lindsey-graham/17.

CHAPTER 8

1. Paul M. Krawzak and Humberto Sanchez, "Senate Passes 'Clean' CR," *Congressional Quarterly Weekly Report*, September 30, 2013, 1614.

2. David Harrison and Humberto Sanchez, "House CR Would Gut Health Care Law," *Congressional Quarterly Weekly Report*, September 23, 2013, 1556.

3. See, e.g., Cohen, "Presidential Leadership"; Edwards, *The Strategic President*.

4. Cohen, "Presidential Leadership."

5. Edwards, *The Strategic President*; Kernell, *Going Public*.

6. Reported by Steve Benen, "Someone Take His Blackberry Away," *Political Animal Blog, Washington Monthly*, July 24, 2009, accessed December 29, 2013, http://www.washingtonmonthly.com/archives/monthly/2009_07.php.

7. Liz Halloran. "Is Grassley Abandoning Bipartisan Health Bill," National Public Radio, August 20, 2009, accessed March 7, 2014, http://www.npr.org/templates/story/story.php?storyId=112044867.

8. Caitlyn Tailor, "Boehner: GOPers Should Vote No on Stimulus," ABC News, January 27, 2009, accessed March 7, 2014, http://blogs.abcnews.com/thenote/2009/01/gopers-should-v.html.

9. Stephanie Haven, "Boehner, King Trade Jabs over Immigration Comments," CBS News, July 25, 2013, accessed March 13, 2014, http://www.cbsnews.com/news/boehner-king-trade-jabs-over-immigration-comments/.

10. Glenn Kessler, "Rep. Darrell Issa Disputes His Four-Pinocchio Ratings," *Washington Post*, March 3, 2014, accessed March 13, 2014, http://www.washingtonpost.com/blogs/fact-checker/wp/2014/03/03/rep-darrell-issa-disputes-his-four-pinocchio-ratings/.

11. A. A. Milne, *The House at Pooh Corner* (New York: Dutton, 1956), 102.

12. James Madison, *The Records of the Federal Convention* (New Haven, CT: Yale University Press, vol. 3, 1937), 479.

REFERENCES

Aldrich, John H., and David W. Rohde. "The Consequences of Party Organization in the House: The Role of the Majority and Minority Parties in Conditional Party Government." In *Polarized Politics: Congress and the President in a Partisan Era*, edited by Jon Bond and Richard Fleisher, 31–72. Washington, DC: CQ Press, 2000.

Arnold, R. Douglas. *Congress, the Press, and Political Accountability*. Princeton, NJ: Princeton University Press, 2013.

Arnold, R. Douglas. *The Logic of Congressional Action*. New Haven, CT: Yale University Press, 1990.

Baum, Matthew A., and Tim Groeling. "What Gets Covered? How Media Coverage of Elite Debate Drives the Rally-'Round-the-Flag Phenomenon: 1978–1998." In *In the Public Domain: Presidents and the Challenges of Public Leadership*, edited by Lori Cox Han and Diane J. Heith, 49–72. Albany: State University of New York Press, 2005.

Baumgartner, Frank R., and Bryan D. Jones. *Agendas and Instability in American Politics*. Chicago: University of Chicago Press, 1993.

Baumgartner, Frank R., and Bryan D. Jones. "Positive and Negative Feedback in Politics." In *Policy Dynamics*, edited by Baumgartner and Jones, 3–28. Chicago: University of Chicago Press, 2002.

Binder, Sarah A. "Elections and Congress's Governing Capacity." *Extensions*, Fall 2005: 10–14.

Boydstun, Amber E. *Making the News: Politics, the Media, and Agenda Setting*. Chicago: Chicago University Press, 2013.

Brownstein, Ronald. *The Second Civil War: How Extreme Partisanship Has Paralyzed Washington and Polarized America*. New York: Penguin, 2007.

Cohen, Jeffrey E. *Going Local: Presidential Leadership in the Post-Broadcast Age*. New York: Cambridge University Press, 2010.

Cohen, Jeffrey E. "Presidential Leadership in an Age of New Media." In *Presidential Leadership: The Vortex of Power*, edited by Bert A. Rockman and Richard W. Waterman, 171–190. New York: Oxford University Press, 2008.

Cook, Timothy. *Governing with the News: The News Media as a Political Institution*. 2nd ed. Chicago: University of Chicago Press, 2005.

Cook, Timothy. *Making Laws and Making News: Media Strategies in the U.S. House of Representatives*. Washington, DC: Brookings Institution, 1989.

Copson, Raymond W. *Congressional Black Caucus and Foreign Policy (1971–2002)*. New York: Novinka Books, 2003.

Davidson, Roger H., Walter J. Oleszek, and Frances E. Lee. *Congress and Its Members*. 13th ed. Washington, DC: CQ Press, 2012.

Davis, Richard. *Typing Politics: The Role of Blogs in American Politics*. New York: Oxford University Press, 2009.

Dodd, Lawrence C. "Re-envisioning Congress: Theoretical Perspectives on Congressional Change." In *Congress Reconsidered*, 7th ed., edited by Lawrence C. Dodd and Bruce I. Oppenheimer, 389–414. Washington, DC: CQ Press, 2001.

Dodd, Lawrence C., and Bruce I. Oppenheimer. "The Politics of the Contemporary House: From Gingrich to Pelosi." In *Congress Reconsidered*, 9th ed., edited by Dodd and Oppenheimer, 23–52. Washington, DC: CQ Press, 2009.

Edwards, George C., III. *Governing by Campaigning: The Politics of the Bush Presidency*. New York: Pearson Longman, 2007.

Edwards, George C., III. "Impediments to Presidential Leadership: The Limitations of the Permanent Campaign and Going Public Strategies." In *Presidential Leadership: The Vortex of Power*, edited by Bert A. Rockman and Richard W. Waterman, 145–170. New York: Oxford University Press, 2008.

Edwards, George C., III. *The Strategic President: Persuasion and Opportunity in Presidential Leadership*. Princeton, NJ: Princeton University Press, 2009.

Eilperin, Juliet. *Fight Club Politics: How Partisanship Is Poisoning the House of Representatives*. Lanham, MD: Rowman and Littlefield, 2006.

Entman, Robert M. *Projections of Power: Framing News, Public Opinion, and U.S. Foreign Policy*. Chicago: University of Chicago Press, 2004.

Evans, C. Lawrence. "Committees, Leaders, and Message Politics." In *Congress Reconsidered*, 7th ed., edited by Lawrence C. Dodd and Bruce I. Oppenheimer, 217–243. Washington, DC: CQ Press, 2001.

Fenno, Richard F., Jr. *Congressional Travels: Places, Connections, and Authenticity*. New York: Pearson Longman, 2007.

Glassman, Matthew Eric, Jacob R. Straus, and Colleen J. Shogan. "Social Networking and Constituent Communication: Member Use of Twitter during a Two-Week Period in the 111th Congress." Congressional Research Service Report 7-5700 R40823 (February 3, 2010), https://www.fas.org/sgp/crs/misc/R43018.pdf.

Groeling, Tim. *When Politicians Attack! Party Cohesion in the Media*. New York: Cambridge University Press, 2010.

Groeling, Tim, and Samuel Kernell. "Congress, the President, and Party Competition via Network News." In *Polarized Politics: Congress and the President in a Partisan Era*, edited by Jon R. Bond and Richard Fleisher, 73–95. Washington, DC: CQ Press, 2000.

Herrnson, Paul S. *Congressional Elections: Campaigning at Home and in Washington*. Washington, DC: CQ Press, 2004.

Hess, Stephen. *Live from Capitol Hill! Studies of Congress and the Media*. Washington, DC: Brookings Institution, 1991.

Hess, Stephen. *The Ultimate Insiders: U.S. Senators in the National Media*. Washington, DC: Brookings Institution, 1986.

Howell, William G., and Douglas L. Kriner. "Congress, the President, and the Iraq War's Domestic Political Front." In *Congress Reconsidered*, 9th ed., edited by Lawrence C. Dodd and Bruce I. Oppenheimer, 311–336. Washington, DC: CQ Press, 2009.

Iyengar, Shanto. *Is Anyone Responsible? How Television Frames Political Issues*. Chicago: University of Chicago Press, 1991.

Iyengar, Shanto, and Donald R. Kinder. *News That Matters: Television and American Opinion*. Chicago: University of Chicago Press, 1987.

Jacobs, Lawrence R., and Robert Y. Shapiro. *Politicians Don't Pander: Political Manipulation and the Loss of Democratic Responsiveness*. Chicago: University of Chicago Press, 2000.

Jacobson, Gary C. *The Politics of Congressional Elections*. 7th ed. New York: Pearson Longman, 2009.

Kedrowski, Karen M. *Media Entrepreneurs and the Media Enterprise in the U.S. Congress*. Cresskill, NJ: Hampton Press, 1996.

Kellstedt, Paul M. *The Mass Media and the Dynamics of American Racial Attitudes*. New York: Cambridge University Press, 2003.

Kernell, Samuel. *Going Public: New Strategies of Presidential Leadership*. 4th ed. Washington, DC: CQ Press, 2007.

LeLoup, Lance T., and Steven A. Shull. *The President and Congress: Collaboration and Combat in National Policymaking*. Boston: Allyn and Bacon, 1999.

Lichter, S. Robert, and Daniel R. Amundson. "Less News Is Worse News: Television News Coverage of Congress, 1972–1992." In *Congress, the Press, and the Public*, edited by Thomas E. Mann and Norman J. Ornstein, 131–140. Washington, DC: American Enterprise Institute and Brookings Institution, 1994.

Lipinski, Daniel. "Navigating Congressional Policy Processes: The Inside Perspective on How Laws Are Made." In *Congress Reconsidered*, 9th ed., edited by Lawrence C. Dodd and Bruce I. Oppenheimer, 337–360. Washington, DC: CQ Press, 2009.

Madison, James. *The Records of the Federal Convention*, vol. 3. New Haven, CT: Yale University Press, 1937.

Malecha, Gary Lee, and Daniel J. Reagan. *The Public Congress: Congressional Deliberation in a New Media Age*. New York: Routledge, 2012.

Mann, Thomas E., and Norman J. Ornstein. *It's Even Worse Than It Looks: How the American Constitutional System Collided with the New Politics of Extremism*. New York: Basic Books, 2012.

Mayhew, David R. *America's Congress: Actions in the Public Sphere, James Madison through Newt Gingrich*. New Haven, CT: Yale University Press, 2000.

Mayhew, David R. *Congress: The Electoral Connection*. New Haven, CT: Yale University Press, 1974.

Milne, A.A. *The House at Pooh Corner*. New York: Dutton, 1956.

Palazzolo, Daniel J. *Done Deal? The Politics of the 1997 Budget Agreement*. New York: Chatham House, 1999.

Petrocik, John R. "Issue Ownership in Presidential Elections, with a 1980 Case Study." *American Journal of Political Science* 40 (August 1996): 825–850.

Plato. *Gorgias*. Translated by James H. Nichols Jr. Ithaca, NY: Cornell University Press, 1998.

Putnam, Robert D. *Bowling Alone: The Collapse and Revival of American Community.* New York: Simon and Schuster, 2000.

Rae, Nicol C. "Republican Congressional Leadership in Historical Context." *Extensions,* Spring 2005: 5–9.

Rivers, Douglas, and Nancy L. Rose. "Passing the President's Program: Public Opinion and Presidential Influence in Congress." *American Journal of Political Science* 29 (May 1985): 183–196.

Rozell, Mark J. *In Contempt of Congress: Postwar Press Coverage on Capitol Hill.* Westport, CT: Praeger, 1996.

Schaffner, Brian F., and Mary Layton Atkinson. "Taxing Death or Estates? When Frames Influence Citizens' Issue Beliefs." In *Winning with Words: The Origins and Impact of Political Framing,* edited by Brian F. Schaffner and Patrick J. Sellers, 121–135. New York: Routledge, 2010.

Schattschneider, E. E. *The Semisovereign People: A Realist's View of Democracy in America.* Hinsdale, IL: Dryden Press, 1975.

Sellers, Patrick J. *Cycles of Spin: Strategic Communication in the U.S. Congress.* New York: Cambridge University Press, 2010.

Sinclair, Barbara. "Hostile Partners: The President, Congress, and Lawmaking in the Partisan 1990s." In *Polarized Politics: Congress and the President in a Partisan Era,* edited by Jon R. Bond and Richard Fleisher, 134–153. Washington, DC: CQ Press, 2000.

Sinclair, Barbara. *Party Wars: Polarization and the Politics of National Policy Making.* Norman: University of Oklahoma Press, 2006.

Sinclair, Barbara. "The Senate Leadership Dilemma: Passing Bills and Pursuing Partisan Advantage in a Non-majoritarian Chamber." In *The Contentious Senate: Partisanship, Ideology, and the Myth of Cool Judgment,* edited by Colton C. Campbell and Nicol C. Rae, 65–89. Lanham, MD.: Rowman and Littlefield, 2001.

Sinclair, Barbara. *Unorthodox Lawmaking: New Legislative Processes in the U.S. Congress.* 4th ed. Washington, DC: Sage/CQ Press, 2012.

Singh, Robert. *The Congressional Black Caucus.* Thousand Oaks, CA: Sage, 1998.

Smith, Steven S., and Eric D. Lawrence. "Party Control of Committees in the Republican Congress." In *Congress Reconsidered,* 6th ed., edited by Lawrence C. Dodd and Bruce I. Oppenheimer, 163–192. Washington, DC: CQ Press, 1997.

Tillery, Alvin B., Jr. "Foreign Policy Activism and Power in the House of Representatives: Black Members of Congress and South Africa, 1968–1986." *Studies in American Political Development* 20 (Spring 1986): 88–103.

Vinson, C. Danielle. "Congress and the Media: Who Has the Upper Hand?" In *New Directions in Media and Politics,* edited by Travis Ridout, 141–157. New York: Routledge, 2013.

Vinson, C. Danielle. "Congress Goes Public: Who Is Using the Media for Policymaking Goals?" Paper presented at the annual meeting of the American Political Science Association, Washington, DC, September 1–4, 2005.

Vinson, C. Danielle. *Local Media Coverage of Congress and Its Members: Through Local Eyes.* Cresskill, NJ: Hampton Press, 2003.

Wattenberg, Martin P. *The Decline of American Political Parties*. Cambridge, MA: Harvard University Press, 1984.

Wolfsfeld, Gadi. *Making Sense of Media and Politics: Five Principles in Political Communication*. New York: Routledge, 2011.

Zaller, John. *The Nature and Origins of Mass Opinion*. New York: Cambridge University Press, 1992.

ABC/ABC News, 91, 112, 152, 177
abortion, 102–103
Abu Ghraib, 157
ACA. *see* Affordable Care Act
accountability, 13, 54, 57, 146, 192, 198
advertising, 2, 95–96
Affleck, Ben, 26
Affordable Care Act, 57, 73, 107, 150,
  183, 188, 190–91, 193–94. *see also*
  health care
Agence France Press, 93
agenda. *see* legislative agenda
agriculture, 41, 103, 107
Alito, Samuel, 157–58, 218n19
American Energy Initiative, 101
apartheid, 131, 140, 146, 148
appointments, 38–39, 211n103, 218n19
  broadcast media coverage of, 87, 213n8
  Congressional Black Caucus
    and, 139–40
  Jim DeMint and, 171
  Lindsey Graham and, 150–51, 153,
    155–58, 218n19
appropriations bills, 168, 211n103
Archer, Bill, 120, 122

bailouts, 54–55, 73, 168
Baker, Howard, 2, 33
Barrett, Keiana, 132
Baucus, Max, 115
Benghazi, Libya, 92, 107, 195
Biden, Joe, 160

bipartisanship, 19–20, 60, 71, 99, 117,
  120–22, 128, 147, 184, 194
  Jim DeMint and, 56, 92, 171, 190
  Lindsey Graham and, 151, 157, 161, 164,
    167, 190
Blitzer, Wolf, 157, 160
blogs, 27, 83, 92–93, 132, 173–74, 176
Boehner, John, 11, 91, 93, 100–101, 105,
  194–95, 214n20
Bolton, John, 157
Boren, David, 56
Boyd, Allen, 215n11
broadcast media, 82–92. *see also* cable
  television; *specific networks;*
  specific shows
  bias towards power of, 85–86
  divided government and, 87
  Lindsey Graham and, 154
  issue coverage in, 87, 213n8
  media coverage and, 15
  political context and, 86–87
  unified government and, 87
  YouTube and, 105
budgets, 38–39, 43, 45, 46, 212n7.
    see also taxes
  broadcast media coverage of, 87, 213n8
  Jimmy Carter and, 129
  Congressional Black Caucus and,
    129, 140
  coverage of during transition
    years, 41–42
  Facebook and, 102–103

budgets (*Cont.*)
  framing issues and, 18
  Lindsey Graham and, 155
  Barack Obama and, 99
  reactions to, 127, 215n37
  Ronald Reagan and, 1–3, 111
  Twitter and, 99–100
  YouTube and, 105, 107
Burke, James, 120
Bush, George H. W., 137, 141–42, 144
Bush, George W., 43, 159
  Congressional Black Caucus and, 137, 142–45, 147
  Jim DeMint and, 168–70, 174
  energy and, 2–3
  Lindsey Graham and, 153, 155–58, 161, 167
  immigration reform and, 92
  No Child Left Behind and, 74
  Social Security reform and, 110, 113–17, 123–24, 189–90, 193, 215n11
business issues, 38, 39, 44–46, 54–55. *see also* economic issues
  bailouts and, 54–55, 73, 168
  coverage of during transition years, 41–42
  Jim DeMint and, 169–70
Butler, Pierce, 5
Byrd, Robert, 2

cable television, 83–84, 90–92, 105, 108, 167, 193, 195, 198. *see also specific networks; specific shows*
campaign finance reform, 38, 71, 139, 212n7
Cantor, Eric, 100–103
Carter, Jimmy, 26, 43
  budgets and, 129
  Congressional Black Caucus and, 129, 137, 140, 141, 143
  Social Security reform and, 110, 113–17, 123–24, 215n6
caucuses, 45. *see also specific caucus*
CBC. *see* Congressional Black Caucus
CBS/CBS News, 91, 112, 152, 163

centralization of power, 10, 30, 197
centralized coordination. *see* coordinated communication
Chaffetz, Jason, 82–83, 91, 105, 214n20
chairs of committees. *see* committee leaders
Cheney, Dick, 43, 159
civility, breakdown of, 10–11, 169–70, 173–75, 182–83, 199
civil rights, 43
  broadcast media coverage of, 87, 213n8
  Congressional Black Caucus and, 131, 139–41, 147
  Facebook and, 102
  Twitter and, 97–99
  YouTube and, 106–107
Clinton, Bill, 26, 43, 57, 68, 74
  Congressional Black Caucus and, 133, 137, 141–44
  Lindsey Graham and, 151
  impeachment trial of, 151–52
Clinton, Hillary, 161
CNN, 91, 152, 157, 160
coalition partners, 9, 59, 70–71, 194, 199
Cochran, Thad, 214n13
Colbert, Stephen, 26, 92
The Colbert Report, 92
Collins, Cardiss, 129, 143
Comedy Central, 83, 92
committee hearings, 5, 8, 26, 39, 41–43, 46–47, 52, 101, 103, 105, 183, 212n8
committee leaders, 11, 15, 30, 32. *see also committees/subcommittees; specific people; specific topics*
  broadcast news coverage of, 84–86
  direct press contact and, 50
  Facebook and, 100–104, 214n18
  goals and, 58–59
  reaction of to president, 112, 114–25
  work-related press contact and, 50
committees/subcommittees, 9, 11, 13–15, 18–19, 26, 30. *see also* committee leaders
  Lindsey Graham and, 151, 153, 182

Congressional Black Caucus, 9, 129–49,
    181, 185
    apartheid and, 131, 140, 146, 148
    Democratic party and, 129, 131,
        134–38, 140–48
    divided government and,
        137–38, 144–46
    early public strategies of, 130–33
    issue ownership and, 139–42
    political context and, 134–36, 140–42
    reaction of to the president, 142–46
    Republican party and, 133–35, 137,
        141–42, 144–46, 148
    unified government and, 137
congressional committees/
    subcommittees. see committees/
    subcommittees
congressional hearings. see committee
    hearings
congressional leaders. see committee
    leaders; majority leaders; minority
    leaders; party leaders
congressional media entrepreneurs, 9–10
Congressional Quarterly Weekly
    Reports, 113
Congressional Research Service, 93
constituent interests, 4, 12
    Facebook and, 101–102
    media coverage and, 15
    new media and, 92
    Twitter and, 95–97
    YouTube and, 105–107
Conyers, John, 100, 102–103
Cook, Timothy, 6
coordinated communication, 12, 18–19,
    31, 46–47, 51, 88, 122, 127–28, 131–32,
    198–99, 203
    of committees/subcommittees, 19
    special orders speeches and, 47
    Twitter and, 98
Cottle, Michelle, 127
coverage. see media coverage
Cranston, Alan, 26
credibility, 11, 14–15, 71, 147, 149, 165,
    176–77, 191, 196

credit-claiming, 4, 95–96
crime, 38, 41–42
    Facebook and, 102
    Twitter and, 97
crossing party lines, 19–20, 60, 161, 176,
    187, 192
Cruz, Ted, 11, 178, 186, 192, 214n20
    Affordable Care Act and, 183, 188
    new media and, 101, 103–104
C-SPAN, 47, 93
Culberson, John, 93

The Daily Show, 92
debate framing. see framing
defense issues, 8, 38–40, 43, 45–46
    Facebook and, 103
    Lindsey Graham and, 151, 153–57
DeLauro, Rosa, 53
DeLay, Tom, 117, 158
deliberation, 200
DeMint, Jim, 56, 74, 92, 151, 167–77,
    181–82, 191–92, 199
    Affordable Care Act and, 150, 190
    breakdown of civility and, 169–70,
        173–75, 182–83, 199
    George W. Bush and, 168–70, 174
    Democratic party and, 169–72, 174–75
    goals of, 171–72
    number of news stories about, 153
    Barack Obama and, 168–72, 174
    Republican party and, 169–70, 172–77
Democratic party, 1–2, 7, 10–11, 20, 26,
    30, 33. see also majority; minority;
    party; specific members
    Congressional Black Caucus and, 129,
        131, 134–38, 140–48
    Jim DeMint and, 169–72, 174–75
    Lindsey Graham and, 155–67
    MSNBC and, 91
    reaction of to president, 110–12, 114,
        117, 120–23, 127
    Twitter and, 93–100
    YouTube and, 104–108, 214n20, 214n21
Dirksen, Everett, 5
district outreach, 95–96

divided government, 16–17, 29
  broadcast media and, 87
  Congressional Black Caucus and,
    137–38, 144–46
  direct press contact and, 50–51
  goals and, 62–63
  political context and, 35–36
  reaction to the president and, 112
  work-related press contact and, 50–51
Dodd, Lawrence, 12
Dole, Bob, 68, 86, 89
domestic issues, 8, 93, 141, 151, 153–56
domestic surveillance, 103, 106, 108, 153,
    156, 158, 164
Dunlop, John, 140

economic issues, 38, 43, 44. see also
    business issues
  bailouts and, 54–55, 73, 168
  Congressional Black Caucus and,
    129, 140
  Jim DeMint and, 169–70, 172
  Lindsey Graham and, 155–57, 156–57
  Barack Obama and, 129, 156–57
education, 42, 44
  on issues, 5, 56, 95–96, 171
  No Child Left Behind, 74
  Twitter and, 95–96
Eilperin, Juliet, 11
elections. see transition years;
    voting rights
Emanuel, Rahm, 122
energy, 38, 40, 43–44, 46, 57, 93
  American Energy Initiative and, 101
  George W. Bush and, 2–3
  H-Prize legislation and, 14
  Twitter and, 93
environmental issues, 38, 43, 46, 102
ethics, 38, 140, 212n7
Evans, Lawrence, 18
executive appointments. see
    appointments

Facebook, 5, 23, 83, 93, 100–104, 186,
    197, 214n16

Face the Nation, 91, 163
Faleomavaega, Eni, 214n13
Family Medical Leave Act, 97
Farm Bill 2013, 107. see also agriculture
Feingold, Russ, 71
filibuster, 12–13, 46
finance. see business issues;
    economic issues
Fitzpatrick, Michael, 116
floor debate, 46–52, 105, 183
food stamps, 103, 107
Ford, Harold, Jr., 122, 140
foreign policy, 8, 38, 39, 45–46, 212n7
  broadcast media coverage of, 87, 213n8
  Congressional Black Caucus
    and, 139–40
  Facebook and, 102
  Lindsey Graham and, 155
Fox and Friends, 83
Fox News, 83, 90–92, 105, 152, 159,
    173, 174
Fox News Sunday, 159
Foxx, Virginia, 99
framing, 7, 9–10, 13, 17–18, 20, 29, 31,
    127, 163–64, 181–82, 187, 190–92,
    197, 200
  broadcast media and, 98–100, 103
  Congressional Black Caucus and, 130
  Jim DeMint and, 170, 172
  going public and, 55–56, 59, 80
  new media and, 98–100, 103
  reaction to the president and, 120–23
Freedom Caucus, 9
Frist, Bill, 166
Fudge, Marcia, 214n20

Gallup Poll, 124
gay marriage, 92, 106
Geithner, Tim, 169
Gingrich, Newt, 10, 20, 26, 47
  negative media coverage and, 16
  use of media by, 33
goals, 191–92
  bypassing committees and, 19
  of Jim DeMint, 171–72

determinants of going public
  on, 64–67
divided government and, 62–63
of going public, 54–67
of Lindsey Graham, 161–65, 219n30
institutional power and, 57–60
polarization and, 63–64
policy, 10, 19
presidential, 60–61
unified government and, 62–63
going public, 1–3, 187–96, 196–201
  Congressional Black Caucus and (*see*
    Congressional Black Caucus)
  decline of traditional intermediaries
    and, 6–7
  defined, 3–5
  direct contact and, 46–51,
    212n13, 212n14
  during elections (*see* transition years)
  goals of, 54–67
  with inaccurate information, 195–96
  increase in, 27–29
  individualism within Congress
    and, 9–10
  influences on, 180–87
  institutional power and (*see*
    institutional power)
  institutional weakness and (*see*
    institutional weakness)
  issues suitable to, 5, 8, 18, 38–46
  legislative agenda and, 7
  limitations of, 192–96
  mechanisms for, 46–51,
    212n13, 212n14
  media coverage and (*see* media
    coverage)
  new media and (*see* new media)
  political context of (*see* political
    context)
  political polarization and (*see*
    polarization)
  position in Congress and, 180–81
  public opinion and, 7–8
  to react (*see* reaction/response)
  reasons for, 6, 53–81, 165–66

during transition years (*see*
  transition years)
work-related activities and, 46–51,
  212n13, 212n14
Goodlatte, Robert, 100
Gorgias (Plato), 4
governmental affairs, 38–39, 45, 46, 212n7
  broadcast media coverage of, 87, 213n8
  Congressional Black Caucus
    and, 139–40
  coverage of during transition
    years, 41–42
  Facebook and, 102
Gowdy, Trey, 91, 105, 214n20
Graham, Lindsey, 14, 86, 105, 122, 171,
  176–77, 181–82, 186, 190–91
  Samuel Alito and, 157–58, 218n19
  George W. Bush and, 153, 155–58,
    161, 167
  Clinton impeachment trial and, 151–52
  committee assignments of, 151, 153, 182
  Democratic party and, 155–67
  goals of, 161–65, 219n30
  as a maverick, 151, 153, 161
  John McCain and, 152–54
  media coverage of, 150–68, 171,
    176–77, 214n20
  number of news stories about, 153
  Barack Obama and, 156–57, 161,
    164–65, 167, 218n19
  partisanship and, 159–60, 219n26
  party politics and, 157–67
  reactions to Democrats by, 157–58
  reactions to Republicans by, 158–59
  reactions to the president by, 155–57
  Republican party and, 151–52, 155–59,
    162–64, 166–67
  Sonia Sotomayor and, 150, 218n19
Grassley, Charles, 100, 117, 194
Griffin, Robert, 2
Gutierrez, Luis, 214n20
gun control, 53, 57, 102–103, 182

Hagel, Chuck, 123
Hall, Tony, 26

Halleck, Charlie, 5
Halloran, Liz, 194
Hamilton, Alexander, 5
Hastert, Dennis, 11, 88
health care, 38–39, 43–44, 46
    Affordable Care Act and (*see*
        Affordable Care Act)
    broadcast media coverage of, 87, 213n8
    Twitter and, 97
hearings. *see* committee hearings
Helvidius (James Madison), 5
Heritage Foundation, 152, 171, 175, 192
Hess, Stephen, 84
holds, 13, 171
Hollings, Ernest "Fritz", 151
House of Representatives. *see also specific
    members*
    broadcast news coverage of, 84–86
    direct press contact and, 50
    Facebook and, 100–104, 214n18
    influence on Senate by, 14
    institutional power and, 12–14
    media coverage and, 31, 48
    minority leaders in, 34
    new media and, 93, 214n16
    reaction of, 70
    reaction of to president, 111–12,
        121–23, 127–28
    Twitter and, 93–100
    work-related press contact and, 50
    YouTube and, 104–108, 214n20, 214n21
    YouTube *vs.* Twitter and,
        106–108, 214n21
H-Prize legislation, 14
Hunt, Al, 194

immigration, 26, 56, 92, 96–97, 139,
    189, 195
    Jim DeMint and, 168–72, 174
    Facebook and, 102–4
    Lindsey Graham and, 151, 153, 155, 158,
        161–64, 167, 177
    YouTube and, 105–8
impeachment, 151–52
individualism, 9–11

individualized pluralism, 9
Inglis, Bob, 14
institutionalized pluralism, 9
institutional power, 11–14, 34–35, 191–92
    centralization of, 10, 30, 197
    goals and, 57–60
    limitation of, 11–14, 53–54
    minority party and, 37
    network bias towards, 85–86
institutional weakness, 6, 34–35, 129–49
intercoder reliability, 206, 212–13n3,
    212n7, 214n16
interest groups, 6, 10, 56, 177
intermediaries, traditional, 6–7
international opinion, 8
interparty opposition, 12
intraparty opposition, 12
investigations/scandals, 16, 38, 212n7
    broadcast media coverage of,
        87, 213n8
    IRS and, 91–92, 107
Iran-Contra, 39
Isakson, Johnny, 99
Israel, 39
Issa, Darrell, 195–96
issue ownership. *see also specific issues*
    Congressional Black Caucus and,
        139–42, 147
    defining issues and, 13
    party leaders and, 18
    Twitter and, 98–99

Jacobs, Lawrence, 23–24
Jay Treaty, 5
Jeffords, Jim, 45
judicial appointments. *see* appointments;
    Supreme Court

Kedrowski, Karen, 9–10
Kennedy, Edward, 110
Kernell, Samuel, 3
Kerry, John, 167
Kessler, Glen, 195
King, Steve, 195
Klobuchar, Amy, 101

Labrador, Raul, 101, 103
Late Edition with Wolf Blitzer, 157, 160
leadership. *see* committee leaders;
    majority leaders; minority leaders;
    party leaders
Leahy, Patrick, 100, 103, 158, 160
Lee, Mike, 107, 183, 214n20
legislative agenda/legislation, 7, 13–14,
    40–44
  influencing, 189–90
  minority party and, 17
  new media and, 27
  passing, 55–67
  press conferences and, 26–27
  real-world events and, 44
  setting of, 7, 12
  stopping, 55–67
legislative cycle, 22, 39, 211n103
Levin, Carl, 214n20
Lewis, John, 135, 138, 147–49
Lipinski, Dan, 14
Long, Russell B., 120
Lowey, Nita, 53

Madison, James, 5, 200
majority leaders, 31–36. *see also* majority
    party; party leaders; *specific parties;*
    specific people
  broadcast news coverage of, 84–86
  bypassing, 13–14
  centralization of power and, 10
  Facebook and, 100–104, 214n18
  factions within parties and, 9
  goals and, 58–59
  issue choices from, 45
  media coverage of, 15
  reaction of to president, 110–28
  YouTube and, 104–108, 214n20, 214n21
majority party, 8, 30. *see also* majority
    leaders; *specific parties*
  broadcast news coverage of, 84–86
  control of White House and, 16–17
  direct press contact and, 51
  divided government and, 16–17
  divisions within, 18, 26

  Facebook and, 100–104, 214n18
  goals and, 57–60
  institutional power and, 12–14
  narrow margins and, 16
  reaction of, 70–71
  reaction of to president, 110–28
  Twitter and, 93–100
  unified government and, 16–17
  unified voice and, 12
  work-related press contact and, 51
  YouTube and, 104–108, 214n20, 214n21
markups, 13
Mason, S. T., 5
mavericks, 151, 153, 161
  Lindsey Graham as, 151, 153, 161
  John McCain as, 86
  media coverage of, 15
Mayhew, David, 21
McCain, John, 71, 86, 152–54, 160
McCarthy, Carolyn, 53
McCarthy, Joseph, 5
McCaskill, Claire, 214n20
McConnell, Mitch, 100–101, 105, 107,
    166, 214n20
McCrery, Jim, 115
media coverage, 11, 15–16, 23–24. *see also*
    new media
  attracting, 11, 15–17, 46–51,
    212n13, 212n14
  balance in, 24
  cultivating reporters and, 23
  direct contact with reporters
    and, 23–24, 26, 46–51,
    212n13, 212n14
  of Lindsey Graham, 150–68, 171,
    176–77, 214n20
  of House members, 31
  issues suitable to, 38–46
  media's own interests and, 24,
    39, 181–84
  online expansion of, 27, 83
  of Senate members, 31
  variations in, 40–44
  work-related activities and, 46–51,
    212n13, 212n14

media events, 23, 82–83, 94
Meet the Press, 21–22, 85–88, 108, 160,
    211n102, 213n7
message politics, 10, 18–19
Middle East, 39, 103, 155
midterm elections. *see* transition years
Miers, Harriet, 156
military. *see* defense issues
minority leaders, 31–36. *see also* minority
    party; party leaders; *specific parties;*
    specific people
    broadcast news coverage of, 84–86
    divided majority and, 18
    Facebook and, 100–104, 214n18
    goals and, 58–59
    in the House, 34
    issue choices from, 45
    press conferences by, 5
    reaction of to president, 110–28
    in the Senate, 34
    YouTube and, 104–108, 214n20, 214n21
minority party, 8, 30, 32. *see also*
    minority leaders; *specific parties*
    broadcast news coverage of,
        84–86, 88
    control of White House and, 16–17
    direct press contact and, 50–51
    electoral prospects of, 12
    Facebook and, 100–104, 214n18
    framing and, 17
    goals and, 57–60
    institutional power and, 12–14, 37
    legislative agenda and, 17
    rank-and-file members of, 36–37
    reaction of, 70–71
    reaction of to president, 110–28
    in the Senate, 12–13
    Twitter and, 93–100
    work-related press contact and, 50–51
    YouTube and, 104–108, 214n20, 214n21
Mitchell, George, 89
moderates, 10, 17, 56, 75, 119, 176
Mondale, Walter, 113
Moynihan, Daniel Patrick, 31, 74, 121
MSNBC, 90–92

NAFTA (North American Free Trade
    Agreement), 39
National Public Radio, 194
national security, 38–40
    broadcast media coverage of, 87, 213n8
    Facebook and, 102–103
    Lindsey Graham and, 151, 153, 156–57
    YouTube and, 106, 108
National Security Agency, 106, 108
NBC/NBC News, 91, 125, 152, 160
negative media coverage, 16
negotiation
    framing and, 17, 187
    impediments to, 92, 194–96
    participating in, 151, 163, 167, 177
    political polarization and, 10–11
network television. *see* broadcast media
Neutrality Proclamation, 5
new media, 5, 6–7, 23, 92–108, 183–84,
    214n16. *see also* media coverage;
    specific medium
    attracting media attention and, 27
    legislative agenda and, 27
New Republic, 127
news coverage. *see* media coverage; press
    conferences
NewsHour with Jim Lehrer, 112, 215n5
newspapers. *see* media coverage; print
    media; *specific titles*
New York Times, 180
    analysis methodology, 203–206
    Congressional Black Caucus coverage
        in, 133, 135–38, 217n16
    coverage of congressional reaction by,
        110, 124
    intercoder reliability and, 206,
        212–13n3, 212n7, 214n16
    sampling data from, 21–22, 27, 38,
        47, 55–56, 83, 85–86, 112, 212–
        13n3, 212n7, 212n8, 212n13, 213n7,
        213n8, 215n5
niche media, 6
No Child Left Behind, 74
North American Free Trade Agreement, 39
NPR (National Public Radio), 194

Obama, Barack, 195–96
  Affordable Care Act and, 57, 73, 107,
    150, 183, 188, 190–91, 193–94
  attacks on, 103, 107
  budgets and, 99
  Congressional Black Caucus and, 129,
    137, 143–44
  Jim DeMint and, 168–72, 174
  economy and, 156–57
  Lindsey Graham and, 156–57, 161,
    164–65, 167, 218n19
Obamacare. see Affordable Care Act
obstructionism, 13, 172, 183
O'Neill, Tip, 1–3, 47, 121

partisanship. see bipartisanship;
    polarization/partisanship
party identification, 6
party image, 10, 12, 16
party leaders, 30, 31–33. see also
    majority leaders; minority leaders;
    party members; specific parties;
    specific people
  broadcast news coverage of, 84–89
  bypassing, 13–14
  centralization of power and, 10
  direct press contact and, 50
  Facebook and, 100–104, 214n18
  factions within parties and, 9
  goals and, 58–59
  issue choices from, 45–46
  issue ownership and, 18
  media coverage of, 15
  party image and, 10
  party members and, 9–10
  polarization and, 18–19, 32
  press conferences and, 26
  reaction of to president, 110–28
  subjugation of committee chairs
    to, 18–19
  Twitter and, 95
  work-related press contact and, 50
  YouTube and, 104–108, 214n20, 214n21
party members, 9–10, 60–61. see also
    party leaders; specific parties

rank-and-file (see rank-and-file party
    members)
party message, 10, 12, 18–19
party politics, 39, 44, 46
  broadcast media coverage of, 87, 213n8
  coverage of during transition
    years, 41–42
  Lindsey Graham and, 157–67
  print media coverage of, 87, 213n8
  reaction to the president and,
    71–80, 88–89
passing legislation, 55–67
Pastor, Ed, 214n13
Paul, Rand, 175, 178, 192
PBS, 112
Pelosi, Nancy
  new media and, 91, 93, 95, 100–103,
    105–7, 214n20
  partisanship and, 10–11, 122, 159, 194
Pepper, Claude, 121
permanent campaign, 7
persuasion, 4–5, 56–57, 141, 177
Peterson, Collin, 214n13
Petraeus, David, 156
Pickle, J. J., 121
Plato, 4
pluralism, 9
polarization/partisanship, 10–11,
    18–21, 185–87
  bipartisanship and, 19–20
  breakdown of civility and, 10–11,
    169–70, 173–75, 182–83, 199
  broadcast media coverage and, 88–90
  crossing party lines and, 19–20
  Facebook and, 102–103
  goals and, 63–64
  Lindsey Graham and, 159–60, 219n26
  partisanship and, 19–20
  party leaders and, 18–19, 32
  rank-and-file party members and, 37
  in reactions to the president,
    75–76, 88–89
  reaction to the president and,
    117–23, 215n15
  Social Security reform and, 110–12

polarization/partisanship (*Cont.*)
  subjugation of committee chairs
    and, 18–19
  Twitter and, 98–100
  YouTube and, 107–108
Policy Agendas Project, 39, 113, 212n8
policy goals. *see* goals
Polis, Jared, 91, 214n20
political context, 16–17, 28–29,
    33–36, 184–85
  broadcast media and, 86–87
  Congressional Black Caucus and,
    134–36, 140–42
  reaction to the president and, 123–27
political polarization. *see* polarization
Politico, 82, 129, 175
position taking, 95–96
Powell, Adam Clayton, 131
power. *see* institutional power
president. *see also specific presidents*
  agenda of (*see* legislative agenda)
  appointments of (*see* appointments)
  congressional districts visits by, 15
  criticism of, 8
  determinants of reaction to, 76–80
  goals of, 60–61
  party members and, 60–61
  polarization and, 75–76
  press conferences and, 15
  press secretaries of, 2
  public addresses of, 2
  reaction to, 71–80, 88–89, 110–28,
    142–46, 155–57
presidential elections. *see* transition years
press conferences, 3, 5, 14–15, 26–27, 40,
    48, 121
  Congressional Black Caucus and,
    129, 148
  new media and, 101, 105
press releases, 23, 46
press secretaries, 2, 5, 132, 179
priming, 7
print media. *see also specific titles*
  Lindsey Graham and, 154
  issue coverage in, 87, 213n8

limited space of, 27–28, 83
network bias towards power and, 85
Sunday shows and, 86–87

race, 139–40, 142, 147, 182. *see also*
  Congressional Black Caucus
Rangel, Charles, 133, 140
rank-and-file party members, 10, 28–32
  broadcast news coverage of, 84–88, 90
  Facebook and, 100–104, 214n18
  goals and, 58–59
  issue choices of, 45
  media coverage and, 48
  of minority party, 36–37
  polarization and, 37
  reaction of, 70, 114–15
  Twitter and, 95
  YouTube and, 104–108, 214n20, 214n21
reaction/response
  of Congressional Black Caucus, 142–46
  determinants of, 76–80
  framing and, 120–23
  members who initiate, 70–71
  polarization and, 75–76, 88–89,
    117–23, 215n15
  political context and, 123–27
  to the president, 71–80, 88–89, 110–28,
    142–46, 155–57
  to Social Security reform, 110–28
  during transition years, 77–78
  Twitter and, 96
Reagan, Ronald, 7, 102
  budgets and, 1–3, 111
  Congressional Black Caucus and, 137,
    141, 143–44, 146
  Social Security reform and, 113–17,
    123–24, 215n6
  taxes and, 43, 111
real-world events, 40, 44
regulation, 38–39, 41, 45, 169
Reid, Harry, 11, 123, 157, 166, 183
  new media and, 86, 100, 101, 103, 105,
    108, 214n20
Remmel, Megan S., 110
reporters. *see* media coverage

Republican party, 1–2, 5, 10–11, 19–20, 30,
     32–33. *see also* majority; minority;
     party; *specific members*
   blogs and, 93
   Congressional Black Caucus and,
     133–35, 137, 141–42, 144–46, 148
   Jim DeMint and, 169–70, 172–77
   Fox News and, 91
   Lindsey Graham and, 151–52, 155–59,
     162–64, 166–67
   reaction of, 70
   reaction of to president, 110–12,
     117, 120–23
   Twitter and, 93–100
   YouTube and, 104–108, 214n20, 214n21
response. *see* reaction/response
Richmond, Cedric, 101
Roosevelt, Franklin, 2
Rubio, Marco, 175, 178
Rumsfeld, Donald, 157
Russert, Tim, 160
Ryan, Paul, 105

Sandy Hook shooting, 102
scandals. *see* investigations/scandals
Schumer, Charles, 86, 161, 166, 214n20
Schweiker, Richard, 113
self-promotion, 4
Sellers, Patrick, 18, 24
Senate. *see also specific members*
   broadcast news coverage of, 84–86
   direct press contact and, 50–51
   Facebook and, 100–104, 214n18
   influence on House of
     Representatives by, 14
   institutional power and, 12–14
   media coverage and, 31, 48
   minority leaders in, 34
   narrow margins in, 17
   new media and, 92–93
   procedural tools of, 12–13
   reaction of, 70
   reaction of to president, 112, 120–21,
     123, 128
   Twitter and, 93–100

   work-related press contact and, 50–51
   YouTube and, 104–108, 214n20, 214n21
   YouTube *vs.* Twitter and, 106–108, 214n21
seniority, 11, 132, 135, 151, 167, 178
Sessions, Jeff, 106–107, 169, 214n20
Shapiro, Robert, 23–24
Shaw, E. Clay, Jr., 117
shutdowns, 183, 188
Skelton, Ike, 54
Slaughter, Louise, 95, 98
Smith, Ben, 82
social media. *see* new media
social policy, 38–39, 44, 46
   broadcast media coverage of, 87, 213n8
   YouTube and, 107
Social Security, 39, 44. *see also*
     social policy
   Jim DeMint and, 172
   Lindsey Graham and, 151, 155
   reaction to reform of, 110–28, 189–90,
     193, 215n6, 215n11
Solarz, Stephen, 31
Sotomayor, Sonia, 150, 218n19
special interest groups, 10, 56, 177
special orders speeches, 47
Specter, Arlen, 194
State of the Union address, 40
States News Service, 93
stopping legislation, 55–67, 64–66, 172
subsidies, 82–83, 213n3
Sunday shows, 84–90, 213n7, 213n8. *see
     also specific show*
   Lindsey Graham and, 154
   print media and, 86–87
Supreme Court, 92, 157–58, 218n19
   Facebook and, 102
   Lindsey Graham and, 150–51,
     153, 155–56
   Sonia Sotomayor and, 150
   YouTube and, 106

taxes, 38–39, 43, 46, 212n7. *see also*
     budgets
   broadcast media coverage of,
     87, 213n8

taxes (*Cont.*)
   Jim DeMint and, 169–70, 172
   Facebook and, 102
   IRS scandal and, 91–92, 107
   Ronald Reagan and, 43, 111
   Twitter and, 98–99
Tea Party, 91–92, 107
terrorism, 39, 54, 151, 153–55
think tanks, 9–10, 152, 171, 175, 192
This Week, 177
Thurmond, Strom, 151, 160
traceability, 13, 56–57, 146, 187, 191
transition years, 22, 28–40, 43, 45, 48–51,
     55, 59, 67, 79, 180, 203, 206
   broadcast media coverage
     during, 86–87
   Congressional Black Caucus and, 138
   direct press contact during, 49–51
   passing legislation and, 64–66
   reaction to the president during,
     77–78, 124–26
   stopping legislation and, 64–66
   top issues covered during, 40–43, 45
   work-related press contact
     during, 49–51
Twitter, 5, 23, 27, 83, 93–100, 195, 197,
     214n16, 214n21
   coordination of activities and, 98
   issue control and, 97–98
   issue ownership and, 98–99
   polarization and, 98–100
   types of message, 95–98
   YouTube *vs.*, 106–108, 214n21

Ullman, Al, 122
unified government, 16–17, 29
   broadcast media and, 87
   Congressional Black Caucus and, 137
   goals and, 62–63
   political context and, 35–36
   reaction to the president and, 112, 120
unified voice, speaking with, 12

veto power, 53, 60, 62, 156–57
Violence against Women Act, 97–100
voting rights, 98–99, 102, 106
Voting Rights Act, 106

Wallace, Chris, 159
Warren, Elizabeth, 11, 105, 178, 214n20
Washington, George, 5
Washington Post, 152, 168, 195
   sampling data from, 112, 215n5
Waters, Maxine, 129
Webb, Jim, 161
Weiner, Anthony, 82–83
welfare, 41, 44, 74. *see also* social policy
White House Office of
   Communications, 2
work-related activities, 46–51,
     212n13, 212n14
Wright, Jim, 122

YouTube, 23, 83, 93, 104–108, 214n16,
     214n20, 214n21
   cable television and, 91
   Twitter *vs.*, 106–108, 214n21